The Difference Between Fichte's and Schelling's System of Philosophy

G. W. F. Hegel

The Difference Between

Fichte's and Schelling's

System of Philosophy

Translated by H. S. Harris

and Walter Cerf

State University of New York Press

Albany   1977

Published by State University of New York Press
99 Washington Avenue, Albany, New York 12246

Library of Congress Cataloging in Publication Data

Hegel, Georg Wilhelm Friedrich, 1770–1831.
  Difference between Fichte's and Schelling's System
of Philosophy in connection with the first fascicle of
Reinhold's *Contributions to a more convenient sur-*
vey of the state of philosophy at the beginning of
the nineteenth century, first fascicle.

  Translation of Differenz des Fichte'schen und
Schelling'schen Systems der Philosophie in Bezie-
hung auf Reinhold's *Beyträge zur leichtern Übersicht*
des Zustands der Philosophie zu Anfang des neun-
zehnten Jahrhunderts, erstes Heft.
Includes bibliographical and analytical indexes.
1. Fichte, Johann Gottlieb, 1762–1814. 2. Schelling,
Friedrich Wilhelm Joseph von, 1775–1854. 3. Faith
and Reason. I. Title: Difference between Fichte's and
Schelling's System of Philosophy . . .

B2848.H3313   193   76-9821
ISBN 0-87395-336-3
ISBN 0-87395-337-1 microfiche

Contents

Translators' Preface

The occasion for the initial attempt to translate Hegel's essay on the *Difference between Fichte's and Schelling's Systems of Philosophy* (1801)[1] into English, was the giving of graduate courses on "The Young Hegel" and on "Post-Kantian Philosophy" by Walter Cerf at the University of the City of New York and the University of Wisconsin during the 1960s. Our first thanks must go to the students in those courses, who never tired of suggesting improvements, and to the City University of New York, which contributed $100 to help cover the expense of typing and mimeographing that first draft.

The mimeographed translation was duly registered with the Translation Center of the University of Southern Illinois. We owe a great debt of gratitude to Professor Fritz Marti whose brainchild this Center is. He never wavered in his interest in, and encouragement of, our translation and he put at Walter Cerf's disposal certain pages of his own translation. Had it not been for Marti's Translation Center, it is very doubtful that H. S. Harris (at Glendon College of York University in Toronto) would ever have learned of the existence of the Cerf translation, and Cerf is certain that without the cooperation of Harris the translation would not have reached the stage of publication.

Harris became involved during a sabbatical leave from York University in 1971–72. Thanks are due both to York University and to the Canada Council for providing the leisure that made his participation possible. The research grant that went with his Canada Council Leave Fellowship also paid for the typing of the final draft of the translation.

We also wish gratefully to acknowledge the help of Sir T. Malcolm Knox, who went over the whole body of our second draft and made many useful suggestions.

Our cooperative effort was from beginning to end under a lucky star of complementarity. Translating the *Difference Essay* fitted in nicely with Harris' research for the second volume of his *Hegel's Development*.[2] Cerf's interest in Hegel, on the other hand, has been mo-

---

1. As likewise *Faith and Knowledge* (1802), Albany: State University of New York Press, 1977.

2. The first volume—*Toward the Sunlight, 1770–1801*—was published by the Clarendon Press, Oxford, in 1972.

tivated more by his studies of Kant. The reader will find therefore, that Harris' introduction to the *Difference* essay seeks both to connect it with the earlier and later thought of Hegel, and to offer explanatory comments on the detail of the rather difficult text. Cerf's introduction, on the other hand, is directed to readers who may not be too familiar either with Kant's Critical Idealism or with Schelling's Philosophy of Identity.[1] He deals in the main with the difference between reflective and speculative philosophy and with the concept of intellectual intuition. We have each studied and criticized the other's contribution, and both of us have profited greatly (though of course we have not always agreed perfectly).

Harris is a native speaker of English, but his knowledge of German is by no means perfect. Cerf is a native German whose forty years of sojourn in the United States have not prevented German from remaining in the full sense his mother tongue. Cerf must therefore bear the main responsibility for mistakes in the rendering of Hegel's text. But Harris assumes a full share of the responsibility for any errors of interpretation, since he will not allow the fault to rest with Hegel (though Cerf maintains, and Hegel's own first audience agreed, that Hegel's German offers difficulties frequently insurmountable even to a native German).

We were agreed on making a translation that would be as faithful to Hegel's German as could be reconciled with its readability in English. Harris was more inclined to sacrifice readability to faithfulness, Cerf faithfulness to readability. Moreover, while Harris believed he could detect in the language of the *Essays* a consistency and precision commensurate to their content, Cerf tended to detect in it speculative insouciance and even simple carelessness, the latter no doubt due to the extraordinary speed with which Hegel wrote the *Essays*. The translators hope that they have hit an acceptable balance in trying to reconcile their divergent tendencies. Our paragraphing generally follows that of Lasson rather than Hegel. The frequently monstrous sentences of the original, some of which cover more than a full page of small print, were ruthlessly cut into manageable pieces. But Hegel's

---

1. Cerf wrote two introductions: one inquiring into ways of making the Hegel of the *Essays* interesting to contemporary analytic philosophy, the other putting the accent on existentialism's relation to Hegel. The first one, of which there was only one copy, was lost in transit between Toronto and Brandon. But as the second introduction was also meant to be useful to readers having little acquaintance with either critical or speculative philosophy it was decided to print it with each of the two *Essays*.

actual language has been rendered with a sort of flexible rigidity. That is to say that although there are many cases where the same German expression is rendered by two different English expressions, there are almost no cases where the same English word is used for two different words in German. Our desire to maintain this much consistency has led us to adopt the artificial expedient of marking three breaches in it with daggers. The English words "formal," "ideal," "real" are, in most contexts, the only possible representatives of the three *pairs* of terms *formal/formell†, ideal†/ideel* and *real†/reell*. For the most part Hegel appears to use these pairs as synonyms; but there are occasions where we suspect that he intends some distinction of meaning between them. We have therefore marked the occurrence of the *less frequent* member of each pair with a dagger (i.e., the daggers in our translation indicate the German words here marked). We must draw the reader's attention to our using "Reason" for the peculiarly Hegelian conception of what Kant called *Vernunft*, and "intellect" for his conception of what Kant called *Verstand*.

For both of us, the labor of translation was far greater than we had expected at the outset. The work had to be relegated to hours that we could spare from other assignments; and our lucky star was often hidden behind the clouds of a postal service that ranged from dead slow at the best to dead stop during the Canadian postal strikes. We are all the more grateful therefore to Caroline Gray, who helped with the Bibliography, and to Lawrence Lyons, who did much of the dullest work for the analytical Index. Nor should the labor of several willing and able typists be forgotten, though their names are not here recorded. Above all, we wish to thank our respective spouses whose love and patience sustained us over the years.

Finally, acknowledgment is due to Professor Marvin Farber, editor of the series Modern Concepts of Philosophy, and Warren H. Green, the publisher of the series. After years of patiently waiting for our translation they very graciously permitted us to transfer the publication to the State University of New York Press whose director, Norman Mangouni, and editor, W. Bruce Johnson, have been most cooperative and helpful.

H. S. Harris
Walter Cerf

Brandon and Toronto, Lady Day, 1976

Speculative Philosophy and Intellectual Intuition: An Introduction to Hegel's *Essays*.

"Speculation" is a bad word nowadays. On the stock market speculators are people who, wanting to get rich fast and without work, invest their money in untested stocks or on the basis of information that gives the prediction of success only a hazardously low degree of probability. And so, when we believe that a scientific hypothesis or a presumed psychological insight or indeed even a statement claiming to be "factual" has no evidence or hardly any evidence that could serve as foundation of its truth claims, we say: "This is mere speculation."

Yet when the congressional committee investigating the wild girations of the stock market asked Bernard Baruch what he did for a living he is supposed to have answered proudly, "I am a speculator." Rather surprisingly, old Bernard Baruch and the young Hegel of these *Essays* have one thing in common: they were proud of being engaged in speculation. Of course they meant two different things by "speculation"—even though the latter-day use of the word is connected in some bizarre way with the earlier meaning.

The term "speculation" comes from "speculare," which is taken to be synonymous with "intuire" (from which comes "intuition"). In a very preliminary way we can describe what the author of the *Essays* meant by speculation as the intuition or vision of the true nature of the relations among God, nature, and self-consciousness or reason. "Self-consciousness" and "reason" are interchangeable on the basis of the Kantian "I think"—"I think the categories"—rather than on the basis of the Cartesian "cogito," which comprises acts other than those of thinking, let alone "pure" thinking. It was Schelling who tried to articulate this vision of the true nature of the relation of God, nature and self-consciousness in his Philosophy of Identity—so called because the relation was to be one of identity, a basically simple design trying to hold together a complex composition. The vision was of course not a sensuous intuition, but an intellectual intuition.[1] When Hegel speaks of speculative philosophy he has the Philosophy of Identity in mind and its intellectual intuition of the all-comprising and ultimate whole of God, nature, and self-consciousness.

The Philosophy of Identity had to have the form of a system whose organic wholeness, reflecting the wholeness of the vision, was to be the test of the truth of the vision. The system consisted of two parts: the Philosophy of Nature and the Transcendental Philosophy, a division obviously at odds with the Kantian as well as the pre-Kantian divisions of philosophy. At the time when Hegel wrote the *Essays* Schelling had published several drafts of the Philosophy of Nature[2] and one of the Transcendental Philosophy.[3] Although Schelling was forever revising his system, the holistic vision behind it is clear. It was a singularly beautiful vision. If ever the time should come when philosophy is judged in terms of æsthetic criteria, the general scheme of the Philosophy of Identity (rather than the detailed execution) would surely be among the crowned victors. Its vision of the whole is the vision of an unconscious God (Spinoza's *natura naturans*) revealing Himself in the ever ascending levels of nature (*natura naturata*) until self-consciousness emerges in rational man. This is the story the Philosophy of Nature tells. The Transcendental Philosophy, on the other hand, claims to trace God's coming to know Himself in a sequence of stages that culminate in art, according to Schelling; in religion or rather, a re-union of art and religion, according to the young Hegel; and in philosophy, according to the mature Hegel. For although Hegel's mature thought and system became more complex and subtle, they never completely lost their connection with the basic vision and division of the Philosophy of Identity. His Philosophy of Nature, like Schelling's though critical of it, was still meant, if not to replace the natural sciences altogether, at least to provide them with the basic framework without which they lose themselves in the infinite chaos of experience and remain atomistic and mechanistic instead of becoming holistic and dynamic. And Hegel's *Logic*, his *Philosophy of History*, and perhaps even his *Phenomenology*, may be said to explicate themes that Schelling's Transcendental Philosophy was unable to shelter and develop in its relatively simplistic frame. Further, Hegel could integrate these themes into the total vision.

In any case, the Hegel of the *Essays*, following Schelling though not without reservations, is convinced that philosophy has finally come into its own as speculative philosophy envisioning the inner unity of God, nature, and self-consciousness, and it has gained its systematic presentation in the Philosophy of Identity with its two organic parts, the Philosophy of Nature tracing the emergence of self-consciousness, and the Transcendental Philosophy tracing the emergence of God's knowledge of Himself.

None of this is likely to sound convincing to a reader with an analytically trained intellect. I shall try in Section III of this Introduction to make the conception of speculative philosophy appear less strange by pointing out how speculative philosophy takes care of objections which non-speculative philosophy raises against it. Nor will speculative philosophy make sense to any historian of philosophy who knows that "speculation" is just another term for "intellectual intuition" and is aware of what Kant did to that concept. In Section IV I hope to show where in Kant's work the speculative philosophers believed to find justification for reintroducing intellectual intuition into the cognitive enterprise of philosophy. In Section II, however, I shall try my hand at an entirely different approach to the Philosophy of Identity, an approach by way of the human or, to use a fashionable term, existential motivations that drove Hegel into the arms of Schelling's Philosophy of Identity.

But first we must return for a moment to the term "speculation." It was of course precisely its Philosophy of Nature that brought speculative philosophy into disrepute. The triumphant march of the natural sciences throughout the nineteenth century turned speculation *qua* intellectual intuition into speculation *qua* unwarranted by any acceptable evidences. In their Philosophy of Nature Schelling and Hegel were like two brave medieval knights fighting a division of tanks. The battle was lost before it began. Yet the thought is perhaps not without some twilight charm that someday the sciences themselves will feel a hankering after a unity that could not be satisfied by the logical reconstruction of the language of science and to which the holistic passion that shaped these now forgotten Philosophies of Nature may be congenial. To be sure, the fuzzy-heads that make up the small but noisy army of today's anti-science and anti-technology prophets may joyfully return to the speculative Philosophy of Nature and claim it as an ally. But its sound re-appropriation, if there is to be another one after the débacle of Bergson's *élan vital*, will have to arise from a need within the sciences themselves.

II. HEGEL AND THE PHILOSOPHY OF IDENTITY

In his introduction to the *Difference* essay Hegel writes that philosophy becomes a need in times when the simple and beautiful harmony of existence is sundered by the awareness of basic dichotomies and antinomies, when the believers become alienated from the gods, man from nature, the individual from his community. In historical situations of this sort philosophy is born and re-born in order to prepare through its systematic thought the revolution through which civilization's many-dimensional alienation will be overcome in a higher cultural synthesis.

We can see by inference from his early theological writings[4] and by what we know of the circumstances of his first thirty years that these views reflect Hegel's own existential situation. On the level of values he was torn apart by clashing loyalties, loyalties to Greek Apollo, Christian Jesus, and Judeo-Prussian Kant. Liberated in mind by the French Revolution like every young German worth his salt, he yet remained in political bondage to the absolutist Duke of Württemberg. He was tied down to the study of dogmatic theology, although there was probably little that interested him less at the time. He who later drew the wide panorama of human history and civilizations into his philosophy lived as a young man in exceedingly narrow conditions of financial, social, and sexual deprivation as stipendiate in Tübingen and as tutor in private homes of the moderately wealthy in Bern and Frankfurt. Only an iron self-discipline can have kept him from exploding and going mad as his friend Hölderlin did. His was a thoroughly alienated existence in which the clash between the life he led and his aspirations, between what was the case and what should and could be the case drove him, as it drove so many of his generation, to dream the idealizing dream of the Hellenic age and of the Christian Middle Ages and to trust in philosophy to prepare the revolution of the German situation. It is important to be aware of the personal urgency in Hegel's commitment to philosophy. What motivated and energized his philosophical beginnings were not at all intellectual puzzles, but the deeply felt disturbances of the situation in which he found himself and his generation, with the clash between Apollo, Jesus, and Kant the most articulate of these personal aspects of the general malaise. At least that much the young Hegel and our own existentialists have in common: matters of personal urgency rather than an interest in intellectual puzzles motivated their philosophizing. And when Kierkegaard compared the later Hegel's Logic with a dance of skeletons he was not aware—and in fact could not have been aware—of how similar the personal problems behind his *Either-Or* were with the clash of value constellations that split the young Hegel. Although their motivational situation was similar they took off in very different directions indeed, doing so on the basis of the sort of decision which is not exactly made by men, but which rather makes men: Kierkegaard to explore, and lead his public into what, in this time and place of his, it should mean to be a Christian in Christianity, and Hegel to explore and finally present what, in this time and place of his, the system of *philosophia perennis* is.

How did the existential situation of the young Hegel lead him in the *Essays* to embrace Schelling's Philosophy of Identity?

To be sure, Hegel might never have become a Schellingian if the accidents of life had not brought him together with Schelling in Tübingen and made them good enough friends to remain in contact even after they went their different ways from Tübingen, Schelling to fame and professorship in Jena, Hegel to the obscurity of a private tutorship in Bern and Frankfurt. Nor must it be forgotten that Schelling, in making Hegel his neighbor and his colleague at the University of Jena, freed Hegel from the social and financial—if not sexual— frustrations of the preceeding decades. It is not cynical to ascribe importance to biographical data of this sort. On the other hand, there must have been something in Schelling's Philosophy of Identity that made it look attractive to Hegel as philosophy from the perspective of his own existential travail.

Kant's Critical Idealism lay before the public in its whole extension and depth. There was Fichte's philosophy as *Wissenschaftslehre*. Hegel was familiar with both. In the rich firmament of Goethe's Germany there was a multitude of other philosophers, now known only to specialist scholars but then quite visible stars, a few of them generally believed at the time to be stars of the first magnitude. What Hegel could see in Schelling's philosophy and in none of the others was the construction—or at least the sketch for it—of a harmonious whole in which Hegel's own basic conflicts, though expressed in the most abstract terms, found their solution. He was able to project the longing after harmony that was energized by his personal turmoil into Schelling's philosophy, a philosophy which aimed at overcoming and bringing into systematic unity the basic conceptual dichotomies and antinomies that had evolved in modern metaphysics from Descartes to Kant around the relation between the infinite and the finite (God and His creation) and between the subject and object (man and nature, the knower and the known). It was not at all impossible to project one's own alienations into these and connected dichotomies and to consider the Philosophy of Identity, with the interdependence of its two parts and their intrinsic relation to the Absolute, as the vehicle of one's own reconciliation with God, nature, and society. Thus Hegel, quite unlike Kierkegaard, took the first and decisive step away from his existential motivations and moved toward the grand tradition of modern philosophy—whose Plotinus he was destined to become. His *Essays* are the documents marking the beginning of his career. Without this first step Hegel rather than Kierkegaard might have become the father of existentialism. His gifts— among which ordinary logical thinking was conspicuously absent —might have well prepared him for this; and the influence which parts of the *Phenomenology* had, for example on Sartre, corroborate it.

III. SPECULATIVE VERSUS REFLECTIVE PHILOSOPHY

Our excursion in the preceding section was intended to aid in an understanding of how the general scheme of Schelling's system— with its view of the Absolute revealing itself in nature and rational self-consciousness and revealing itself to itself in the two parts of the Philosophy of Identity—found a ready response in Hegel. The schisms characteristic of his situation and that of his generation, when expressed in philosophical dichotomies such as those of the infinite and finite and of subject and object, could find their harmonious solution in the Philosophy of Identity, which seemed to offer on the academic level a view of the whole uniting in harmony all sorts of opposites. As such, it could serve as a philosophical basis for the revolution that would turn modern civilization, sick from and of its schisms, into a truly integrated culture to be described in metaphors taken from the romantic conception of nature: a living whole of which the individuals were organs rather than atoms. As each part was sustained and enriched by the whole, so each part functioned to sustain the whole.

But here a problem arises. If speculative philosophy, having its sight on that final whole of God, nature, and self-consciousness, is philosophy as it has finally come into its own truth, then what about all those philosophical efforts that cannot be said even by the most tolerant historian to anticipate speculative philosophy at least germinally? That is, what about all non-speculative philosophy? And what about the interrelations, if any, between speculative and non-speculative philosophy? These questions are among the questions which Hegel himself takes up in his Introduction to the *Essays*.

The *Essays* have a name for non-speculative philosophy: reflective philosophy. The term has here only an indirect connection with the various uses Kant assigned to 'reflection' and 'reflective' in *The Critique of Pure Reason* and *The Critique of Judgment*. Basically, Hegel uses it as Schelling had done in his *System of Transcendental Idealism* (1800), where reflection was what the second of the three "epochs" in the "history of self-consciousness" led to, reflection going hand in hand with analysis, both being opposed to the "productive intuition" and "synthesis" that characterize the first epoch. And Kant's philosophy was taken to be the typical culmination of the epoch of reflection. (The third epoch was that of "the absolute act of will.") But as no concept remained quite the same when Hegel took it up in his own thought, we can understand what Hegel meant by 'reflective philosophy' without discussing Schelling's view.

The distinction between reflective and speculative philosophy is not meant to be a distinction between different schools of philosophy. To Hegel, English empiricism from Locke on as well as continental rationalism (with the exception of Spinoza) were reflective philosophies. The whole philosophy of the Enlightenment was reflective. And so was most of Kant's transcendental idealism. Reflective philosophy is philosophy that has not come to the true conception of philosophy, philosophy that is not really philosophy—inauthentic philosophy over against authentic philosophy which is, and cannot but be speculative. In terms of the Kantian faculties, reflective philosophy is philosophy of the intellect (*der Verstand*), speculative philosophy is philosophy of Reason (*die Vernunft*), but of a Reason which has been allowed to trespass on territory Kant believed to be inaccessible to finite man. It is typical of reflective philosophy, though it does not exhaust its nature, that it relies on arguments, proofs, and the whole apparatus of logic, that it insists on clear-cut dichotomies in terms of abstract universals, dichotomies such as those of the infinite and the finite, subject and object, universal and particular, freedom and necessity, causality and teleology, etc., etc.; that it tries to solve intellectual puzzles rather than give the true conceptual vision of the whole; that it sticks to the natural sciences as the source of the only reliable knowledge of nature, thus committing itself, in the first place, to a concept of experience reduced to sense perception and to a concept of sense perception reduced to some causal chain, and in the second place, to a pervasive atomism that reduces the whole to the sum of its parts, and to a mechanism that excludes teleology from a positive role in cognition. No reflective philosophy need have all of these characteristics although any one of them would be the indication of a philosophy that has not reached the one authentic conception of philosophy.

Hence, any assault that reflective philosophy directs against speculative philosophy can be taken care of simply by pointing out that it is a reflective assault. Answering it by counterarguments would turn the speculative philosopher into a reflective one. What is wrong with the attack is that it is reflective; it is made in a style of doing philosophy that is not truly philosophical. Whatever the argument may be which a reflective philosopher uses against speculative philosophy, his very arguing shows that he is not really a philosopher. Contempt is the only answer to all reflective assaults. No dialogue is possible.

We shall soon observe that this is only one side of Hegel's attitude toward reflective philosophy. But before we come to the other side we may want to illustrate this conception of the relation between reflective and speculative philosophy by way of a contemporary parallel. I mean the relation between existentialism and analytic philosophy.

There can be no doubt at all that our own contemporary analytic philosophy, in its narrowest as well as in its widest meaning (which excludes only the existentialists, the Whiteheadians, and the Thomists), would be judged by Hegel to be a very typical reflective philosophy. There must be considerable doubt, however, whether or not Hegel would acknowledge existentialism to be speculative philosophy. From the viewpoint of the Philosophy of Identity, existentialism spoiled its chance of being authentic philosophy by concentrating not just on man but on man as condemned to finitude. And from the viewpoint of existentialism Hegel spoiled his chance of being the first modern existentialist when he permitted the urge that drove him into philosophy to find satisfaction in the more or less traditional apparatus of the Philosophy of Identity. Yet there are several aspects of existentialism in which the Hegel of the *Essays* could recognize himself. Besides the already mentioned motivational factor (one does not do philosophy to solve intellectual puzzles, though a positive version would have to have recourse to some colorless formula such as searching for meaning in a world become meaningless, which fits neither Hegel nor existentialism), Hegel would recognize his contempt for the philosophy of the intellect in existentialism's contempt for a civilization in which the empirical sciences and technology have become predominant and where philosophy has very largely become the handmaiden of science. He would recognize, as we already did, his distinction between reflective and speculative philosophy in the distinction so dear to existentialists, the distinction between what is authentic and what is inauthentic, between *eigentlich* and *uneigentlich*. And speculation itself, intellectual intuition as vision of the whole, has its analogue or rather, its subjective caricature in the cognitive function existentialists ascribe to moods, the mood of boredom, for example, being said to reveal the Whole of Being or Being as a Whole. In any case, whether or not existentialism is what speculative philosophy would have come to be in our own day, it is quite certain that the reaction existentialism has shown towards even the most devastating attacks launched against it by analytic philosophers is very much the same as the reaction of speculative philosophy towards reflective attacks. These attacks are attacks that need not be answered except by classifying them as analytic, that is, as basically unphilosophic, as philosophically inauthentic. From the side of existentialism no dialogue is possible between it and analytic philosophy, just as from the side of speculative philosophy no dialogue is possible between it and reflective philosophy. (From the side of analytic philosophy as from the side of reflective philosophy in general, the situation is of course quite different as they are committed to the idea of rational discourse. It seems to them incomprehensible that there are philosophies which in principle refuse to argue or, if they condescend to argue, know that they are lowering themselves to a pseudo-philosophical level.)

We had mentioned that the contempt for reflective philosophy will turn out to be only one side of Hegel's attitude toward reflective philosophy. To the reader of the *Essays* it may appear to be the most prominent part, as they abound with ferocious sarcasms directed at reflective philosophy in general and at this or that reflective philosopher in particular. Yet there is something authentically inauthentic, so to speak, about the very dichotomy of reflective and speculative philosophy. For like all the other dichotomies mentioned before, the dichotomy of reflective and speculative philosophy is itself typical of the style of reflective philosophy, and not at all typical of speculative philosophy, in which the reflective dichotomies are overcome in a vision of the organic whole that builds up its richness of harmony out of the tensions between its constituents. To be sure, unlike the reflective dichotomies separating the infinite from the finite, subject from object, freedom from necessity, etc., the dichotomy separating reflective from speculative philosophy is not a dichotomy *in* philosophy, but a dichotomy *about* philosophy, a second-level dichotomy. But this should make no difference at all; for meta-philosophy is itself an essential part of philosophy and the meta-philosophical dichotomy is philosophical—although Hegel should have called it a reflective philosophical dichotomy, a dichotomy which sets speculative philosophy the task of overcoming it as it is to overcome the first-level dichotomies that reflective philosophy prides itself of.

Here we reach the positive side of Hegel's attitude toward reflective philosophy. It is historical or at least, it is historical in a way. Only after reflective philosophy has gone through all its paces and realized its major possibilities can philosophy come into its own as speculative philosophy. The analytic gifts of the intellect must have bloomed and so made all the dichotomies of the time explicit before the bud (ever present?) of speculation can open up in its full glory. In particular, reflective philosophy must have reached the stage where it sees itself split into unsolvable antinomies and is forced into scepticism concerning the very problems that form its traditional core. It is at this historical point when philosophy despairs of metaphysics —as it does in Kant's Dialectic of Pure Reason—and forbids pure Reason to have any but a methodological ("regulative") role in cognition, that philosophy can and must come into its own as speculation. In Hegel's style of speculative philosophy this necessity is at once historical and conceptual—without much awareness of this reflective distinction. Rather it is taken for granted that the logical dependence of the concept of speculative philosophy—the overcoming of the dichotomies—on the concept of reflective philosophy is *eo ipso* a temporal sequence or, to express it in a somewhat different way, as if the teleological unfolding of philosophy is identical with the causal chain of historical events. (It needs no stressing that this sort of identification as it occurs in the *Essays,* is at the very heart of the later Hegel's elaborate and subtle historical dialectic.)

(In the *Essays* Hegel's view of the history of philosophy is rather ambivalent. At times he does seem to view the history of philosophy as leading "necessarily" in its last stages from reflective philosophy to speculative philosophy. At other times he seems to think that any philosophy which deserves the name is germinally speculative, but kept from knowing itself as such by the cultural situation in which it makes its appearance. Yet there is Spinoza, the great inspirator of the Philosophy of Identity. It seems difficult for either of these views to account for Spinoza's system appearing at the time when it did appear.)

There are two images that the *Essays* occasionally use for the relation between reflective and speculative philosophy, and they show how ambiguous Hegel's concept of this relation is. In one image, what philosophy is about is compared with a grove. To speculative philosophy the grove is where the god dwells. To reflective philosophy, the grove is a number of trees. In the other image, philosophy is compared with a temple. Speculative philosophy dwells in it, but reflective philosophy remains in the forecourt.

The first image appears to make the difference between reflective and speculative philosophy so radical as to exclude all relation, let alone dialogue, between them. Yet in his earlier theological writings Hegel also uses the image of the hallowed grove for the youthful organic and holistic culture of Hellas, in which nature and the divine were not yet split one from the other nor the individual from his community. If we remember this, then we may also interpret the hallowed grove image with respect to speculative philosophy in a dialectical way: reflective philosophy had to separate the sacred grove into its component trees so that in speculative philosophy the divine, the natural, and the rational could achieve consciousness of their unity.

Exactly the opposite holds for the other image, that of the temple and its forecourt. Obviously, if there is a forecourt one cannot enter the temple of speculative philosophy without passing through the forecourt of reflective philosophy. On the surface, then, the second image seems to be that of a necessary connection between reflective and speculative philosophy. But why does there have to be a forecourt at all? And in fact, Hegel stresses that there is no approach to speculative philosophy but a *salto mortale, à corps perdu,* by a jump that must be lethal to reflective philosophy if it is to be resurrected as speculation.

Besides the rather hedged-in admission that reflective philosophy had to run its full course before the true conception of authentic philosophy could arise, the *Essays* contain a second positive appraisal of reflective philosophy. For it would seem that Hegel concedes that the very language of speculative philosophy must for purposes of communication be to a large extent the language of reflective philosophy and even the language of ordinary discourse. There are certain indications that the writer of the *Essays* had already given considerable thought to the problem of how to communicate speculative philosophy. He is convinced that it should not be done *more geometrico*, not even in the very attenuated form in which it occurs in Fichte's *Science of Knowledge* and Schelling's publications up to 1801. This logical apparatus is hopelessly reflective. Nor would Hegel's own inclinations and logical gifts be appropriate to it. But then, how can speculation, extra-ordinary and extra-reflective as it is, be communicated at all? How can ordinary language and reflective philosophical discourse be made to do an extra-ordinary and non-reflective job? There is quite a similarity here between the speculative philosopher and Kierkegaard. Kierkegaard focused in on this sort of problem very early and his whole literary style is a deliberate answer to it, an answer full of astonishing deviousness. Even the most prejudiced Hegelian will have to admit, I think, that in this respect Kierkegaard was much the greater craftsman of the two. Hegel found the full measure of his style only in the *Phenomenology* (1807) when he was 37 years old, and it consisted mainly in various singular ways of adapting the grammar and terms of ordinary and reflective discourses to the presentation of an ever ongoing movement of concepts fed by dialectical tensions. Kierkegaard was an artful spider weaving intricate nets to catch his readers, Hegel a busy bird bravely bending and stretching the available material to build a fine nest for his dialectical eggs, and the reader be damned. Some of this bending and stretching can already be observed in the *Essays*. Hegel's style in the *Essays* was unlike that of anybody else then writing in German philosophy. This is not necessarily a praise, least of all in Hegel's own judgment, which condemns the idiosyncratic in philosophy. I am somewhat inclined to agree with those critics who say that the main stylistic rule of the *Essays* is this: the more complex the grammatical construction of a sentence and the less clear its meaning, the more speculative it will be. In any case, the uniqueness of his style in the *Essays* seems due less to any clear insight into how speculative philosophy should and could be communicated than to a rather tentative groping in many divergent directions of adapting the linguistic medium to speculative purposes. The reflective dichotomy, for example, of subject and object is overcome linguistically with Schelling's aid by way of the awkward formulas at the heart of the Philosophy of Identity: "the subjective Subject-Object" and "the objective Subject-Object." The latter is dealt with in the Philosophy of Nature, the former in the Transcendental Philosophy. The same procedure might have been used for the reflective dichotomy of the Infinite and the Finite, but neither Schelling nor Hegel does so, though they use "the finitely Infinite" and "the infinitely Finite," neither of which would indicate what it should: the overcoming of the dichotomy in the "identity" of the Infinite and the Finite. To speak of God in epistemological terms as Subject-Object must have seemed less iconoclastic and objectionable than to speak of Him as the Finite-Infinite. One shudders to think of Schelling and Hegel extending the symbolization of the identity of subject and object to other dichotomies such as those of freedom and necessity or causality and teleology.

Parenthetically we may note here that Hegel is rather flexible in relating these two basic dichotomies of subject and object and of the infinite and the finite to one another. Sometimes it is the subject that is infinite and the object finite, sometimes the other way around, a flexibility that only a philosophy contemptuous of reflective philosophy could allow itself.

In any event one has to keep in mind the whole glorious scheme of the Philosophy of Identity to give to the 'objective and subjective Subject-Object' the flesh and blood it seems to lack in the *Essays*. One must keep in mind, moreover, that these abstract identity formulas were alive with the existential agony felt by Hegel and his contemporaries and that the holistic passion at the living core of the Philosophy of Identity was fed by the alienation of the individual from nature, community (*das Volk*), and God.

Speculative philosophy, in sum, defends itself against the attacks of reflective philosophy by labelling the attacks reflective, and not by arguing with them—because it would then abandon itself as speculation and surrender to reflection. On the other hand, reflective philosophers, *cupidi rerum novarum*, see in the speculators an interesting new sort of monkey they would like to get better acquainted with. In fact, if the monkey could convince them that his system is not just another cage but what he claims it to be, the ultimate whole as known in the only sort of knowledge that deserves the name, the reflectors might in the end want to share the cage with him. But instead of trying to convince them in the style they expect from a philosopher, the monkey develops his *salto mortale* rhetoric which is as convincing as telling a healthy man that he must go through cancer of the brain in order to enjoy true health. So what can speculative philosophy actually do to convince reflective philosophy (as well as common sense and the general public) that it is what it claims to be?

Perhaps this is one of the problems, taken in its most catholic scope, that the *Phenomenology*, as the prolegomena to Hegel's system, was later intended to answer. In the *Essays* the answer is an inaudible sigh of regret joined with an affirmation of hope. The sigh of regret: if only THE speculative system existed, not in fragments and sketches as in Schelling, but as an organic whole detailed in its totality! The affirmation of hope: once this system exists, the spirit of the time will reach out toward it, its time will have come, *es wird sein Glueck machen.*[5] For civilization is longing to be cured of the dichotomies that rend it and that reflective philosophy had the task of bringing into the open.

And the spirit did reach out toward it. However, it was not in the Philosophy of Identity that the spirit recognized itself, not in Schelling and not in the Hegel of the *Essays.* It recognized itself in the Hegel of the *Phenomenology*, the *Logic* and the *Philosophy of History.* In them, speculative philosophy, though greatly changed, fulfilled its promises, and died (except in England, where religion found a strong ally in it, and in Italy, where liberalism was the ally and where national pride could claim Vico to be St. John the Baptist to Hegel, the savior).

After all is said and done it must yet be admitted that the *Essays,* notwithstanding Hegel's unwillingness to let speculative philosophy descend to the level of reflective philosophy, give not only a speculative judgment on reflective philosophy, but also a reflective approach of sorts to speculative philosophy. Contemptuous of the forecourt of the temple, the *Essays* manage just the same to spend much time and effort in it—just as Michelangelo did in *la bella rusticana,* the little Quattrocento church on the hills of Florence whose simple static harmonies he was in need of as a foil for the complex dynamic tensions of his own revolutionary style.

IV· INTELLECTUAL INTUITION

We might begin in a cavalier fashion by saying that intellectual intuition furnishes the evidences on which the Philosophy of Identity is built. In saying this we are, however, already victims of reflective philosophy. For the concept of "being based upon . . ." involves some logical relation pertaining to induction or deduction, as if intellectual intuition either furnished the evidences that could verify or falsify the truth claims of statements, or were some set of self-evident axioms at the basis of a body of theorems. In the former case the Philosphy of Identity would be an empirical science with an exceedingly strange sort of evidence as its experiential ground. In the latter case it would be like geometry as traditionally conceived, and hence subject to the threat of the Kantian question whether the apriority of the axioms is analytic or synthetic; and if synthetic a priori, the possibility of their objective reference would have to be made intelligible. But this whole apparatus remains of course in the forecourt of the temple of philosophy and is, or should be, foreign to speculative philosophy—which dwells in the temple itself.

We have already suggested that intellectual intuition became, in Schelling and Hegel, the vision of the whole, a vision in which God, nature, and self-consciousness (or reason) come into their truth. Spinoza's *scientia sub specie æternitatis* becomes *scientia sub specie totalitatis atque harmoniæ*. (In the following generations this vision of the whole will be degraded to *Weltanschauung*, leading to the relativization not only of moral and æsthetic standards but also of the basic theoretical categories, emerging as sociology of sorts in France, and in Germany as Dilthey's typology of *Weltanschaungen*.) Kant, however, had surely meant by intellectual intuition something quite different from this vision of the whole. And he had clearly and decisively disallowed intellectual intuition to have any positive role in human cognition. How was it then that intellectual intuition turned into this holistic vision and organized itself into something that claimed to be THE system of knowledge under the name of the Philosophy of Identity?

I shall let Schelling and Hegel speak for themselves, letting them talk *univoce* without drawing a line between what Schelling said and what Hegel said. Nor shall I draw a line between what they did say and what they might have said. It must of course not be assumed that the way they understand Kant is my own way.

What the speculators said and might have said to Kant is this:

"You admit that the concept of an intuitive intellect or intellectual intuition harbors no logical contradictions and that therefore there could be such a thing as intellectual intuition; but you also assert that as a matter of fact human beings do not possess it. For the basic way in which anything can be knowable to us as an object of experience is by its being given to us, and the only way in which it can be given to us is by its becoming a datum to our senses: it must cause a sensation in us. Having sensations, however, is very different from having knowledge. So you bridge the gap between having sensations and having knowledge by an impressive analysis of the apparatus which our sensibility and the reason (*der Verstand*) contribute on their own account to the objectivity of possible objects of experience. We say '*our* sensibility' and '*the* reason' because you do play with the idea of non-human subjects whose sensibility might have forms different from those human sensibility has. And you do *not* play with the idea of rational beings whose forms of judgment and therewith categories might be different from those of man. This is part of your Stoic background, about which more later. Sensibility contributes (the forms of) space and time; reason contributes twelve basic concepts in accordance with the twelve forms of judgment and, dependent on the categories and their schematization, your twelve 'principles of the pure understanding.' In consequence, what you allow us to have knowledge of in our experience are not the things as they are in themselves but only as they affect us, that is, as they appear to us. You revel in the dichotomy of things in themselves— which are unknowable to us—and their appearances—which are all we are ever permitted to know. Even what you call our synthetic a priori knowledge such as mathematics does not reach beyond the possible objects of experience.

"If we examine the nature of your prejudice against intellectual intuition more closely we find it to be rooted in dubious psychology, theological dogma, and the procedures of the natural sciences. To begin with the last, you state that the knowledge claims of the natural sciences are well founded to the extent that their judgments, from statements of observation to the most general theories, can be tested empirically, that is, by perception; and perception, according to the causal theory of perception which you unquestionably accept, has as its basic stratum visual, acoustic, and similar sensations. So the triumphant course of the natural sciences since Galileo and Newton over against the debacle of the metaphysical knowledge claims of the rationalists leads you to assert that we must claim no knowlege of any object, ourselves included, that cannot be related in certain prescribed ways to something that is given to us either in externally or in internally perceptual experience. (The prescribed ways in which any object we claim to know must be related to what is sensuously given to us are spatial, temporal and those formulated in your principles of the pure understanding.)

"The lesson which the natural sciences taught you goes beautifully hand in hand with your theological bias. This is your conviction of the inescapable finitude of rational man. You find the index of this finitude in the fact that objects can be known to us if and only if they (a) affect our sensibility and (b) conform to the spontaneously imposed conditions of our intellect. Our sensibility is merely passive and our spontaneity is limited to the mere forms of objectivity. Over against this doubly finite relation of the human subject to the objects of his cognitive experiences you conceive of a kind of knowledge which is spontaneity all through. There would be no receptivity in it at all and spontaneity would not be limited to the mere forms. This is what you call intellectual intuition. It is divine creativity seen in the perspective of your epistemological and psychological presuppositions.

"Your psychological presuppositions have already come to the fore. Man has the capacity to receive sensations, and you call this receptivity sensibility. This is one psychological stem from which knowledge grows. The other is the faculty of freely forming concepts, combining them in judgments, and combining judgments in syllogisms. This is reason. What sort of psychology is this? If it were rational psychology à la Wolff and Baumgarten, you yourself would have destroyed it in the Paralogism section of your Dialectic of Pure Reason. If it were empirical psychology you would seem to have founded, at least in part, your explanation of the possibility of empirical knowledge on empirical knowledge and this is hardly a convincing foundation.

"Besides, there is the basic contradiction that you got yourself into. Jacobi summed it up when he said that without the thing-in-itself one cannot get into *The Critique of Pure Reason* and with the thing-in-itself one cannot stay in it. What is it that causes the sensations in us? This cause of our sensations cannot be found in the objects of our experiences, whether we mean by the objects of our experiences ordinary objects like trees and houses or scientific objects like gravity and atoms.[6] The objects of our experiences cannot be the causes of our sensations, for according to your own theory the possibility of any object is rooted in the forms of our sensibility and the forms of the intellect having shaped the sensuous material. So the X that causes the sensation must be the thing-in-itself unknowably hidden behind the veil of appearances. But in making the thing-in-itself the cause of our sensations you have done what is *verboten* by your own *Critique*. You have applied one of the categories, the category of causality, to the thing-in-itself. It is inconceivable in terms of your theory that the thing-in-itself causes sensations. One could more easily receive a letter from outer space, even one written in English.

"Now what would you say if we show you that you yourself un-knowingly make intellectual intuition the ultimate basis of all knowledge claims that you consider soundly grounded? We are of course referring to your transcendental apperception, the 'I think,' of which you say that it is the highest point to which must be fastened the applicability of the categories to time (and space), therewith the possibility of experiencing objects and therewith the possibility of objects of experience. For according to your first *Critique* the unity of nature as the totality of all possible objects of experience depends in the last analysis on the unity of the I in its synthetizing categorial acts of thinking. But precisely in making the thinking I the highest point you give it the characteristic that is definitory of intellectual intuition. To think oneself as thinking—pure self-consciousness—is to *give* oneself existence as pure I. Your transcendental apperception lives up to your own concept of intellectual intuition. You have overcome your dichotomy of receptivity—in which objects are given—and spontaneity—in which they are thought. The pure Ego gives itself to itself in the pure act of thinking itself as thinking. This is how it exists. Naturally, 'existence' does not have the meaning it ordinarily has. It does not have anything to do with being localizable in time and space, which is the reason why the I must not be said to create itself. Fichte prefers to speak of the Ego 'positing' itself. We use 'constructing,' others 'constituting.'

"Your transcendental apperception, however, does not only overcome your dichotomy of receptivity and spontaneity. It also is the beginning of a synthesis of your two most radical and basic opposites, that of the subject and object and that of the infinite and the finite.

"As to the dichotomy of subject and object, it is seen at once that the 'I think' of the pure apperception—the I that thinks itself as thinking—is at the same time both subject and object, or as we prefer to say, the identity of subject and object. *Nous noei heauton.* This, though, is Aristotle. The Greek roots of your philosophy are Stoic rather than Platonic or Aristotelian. So were those of Rousseau, whom you so admired. The light that gave the Enlightenment its name was the *lumen naturale*, the Stoic spark of reason, the representative part of divine reason in all rational beings making them all free, equal, and brothers, as the French Revolution concluded.

"The metaphysical rationalism of Stoicism also forms the hidden background of your transcendental apperception. For the 'I' of your 'I think' is not at all that of any I-saying individual, who is no less appearance than the objects he experiences. One might rather say that the I of the pure apperception is that of the Leibnizian monad which, as the I-in-itself, is hidden behind the subject as it appears to itself. This monadological background of the pure apperception would seem to be undeniable. Yet it must not ever be forgotten that the monadic subject-in-itself is given, in the spirit of the age, the features of the Stoic spark of reason, the same divine reason in each rational individual. So there is occasion for a secret tug-of-war between the Leibnizian and the Stoic background. In any event, at the bottom of your *Critique* there is the Stoic philosophy of identity. It is a very limited one in comparison with ours. It excludes all of nature. For though divine reason is said by Stoic metaphysic to rule over nature, the laws of nature being decrees issued by it, Stoicism does not allow divine reason to be present inside nature as the unconscious urge driving it toward the emergence of self-consciousness. Thus your Stoic identity is limited to the divine reason ruling the universe and its representative sparks residing in human individuals, and through that very residence standing in constant danger of being infringed and becoming polluted. To this extent, then, and only to this extent, your transcendental apperception is also the overcoming of the finite-infinite dichotomy. Without this Stoic identity between infinite and finite reason, each monadic subject would have its own world and you would have to appeal to the hypothesis of a preestablished harmony to explain the illusion of a world shared by all. You would not be able to explain that our experience, instead of being a flux of private sensations, gives us knowledge of a common world. On the other hand, your monadological background might have permitted you a more subtle way of accounting for the prepersonal individuation of the sparks of reason—of the indexing function of the I of the transcendental apperception—than Stoicism itself would have been able to do. In either case, though, for either monad or spark of reason the use of language, in any of the customary senses of 'language,' is a disquieting problem, though not within the Philosophy of Identity as it knows God's becoming man.

"Here we must return for a moment to what we have said about your overcoming of the subject-object dichotomy. For the 'I think' of your transcendental apperception is not just the Ego's thinking itself as thinking—and thus in this very narrow sense the identity of subject and object. Your 'I think' is an incomplete expression. You yourself stress that what the I thinks are the categories and through them the twelve principles of the pure understanding to which the objectivity of the objects of our experience is due. 'I think the categories' is, in terms of our Philosophy of Identity, a formula for the identity of that part of the subject which you call *Verstand* and the form of objectivity. In claiming that the twelve principles are the conditions furnished by reason which allow our experience to be of objects you may also claim, as we would express it, the identity of the rational self with the form of objectivity.

"In sum, then, your transcendental apperception is indeed intellectual intuition unilaterally defined from the perspective of the dichotomy of receptivity and spontaneity as the overcoming of this dichotomy. At the same time, however, and again without your recognizing the fact, the transcendental apperception is the very limited overcoming of the dichotomies of the subject and object and of the infinite and the finite that your philosophy allows. And intellectual intuition does all this right at the most crucial point of your philosophy, where you deny the possibility of intellectual intuition to the finite beings men are. From all this we conclude that your concept of intellectual intuition is much too narrow. Intellectual intuition must be conceived as the construction of the identity underlying all the dichotomies you reflectors have been proud of establishing, and particularly the subject-object and infinite-finite dichotomies. It is this enlarged concept of intellectual intuition which we call speculation and which thus becomes the holistic vision of the complex identity of subject and object and of the infinite and the finite or—in terms that join these basic dichotomies—of God, nature and self-consciousness.

"Transcendental apperception as intellectual intuition, however, is not the only motive in your Critical Idealism that leads directly into the speculation of our Philosophy of Identity. We have always been fascinated by an aside of yours that you let slip in an unguarded moment. This is your remark that perhaps the two stems of our cognitive faculties, sensibility and reason, have the same root.[7] You must have had in mind something like an unconscious intellectual intuition, an identity of receptivity and spontaneity prior to their reflective separation. We think we are justified in seeing this as an anticipation of the unconscious God revealing Himself in nature. For one inspired moment you came close to our philosophy of nature.

"We also like to connect this aside of yours with your equally inspired conception of the role of productive imagination in your Transcendental Deduction of the Categories. The role productive imagination is given in your Deduction is that of synthetizing the pure manifold of time in accordance with the rules as which the categories function in the objectification of experience. Pure imagination, as the great synthetizer, is the mediator between time and the categories. It does not seem to us far-fetched to see in the role you ascribe to imagination an anticipation of the speculative construction of the identity of these opposites. Productive imagination, instead of merely putting two different pieces in an external unity, is their inner unity, their 'common root' raised from its unconscious pre-reflective status to post-reflective awareness.

"The role you ascribe to productive imagination in your Deduction anticipates our speculative philosophy, or is at least a step in the right direction, also with respect to the finite-infinite dichotomy. For in overcoming through productive imagination your own rigorous confrontation of receptivity and spontaneity, you are also undoing, however cautiously and limitedly, your stubborn insistence on the finitude of man. And at the same time you are advancing beyond the Stoic philosophy of identity with its restriction to the sparks of reason as the only divine element in man. To be sure, you still exclude the sense data from the Ego's productivity. It was Fichte to whom we owe this giant step. But in making productive imagination the great synthetizer you have given to the pure Ego, at least within the cognitive sphere, a spontaneity that goes far beyond the mere thinking of the categories. The Ego is now coming close to being a 'finitely infinite.' By the same token you have transcended the limitations of your Stoic background. To the Stoic reason which is pure thought you have added productive imagination to do the work which reason cannot do, the work of synthetizing the pure manifold of time. Though there is no labor involved in this sort of work, it is at least doing something while the pure manifold of time, on the left of productive imagination, and the pure thinking of the categories, on its right, are in one sense and another not doing anything at all. You have gone beyond the contemplative god of Stoicism; yet you have not come closer to the active God of Christianity.

"In your theoretical philosophy God functions as a merely methodological rule in the ongoing business of exploring the world: do not ever stop exploring. In your practical philosophy God is a postulate, though a necessary one, to guarantee justice in distributing blessings according to deserts. Your Stoicism turns Judaic in the moral sphere. You totally separate reason and the universal moral law grounded in it from the beautiful sphere of human passions. Moreover you are unable to explain how the universal moral law can actually function as such in human life and you admit that even if it does no one can ever be sure that it is doing so. This is what the Father, the Son and the Holy Spirit have come to in your philosophy. Your hidden metaphysical Stoicism is Hellas' revenge on Christianity.

"We regret to have to say this. Our Philosophy of Identity has as much of the Christian God as any metaphysic can possibly have that claims to be knowledge. You must not suspect us of being frivolous when we see the total relationship of God, nature and self-consciousness in analogy with the Father, the Son and the Holy Spirit.[8]

"But quite apart from this somewhat esoteric analogy taken from the tradition of Christian theology—not for nothing did we spend years in the *Stift* in Tübingen—speculation achieves its overcoming of all the basic reflective dichotomies in the organistically conceived vista of THE WHOLE as presented in the Philosophy of Identity. Its Philosophy of Nature deals with the objective Subject-Object, whose unconscious self-revelatory dynamics replaces your dichotomy of the thing-in-itself and its appearances. The Transcendental Philosophy deals with the subjective Subject-Object and solves the problems, unsolvable within your Critical Idealism, of the relation of the pure apperception to God on the one hand, and to the (logico-historical) development of rationality in man on the other. The God who reveals Himself in nature is not, as such, the God who comes to know Himself as having revealed himself in nature. That God He becomes only in the evolution of human rationality. Man's re-construction of God's creativity in nature is thus itself a chapter—the last one?—of God's creation of Himself.

"It surely cannot be said against our system with its superb balance of idealism and realism that there is still a vestige of an idealistic imbalance in it because the Philosophy of Nature was not written by nature itself but had to wait for the birth and development of rationality in man. One could just as well talk about an imbalance in favor of realism in that the whole ascending chain of God's unconscious revelations in nature was needed to bring forth that rationality in man which becomes the instrument of God's knowledge of Himself.

"To use an analogy which is not at all congenial to us but may become fashionable someday, your *Critique* sets new rules for the game of METAPHYSICS. Yours is a game somewhat like tennis. The ball must always pass above the net of empirical statements. The game begins with a rally in which the ball must hit the ground in the narrow part of the area that you call the synthetic a priori, namely, that part of the synthetic a priori that gives 'the conditions of the possibility of objects of experience.' This is the rally of meta-metaphysics. Once this rally is over and the properly metaphysical part of the game begins, the ball must hit the ground in the area of analytic judgments and logical inferences and, strangely enough, also in an area adjacent to the synthetic a priori but having certain empirical ingredients—as in your *Metaphysische Anfangsgründe der Naturwissenschaft* (1786) and *Die Metaphysik der Sitten* (1797). We say, strangely enough,' for after you had drawn a line of absolute opposition between the empirical and the a priori you yet proceed as if there were a gradual transition from one to the other. This may very well serve as another example of your overcoming your own dichotomies; but it is not of the same interest to us as the examples of the transcendental apperception and productive imagination.

"Our game is quite different: it is rather like doing a jigsaw puzzle. Directed perhaps by what we retain from the picture when we first saw it before it was taken apart, we reconstruct it by finding the proper place for each part within the whole, the only rule being that we have to follow faithfully the outline of each part so that they fit together as their maker meant them to. There is only one solution to the jigsaw puzzle, and it is ours.

"From the viewpoint of our system as a whole your *Critique of Judgment* with its discussion of the role of teleology in cognition is almost as important to us as your first *Critique*. For the process as which we see the whole cannot but be teleological, and so we had to undo your typically reflective position with respect to teleology in your *Critique of Judgment*. However, as we aim in this speech of ours to show the germs of true speculation in your philosophy, we have no reason to go into your treatment of teleology where you stubbornly insist on the finitude of human cognition. (Just the same, we wish to advise anyone who wants to understand our Philosophy of Identity from the inside out to study carefully the Critique of the Teleological Judgment—Part II of the *Critique of Judgment*—and particularly §§ 74–78.)

"However, there is one famous remark of yours that we wish to comment on. You are convinced that there never will be a Newton able to explain as little as the origin of a blade of grass according to laws of nature that were not arranged by design (*Absicht*)[9]. In other words, you believe the biological realm to be ultimately impervious to that atomistic-mechanistic approach that is celebrating triumph after triumph in physics and chemistry. And yet at the same time you seem to resign yourself to the fact that biology as science has no choice but to use the methods of physics and chemistry as far as they can go, and beyond that point there is no knowledge that is scientific. This is absurd. To us biology in its largest sense is truly theogony and instead of reducing it as much as possible to physics and chemistry we extend to the subjects of physics and chemistry the holistic and dynamic vision of theogonic biology.

"May we now talk to you about Fichte, your erstwhile disciple and our erstwhile mentor and friend. Knowing how he annoyed you with his interpretation of your first *Critique*, we shall talk about him only for a moment, though we have much to say about him in the *Essays*.

"We have already mentioned the importance of his translating your 'I think' into 'The Ego posits himself.' This translation made it clear to us that your transcendental apperception is intellectual intuition. Prompted by us, Fichte accepted this. The ultimate basis of your *Critique* and his *Science of Knowledge* is intellectual intuition. His second important merit was his radical elimination of the thing-in-itself, although others had seen its paradoxical role in your idealism before him. He eliminated it, in the first place, through the Ego's second *Tathandlung*: the Ego posits the non-Ego. However, this would not take him any further than your own grounding of the form of objectivity in the subject. The step that leads him radically beyond your 'formal' idealism is his showing that the sensations themselves, far from being caused by the thing-in-itself, as well as their spatial and temporal relations, are doings, though unconscious ones, of the Ego. The historical merit of this doctrine is that it is so paradoxical. Thinking our way through the paradox greatly assisted us in bringing to birth the true system of philosophy. The paradox as presented from the side of the object of knowledge, that is, from the side of nature, consists in the fact that Fichte's doctrine totally de-naturalizes nature so that nature becomes even less than it is in your philosophy. In the *Critique* nature is mere appearance, but it is the appearance of something that is, the thing-in-itself, even though it is unknowable to us and not even definable as to the sense in which it can be said to be. The paradox from the side of the subject is that the Ego has lost your index of its finitude, for it is all spontaneity. Yet it is not allowed to be God nor is *The Science of Knowledge* allowed to be a text about God's acquiring knowledge of Himself. Fichte's third *Tathandlung* posits the definite finalization of the Ego: the Ego's aspirations to become one with God will be fulfilled only in the infinitely distant future, that is to say, they will never be fulfilled.

"Over and against the Fichtean idealism, completely one-sided and perhaps rightly denounced as atheistic, we plead with you to see the profound balance and harmony, based on the speculative viewing of the relations among God, nature and self-consciousness, of our Philosophy of Identity, in which nature is as truly existent in God as God is subsistent in self-consciousness."

Kant had received his guests in his bedroom, seated in a chair by a closed window. When Schelling and Hegel finished with their plea Kant appeared to be asleep. The year is 1803 and he is sick and a little senile. He will die the following year, two years after the publication of the second of Hegel's *Essays.* (*Post hoc*, but not *propter hoc*—although if Kant had read the *Essays*, they might have shortened his life.) The silence continues. Hegel turns rather brusquely toward the door. He finds the stale air in the room oppressive. (Kant did not allow windows to be opened as he believed that bed bugs, which had been torturing him for years, fly in through the window.[10]) Schelling bows elegantly in the direction of Kant. It is then that Kant gets up from his chair with great effort, holding himself by the table next to his chair and, slowly returning the bow, mutters, "I honor humanity in you."[11] Schelling, quite touched, answers with a charming smile, "Sir, we honor divinity in you." He rushes to help the faltering Kant into his chair. But the old man does not want help. And Schelling, bowing once more, follows Hegel into the hall, leaving the great reflector to his bugs.

Walter Cerf

1. Cf. below, pp. XXIV ff.

2. *Ideen zu einer Philosophie der Natur als Einleitung in das Studium dieser Wissenschaft (1797). Von der Weltseele (1798). Erster Entwurf eines Systems der Naturphilosophie (1799). Einleitung zu dem Entwurf eines Systems der Naturphilosophie (1799).*

3. *System des Transcendentalen Idealismus (1800).*

4. First published by H. Nohl in 1907 and in large part translated by T. M. Knox and R. Kroner in 1948 (see Bibliographical Index).

5. See below, p. 82. Also *F & K*, p. 55.

6. These two sorts of objects, the ordinary and the scientific, were at that time not yet so different from one another as to cause much of a problem concerning their relation.

7. *Critique of Pure Reason*, A15, B29.

8. See H. S. Harris' Introduction, p. 22.

9. *Critique of Judgment*, § 75.

10. Hermann Schwarz, *Immanuel Kant, Ein Lebensbild* (Halle a.S., 1907), p. 269.

11. Ibid., p. 378. In the spirit of this imaginary scene I have taken some liberties with the passages in Prof. Schwarz' book.

Note on the Text
and on Conventions

THE TEXT:

Two editions of the text were used in making this translation: that of
Georg Lasson (Philosophische Bibliothek, Leipzig: F. Meiner, 1928;
reprinted, Hamburg, 1962), and that of Hartmut Buchner and Otto
Pöggeler (*Gesammelte Werke*, Band 4, Hamburg: Meiner, 1968). The
latter was taken as basic, and the pagination of this authoritative
critical edition is indicated in square brackets in the translation.

THE TREATMENT OF HEGEL'S QUOTATIONS

When Hegel quotes from other authors, he rarely uses quotation
marks. We have added quotation marks wherever we were able to
trace the quotation (a task which has generally been made easy by
the editors of the two German texts that we have used). In the relatively rare cases where Hegel himself used quotation marks we indicate this in the footnotes.

But whether they are marked by him or by us, Hegel's quotations
from other authors are apt, like those of most other (German?) authors of the period, to fall short of perfect scholarly precision. He
rarely marks his omissions. We have marked his unacknowledged
elisions by inserting "[. . .]". Also, Hegel's emphases are almost always different from those of the original text quoted. Here, we have
not tried to be precise ourselves. Instead of noting every change in
emphasis we rest content with a general warning to the reader that the
emphases in quotations are usually Hegel's, and not those of the author quoted. Other major deviations are indicated in our footnotes.
Occasionally we have also furnished a translation of the original text
from which Hegel's quotations and summaries are taken.

Abbreviations and References:

    The following abbreviations are employed regularly:

    F. & K.=*Faith and Knowledge,* translated by Walter Cerf and H. S. Harris, Albany: State University of New York Press, 1977.

    N.K.A.=Hegel, *Gesammelte Werke,* Hamburg: Meiner, 1968 ff.

    Akad.=*Kants Gesammelte Schriften,* herausgegeben von der Königlich Preussischen Akademie der Wissenschaften, Berlin.

Other references in the notes are usually confined to the author (editor, translator) and short title where needed. The Bibliographic Index supplies the full details of the work cited.

Concerning the use of the dagger (†), see the Translators' Preface.

Introduction to the *Difference* Essay

1. FICHTE, SCHELLING, AND HEGEL

The essay on the *Difference between Fichte's and Schelling's System of Philosophy* was Hegel's first acknowledged publication.[1] He wrote it between the middle of May (probably) and the middle of July (certainly) in the year 1801. It appeared at the end of September, just a month after his thirty-first birthday.[2] For Hegel it represented the first step toward a professional academic career which he had long desired.

At the dawn of the new century, 1 January 1801, Hegel was thirty. He had not achieved anything very remarkable in the world, and no one could have foreseen his later eminence.[3] He came from a family which had spawned teachers, preachers and minor civil servants in the Duchy of Württemberg for several generations. His father was a relatively unimportant financial official in the Stuttgart administration. The youthful Wilhelm showed a scholarly bent from the first. At the Stuttgart Gymnasium he was always at the top of his class, and out of school he read widely and voraciously, always with pen in hand, making copious excerpts and notes. The family expected that he would make his career in the churches or schools of his homeland, and this became a legal obligation when he entered the Theological Seminary at Tübingen as a stipendiary of Duke Karl Eugen of Wurttemberg in 1788.

News of the Revolution in Paris stirred the even tenor of his scholarly way before he achieved his MA in the Faculty of Philosophy in 1790. He rebelled against the prospect of three years of formal study in theology, and tried, unsuccessfully, to persuade his father to let him transfer to law. A theologian he had to be; but a career in the Church he was still determined to avoid. When he graduated in 1793 he applied to the Consistory at Stuttgart for permission to take a teaching post abroad. With their consent he became house-tutor to the children of the von Steiger family in Berne. There he remained for more than three years, meditating on classical antiquity and on the origin and history of Christianity. These meditations continued after he moved to a similar position with a merchant family in Frankfurt at the beginning of 1797. But at Frankfurt he was once more in company with the poet Hölderlin—who had been in his class at Tübingen—and with a group of young men for whom the study of the new idealist philosophy of Fichte was part of an active preparation for a German Revolution. Hegel himself had predicted in his letters from Switzerland that the proper "completion" of the Kantian philosophy would lead to a revolution in German life, and all of his intellectual labours in these years are best understood as contributions to this "completion" of Kant in preparation for the revolution.

From Switzerland he watched the boy-wonder, Schelling—five years younger, yet only two years behind him in the Seminary—take the first steps of what was clearly destined to be a brilliant academic career. Schelling's first published philosophy essay appeared in 1794 when he was in his last year at Tübingen, and still under twenty. In that essay—"On the Possibility of a Form of Philosophy in General"[4] —and in several subsequent ones, Schelling stood forth as a talented and enthusiastic disciple of Fichte. But gradually he moved into an independent position, largely because of his excited interest in the speculative philosophy of nature. Fichte remained decidedly cool toward this aspect of his young champion's work, but it soon attracted the favorable notice of Goethe. In August 1798 Schelling was appointed as an extraordinary professor of Philosophy at Jena, which could at that period properly be called the intellectual capital of Germany.[5]

This was only a few months after the death of Hegel's father—an event which gave Hegel both a small legacy, and the freedom to make plans for its spending which his father might well have frowned at. Not that Hegel did anything very precipitate. For more than eighteen months he continued quietly working at his religious and political essays. When he finally wrote to Schelling in November 1800 that he was now ready to embark on an academic career, and asking advice about where he should spend the next few months before applying for a license to teach at Jena, Hegel was probably hoping for the response that he must certainly have received—an invitation to come straight to Jena, and prepare himself on the spot.

Even after he arrived in Jena, and settled in comfortably, next door to Schelling in the Klipstein Garden, Hegel continued to work for some time on his political studies rather than on anything directly relevant to his career as a philosophy lecturer.[6] It may very likely have been Schelling who urged him to set his revolutionary labors aside and concentrate on something more strictly philosophical. Perhaps he even suggested the topic of the *Difference* essay. We can be sure, at least, that Hegel discussed the project at length with Schelling, when he embarked upon it. For Hegel appeared on the scene at Jena, and was accepted there, as a disciple and coadjutor of Schelling. In the *Difference* essay itself, it is plain that he accepted this role. But he had been following his own way ever since he was eighteen, and although he continually took over new concepts and vocabulary from friends whom he thought of as more advanced in the study of philosophy than himself, he consistently sought to apply the new concepts to his own problems and uses.[7]

Toward Fichte, Hegel had always been rather cool. In his Frankfurt years he was much influenced by Hölderlin, whose purely philosophical fragments show that he was moving toward a type of "Identity-philosophy" as early as 1795. Like Schelling, Hölderlin derived the basic conceptual apparatus for his new position from Fichte. Hölderlin's friend Sinclair—from whose notes we get most of our knowledge of Hölderlin's position at this period—was later characterized by Hegel himself as a "stubborn Fichtean."[8] But the loyalty of Hölderlin and his friends to Fichte was of the same kind as Fichte's loyalty to Kant. It was the sense of an intellectual debt that was to be paid precisely by *transforming* the ideas one had received.

This sort of loyal affiliation tends to be embarrassing, and hence irritating, to the intellectual father figure who is the object of it. Just as Kant had been driven to denounce publicly Fichte's claim to be his true and genuine intellectual heir,[9] so Fichte would finally have been obliged to denounce Schelling in the same way. But in this case Schelling's new "disciple" Hegel proclaimed the apostasy first. The immediate effect of Hegel's *Difference* essay was to make a public breach between Fichte and Schelling, a breach which both parties had so far managed to avoid, and which Schelling still strove to avoid for a time even after Hegel's essay appeared.[10]

2. HEGEL AND THE PHILOSOPHY OF IDENTITY

We cannot be very sure or precise about Hegel's own philosophical position immediately before he arrived in Jena and made himself the champion of what he calls "the Schellingian System." He *did* have a position; and we can be fairly certain that it was spelled out at some length in an essay that he finished in September 1800. But only two sheets (about one twentieth of the whole) remain to us from that essay; and these two sheets—generally referred to as the *Systemfragment*—are not easy to interpret.[11] But three conclusions do seem to be fairly clearly warranted: First, that Hegel held that it was the task of philosophical reflection to overcome or resolve antinomies; secondly, that philosophy cannot bring this task to completion, but must in the end pass over into a higher form of consciousness called religion; and thirdly, that a religious consciousness that does not rise to this higher level, but remains within the bounds of reflection, will be "positive," that is, will involve alienation and authority. In the final paragraphs of his manuscript Hegel used Fichte's theory of the Ego as an example to demonstrate this point.[12]

It is probably fair to say that Hegel became a disciple of Schelling at Jena because Schelling's philosophy of Identity provided him with a bridge across the gulf that he had discovered between theoretical reflection with its Kantian antinomies, and the "beautifully humane" religion in which the infinite and the finite are perfectly reconciled. Because the philosophy of Identity is founded in "intellectual intuition," the gulf between finite reflection and the infinite that is the goal experience in religion does not arise. The principal difficulty that the new philosophy faced lay in the explication of the intuitive foundation to which it laid claim. How can it be the case that we enjoy a kind of awareness which seemed to Kant to be quite evidently out of our range altogether?

Schelling took the first step toward the new philosophy while he was still an orthodox disciple of Fichte. It was probably he who convinced Fichte that the self-positing of the Ego (in the *Science of Knowledge* of 1794) was an intellectual intuition as defined by Kant in § 77 of the *Critique of Judgment*. But this self-intuition of the Ego was only a kind of leap across the gulf between finite and infinite that troubled Hegel. It leaves finite experience behind altogether. The real breakthrough came when Schelling went on to claim in the "Exposition of My System" (1801) that the Ego of Fichte was intuitively identical with the "God or Nature" of Spinoza.

As we can see from his references to Spinoza in the *Science of Knowledge*, Fichte regarded Spinoza as the paradigm of "dogmatic philosophy."[13] A consistent dogmatism must arrive at the morally unbearable position of fatalism because it must posit universal causal determinism. In Fichte's eyes Spinoza was the one dogmatic philosopher who could not be theoretically overthrown because he recognized and accepted this conclusion. The achievement of the Critical Philosophy, as systematized and completed by Fichte himself, was to exhibit the viability of an alternative philosophy of moral freedom. But the decision between the alternatives was essentially a moral choice, not a logical conclusion. To Fichte's young disciples who moved on to a "philosophy of Identity," this absolute option between dogmatic rationalism and moral idealism appeared as the final form of precritical dogmatism in Fichte himself. The antinomy between Spinoza's doctrine of necessity and Fichte's doctrine of freedom must somehow be resolved in a higher synthesis. Hölderlin seems to have been the first to move in this direction; and much of Hegel's speculation at Frankfurt was carried on in the context of this problem. Before he arrived in Jena Hegel seems to have held that there was no *theoretical* solution, but that the problem is resolved *practically* in religious experience. Schelling's "System of Absolute Identity" provided a theoretical solution by claiming to exhibit a perfect parallel between the philosophy of nature as the non-conscious production of objective reality by Reason, and transcendental philosophy as the conscious self-construction of Reason as the absolute subject. What is "intellectually intuited" (that is, revealed to itself in the very process of its genesis) is neither Spinoza's Substance nor Fichte's Ego (Subject) but an infinite *life* which is at once Substance and Subject; and the intuition does not involve a leap *out of* all finite categories, because in the philosophical system the categories of finite experience are themselves exhibited as a chain of successive "powers" of the Absolute Identity.

If we look at this programme from the point of view of Hegel when he finished the manuscript from which the above mentioned "System-fragment" is all that now remains, we can readily see that what would have attracted him about it was the project of grasping objective nature and subjective experience as an articulated whole. The articulation must not be *endless*, and there must be some means of demonstrating that it is *complete*. Otherwise he would be no better off than he was already. This explains his deep concern about the *method* of the new philosophy. Spinoza's geometric method did not please him any more than Fichte's method of postulation. He accepted Schelling's contention that a *philosophy* of the Absolute Identity was *possible*. But some of the general reflections with which the *Difference* essay begins tell just as heavily against Schelling as they do against Fichte or Spinoza.

We should notice, for example, that in Hegel's view nothing could make a more misleading impression than to begin with a *definition* as Spinoza does (105).[14] This remark is interesting because Schelling had declared that Spinoza was the model for the exposition of his "break-through."[15] Hegel goes on to give, in some detail, the reasons why a philosophical system ought not to be deduced from a fundamental principle, and to attack the whole apparatus of the Critical Philosophy as we find it in Fichte. His attitude toward both of these great predecessors, Spinoza and Fichte, who are reconciled in the new dispensation, is here basically appreciative, but the eventual scathing attack upon Schelling's Identity Theory as an empty formalism (in the Preface to the *Phenomenology*) is already implicit in his comments on philosophical method in the *Difference* essay.

Indeed, the criticism of Schelling is so nearly explicit that one wonders how any of Hegel's readers, let alone Schelling himself, could have regarded this unknown "Doctor of Secular Wisdom"[16] as a mere disciple. The explanation seems to be that his contemporary audience simply did not understand what Hegel was saying; and they did not at that point have any reason for thinking that what they did not understand was important.[17] Only Schelling himself was really in a position to know better, for only he could talk to Hegel about what he had already thought and written. Close study of Schelling's writings in this period does show that he learned some things from Hegel.[18] But he was too volatile, too much the type of the romantic genius, to appreciate Hegel's patient struggle with the problems of philosophical method. Schelling was continually subject to new inspirations, and whenever he was seized by one he was apt to begin all over again, so that all of his attempts at a systematic exposition of his Philosophy of Identity remained incomplete. He wrote rapidly and published work still in progress. As the more phlegmatic and methodical Hegel remarked some years later, "Schelling conducted his own education in public."[19]

The quicksilver character of Schelling's speculative thought is one of the major stumbling blocks in the path to an understanding of the *Difference* essay. In his preface Hegel speaks of the systems of Fichte and Schelling as already "lying before the public," but in fact Schelling's system was not properly displayed for public view at this time. The fundamental statement of his position to which contemporary readers would most naturally turn—the "Exposition of My System of Philosophy" of 1801—dealt only with general principles and with the philosophical construction of inorganic nature. In order to get a synoptic view of Schelling's position, we have to supplement this initial statement from various later essays and lectures published or delivered during the next five or six years; and when we put the various statements together we find that even at a quite basic level there is a great deal of wavering in the systematic outline.[20]

Among Schelling's contemporary critics Hegel himself was one of the most perceptive. When he came to deal with Schelling in his first course on the history of philosophy he summed up the problem as follows:

> It is not feasible here to go into details respecting what is
> called the philosophy of Schelling. . . . For it is not yet a scientific
> whole organized in all its branches, since it rather consists in
> certain general elements which do not fluctuate with the rest of
> his opinions. Schelling's philosophy must still be regarded as in
> process of evolution, and it has not yet ripened into fruit.[21]

This was how Hegel saw the matter in 1805. But it was not how he affected to see it in 1801. The title of the *Difference* essay clearly implies that Schelling does have a system; and the essay itself provides some indications of what it will look like when it does finally "lie before the public" as a whole. But the fact that the comparison of Schelling and Fichte is not *preceded* by an exposition of Schelling's system is a tacit admission that Schelling has still to do what Fichte has already done:—provide the raw material for a critical analysis comparable with that which Hegel performs upon Fichte's major works.

3. THE ADVANCE FROM CRITICAL TO SPECULATIVE PHILOSOPHY

Of course, Hegel's slightly curious procedure of using the imperfect as a yardstick for the perfect—analyzing Fichte's System in order to reveal its shortcomings and inadequacies, and then comparing it with his own projection of Schelling's system—is largely jusified by the fact that Schelling's system grew out of Fichte's in the first place. In Hegel's own terms, the two *systems* whose difference is to be exhibited arise from the common root of a single *philosophy* which they both express. We can best begin our own analysis of Hegel's essay, therefore, with a brief characterization of the philosophy that Fichte and Schelling are supposed to have in common, even though their systems are different. This common ground is the "authentic idealism" which is the spirit as distinct from the letter of the Kantian philosophy.[22] Kant himself remained bound to his own "letter" and scarcely rose into the higher realm of truly *speculative* philosophy at all—so that "even the Kantian philosophy had proved unable to awaken Reason to the lost concept of genuine speculation" (118). But Fichte's work, like Schelling's is "the most thorough and profound speculation" (118; cf. 173).

What, then, does Fichte's achievement as a speculative philosopher consist in? Hegel's answer, which is given quite explicitly in the *Difference* essay and confirmed in the *Lectures on the History of Philosophy*, is that Fichte turned Kant's deduction of the categories into a genuine science of knowledge. "In the principle of the deduction of the categories Kant's philosophy is authentic idealism. . . . Fichte extracted this principle in a purer, stricter form" (79).

What Hegel refers to as "the principle of the deduction of the categories" is what Kant calls "the transcendental unity of apperception." Kant himself says that "the principle of apperception is the highest principle in the whole sphere of human knowledge."[23] Fichte "extracted this principle in a purer, stricter form" as the "Ego." The self-positing Ego in Fichte's words is "the primordial, absolutely unconditioned first principle of all human knowledge" and his initial description of it is "that Act [*Tathandlung*] which does not and cannot appear among the empirical states of our consciousness, but rather lies at the basis of all consciousness and alone makes it possible."[24] Fichte sought to show how the categories could be derived from this basic principle without the problematic Kantian thing-in-itself playing any role in the deduction. Only in this way could a proper deduction of the categories be given; and only then would the theory of knowledge be established on a truly "scientific" basis.

Thus, as Hegel said in his lectures, Fichte removed the "unthinking inconsistency" of Kant.[25] But it is precisely when we follow this line of interpretation (which I believe to be essentially just to Fichte's own aims, and which became canonical in any case, through ceaseless repetition by Hegel and his followers in his later years) that the fundamental claim advanced in the *Difference* essay on behalf of Schelling's system becomes most problematic. For if Fichte laid the foundations of a genuinely speculative philosophy by providing an *organic* account of the derivation of the categories from the self-positing of the Ego, how can Schelling's breakthrough to the philosophy of Identity, or his doctrine of a parallel between transcendental philosophy and the philosophy of nature be an *advance* from this position? All of this looks like a gratuitous return to pre-Critical dogmatism. Why is it necessary at all?

In order to understand why Hegel believed that Schelling's system was an advance over Fichte's we must now ask what it was that Fichte got *wrong*. If we examine carefully what Fichte says about Spinoza, we shall soon find the clue. "We shall," says Fichte," "encounter his [i.e., Spinoza's] highest unity again in the Science of Knowledge; though not as something that *exists*, but as something that we *ought to*, and yet *cannot* achieve."[27] This acceptance of a mere *Sollen* is the burden of Hegel's life-long complaint against Fichte. But why should an endless endeavour *not* be the ultimate truth of our condition? Why must Fichte's science of knowledge be counted a failure because *this* is what we *know*? This is the crux.

When we compare Fichte's *Science of Knowledge* with Schelling's *System of Transcendental Idealism*, we can see at once, upon the most superficial survey, that although they have a common aim with respect to the deduction of the categories, there is a fundamental difference between them with respect to Kant's doctrine of our cognitive faculties. Schelling's problem is not just to trace the logical evolution of the categories from the transcendental unity of apperception but to trace the evolution of the faculties of conception, of judgment, of moral choice, and finally of artistic creation, from the original spontaneity of the productive imagination. Fichte finds that the *Critique of Pure Reason* needs to be done over again; but Schelling sets out to do the whole Critical Philosophy over again. The relation of the three Critiques, which remained quite unproblematic for Fichte, has become problematic for Schelling.

In order to understand why this has happened we must consider some of the fundamental doctrines of the "Critique of Teleological Judgment." Kant lays it down (in section 76 of the *Critique of Judgment*) that "Reason is a faculty of principles, and the unconditioned is the ultimate goal at which it aims."[28] But it cannot achieve this ultimate goal because in all of its existential assertions it is dependent on the cooperation of intuition and concept in the understanding. Without its intuitive content, the mere concept is just something possible (as long as it is self-consistent). The intuitive content that gives it existential import, comes to us through the senses; the understanding cannot supply this content for itself. If it could, then the object of its concept would be actualized in the very process of conceiving it. An intuitive intellect of this sort is conceptually possible—it contains no contradiction in itself. But our own understanding cannot operate like this, for it is totally dependent on sensibility to furnish it with content.

However, this rational concept of an intuitive intellect, which must forever remain for us a mere possibility without any application in experience is not, in Kant's view, just one among the infinity of think- able possibilities that we can never experience. It is a *necessary* idea, it plays an essential role in our theory of knowledge. In fact, it is the ultimate ground of the very possibility of systematizing our experi- ence in such a way that we can properly speak of knowledge at all. For without this ground we cannot form the conception of nature as an organic whole; and we cannot reconcile our own moral experience with the constitutive principles of our understanding without regard- ing nature in a teleological perspective.

Kant sums up the situation thus:

> Now the principle of the mechanism of nature and that of its causality according to ends, when applied to one and the same product of nature, *must* cohere in a single higher principle and flow from it as their common source, for if this were not so they could not both enter consistently into the same survey of na- ture. . . . Now the principle common to the mechanical derivation, on the one hand, and the teleological, on the other, is the *super- sensible*, which we must introduce as the basis of nature as phenomenon. But of this we are unable from a theoretical point of view to form the slightest positive determinate conception. How, therefore, in the light of the supersensible as principle, na- ture in its particular laws constitutes a system for us, and one capable of being cognized as possible both on the principle of production from physical causes and on that of final causes, is a matter which does not admit of any explanation.[29]

What becomes of the science of knowledge if this conclusion is al- lowed to stand as Kant states it? Fichte's boasted science becomes the absolute knowledge of our own inescapable ignorance, the knowledge that we cannot absolutely *know* anything. Kant remarked in an aph- orism which was quoted by hosts of competing interpreters that he had "found it necessary to deny *knowledge* in order to make room for faith."[30] Fichte was among the most enthusiastic—and the most self- assured—of all the thinkers who accepted this dictum. But in follow- ing Kant here he abandoned his project of a science of knowledge and so ceased to be a speculative philosopher altogether.[31] For if the ulti- mate conclusion of the supposed science is the recognition that all of our knowledge is grounded in faith, then we cannot claim to have a science of knowledge, we cannot properly claim to *know* what it is to know anything. When we find ourselves faced with this result we are therefore bound to reexamine the "absolutely unconditioned first principle" from which we began.

This "absolutely unconditioned first principle" was *self*-knowledge, the *Cogito* of Descartes, the "I think" of Kant. But in Fichte's science of knowledge this principle is not a dogmatic *conclusion* from thinking being to substantial being as in Descartes; nor yet is it a necessary "form," critically cleansed of all ontic commitment, such as we see in Kant's *Ich denke*. Fichte's "Ego" is a primordial *Act*, a *Tathandlung*, a self-establishing, the self-positing of Reason. Now if in fact we *can* know ourselves as the self-positing of Reason, and if this is the only way that we can know ourselves to be rational at all, then Kant was mistaken in thinking that our understanding does not operate intuitively, for on the contrary, Reason is always intuitive, it "gives" its own object. That is, Reason is always "positing" itself, it is always self-actualizing; and this self-actualization, this intellectual intuition is what is at the foundation of all possible experience. Fichte was thus the founder of speculative philosophy—the intellectual vision of all things in the Universal Logos—on a critical base. But the programme of his science of knowledge will not be properly concluded until we do know ourselves to be identical with the putative but necessary "common source" of natural mechanism and organic teleology. So when Fichte says that "we shall encounter the highest unity . . . as something that we *ought to*, and yet *cannot* achieve" he is admitting that he has not succeeded in what he set out to do. In fact, his initial statement of the problem already indicates the inadequacy of his enterprise; for he declares that the *Tathandlung* we are seeking is one that we must necessarily *think* (he italicizes *denken* himself) "as the basis of all consciousness."

About 1797, Fichte himself began to speak of "intellectual intuition" (*intellektuelle Anschauung*) as "the only firm standpoint for all philosophy."[32] His need to do this was a direct consequence of continued meditation on what was implicitly involved in the characterization of the Ego as the *Tathandlung* of self-positing. Probably he was influenced by his younger friend Schelling—still, in his eyes, a faithful disciple. It must be emphasized, however, that Fichte did not accept the consequence that Spinoza's "unity of the mind with the whole of nature" either had to be, or even could be, demonstrated.

Since this "highest unity" remained for Fichte an unachievable ideal, it is obvious that Fichte did not hold that we must achieve it in order to prove to ourselves that we are indeed rational beings, or in order to know scientifically what our knowledge is. In fact, he held that our rational nature is known to us intuitively in the moral law. To those who jeered at his appeal to "intellectual intuition" he retorted, "I should like to know how they view the consciousness of the moral law; or how they would undertake to construct the concepts of right, virtue, and so forth, which they yet undoubtedly possess."[33]

But the grounding of our knowledge of what *ought* to be in an intellectual intuition, while all of our knowledge of what *is* continues to be grounded in empirical intuition, merely legitimates the breach in human nature which Hegel had been struggling for years to overcome. Long before he joined Schelling at Jena, Hegel had become convinced that the whole Kantian conception of morality as a sort of internal legislation imposed by Reason on our "lower" nature was not rational freedom at all, but the most insidious form of slavery. In formulating the Hellenic ideal of his earliest essays he already envisaged the rational life as a communal and public expression of a spontaneous harmony of *all* aspects of human nature, not a private and personal strenuous assertion of the law of reason against the pulling and pushing of natural desires and instinctive drives.[34] In any case, we do not *know* the Kantian law of Reason. Pure practical Reason does not, and cannot, tell us what to do in any actual situation. Hegel remarked in his Frankfurt manuscripts on the difficulties created for Kant by "conflicts of duty." In *Faith and Knowledge,* he gives free rein to his irony against Fichte on this topic. Fichte's *Science of Rights* and *System of Ethics* were in his eyes the *reductio ad absurdum* of all the ethical theories that begin from the established opposition of human reason and human life.

"The sole interest of Reason," says Hegel, "is to suspend such rigid antitheses." (90) The *Gegensatz* of "reason" and "the passions"—to speak of it in the way that is probably most familiar in English, though Hegel does not refer to it thus—is the obvious one which we must overcome before we can claim to have an intuitive knowledge of ourselves as rational organisms. The self-intuition of Reason is the intellectual intuition on which genuine speculation is founded; it must not find itself faced by an incomprehensible *opposite*, an independent reality or thing-in-itself. What Hegel calls *Vernunft* is not a distinct faculty which we discover, and which we then show by analysis and comparison to be the defining characteristic of the class of animate organisms called man. *Vernunft* is not something discovered and classified in that way at all. To speak of the antithesis between reason and the passions would be awkward for Hegel, because it would involve the abandonment of the *speculative* standpoint at the very beginning, and the complete assimilation of intellectual intuition—the self-constitutive activity—into the empirical or sense intuition through which we *discover* something other than ourselves. It was Kant's great achievement that he showed us how much of the process of *discovering* objects of experience must be credited to our own activity as rational subjects. But what he failed to recognize, according to Hegel, was that the critical activity by which we distinguish between activity and passivity, form and matter, concept and sensation, both requires and exemplifies a non-sensuous intuition. Only our sense-knowledge is accounted for by Kant's account of intuition. The knowledge of our own rational *activity* that the *Critique of Pure Reason* puts before us remains yet unaccounted for as *knowledge* in the *Critique*.

The recognition that the Critical Philosophy is itself knowledge was the crucial step that Fichte took in proclaiming his science of knowledge. It was natural enough that he should express this discovery in terms of a new kind of *intuition*. To speak of it thus was the simplest, most minimal, adjustment of the Kantian perspective. The establishment of the science of knowledge was just a matter of adding to Kant's account of experience, the one thing required to legitimate the scientific status claimed for the critical account of experience itself. We have merely to notice that when we are engaged in the critique of our own rational capacities we do have an indubitable awareness of our own rational activity; that this awareness is an essential element in the activity because it is just what makes it self-*critical*; and that this activity of pure reason is a *self-constitutive* activity (as our critique itself shows). Thus we are led to recognize in our critical philosophy that we have an *intellectual* intuition of ourselves, because the activity that is the *content* of this intuition is the one that *constitutes* the formal structure of our ordinary empirical consciousness. The activity that is the form or concept in the synthesis (which is our philosophic consciousness) is our own comprehending of this truth about ourselves. But if we preserve the original Kantian analysis of experience in this Fichtean way, and are content simply to supplement it as Fichte did, then our conception of our own nature will have two sides which must remain essentially sundered and opposed. For we now claim to have one kind of intuitive knowledge of ourselves as *rational*, and another kind of intuitive knowledge of ourselves as *animal*. If we could simply say that we have intellectual intuition of ourselves, and empirical intuition of the outside world, we might perhaps be satisfied with our science of knowledge, for the opposition between "self" and "other," the "inside" and the "outside," is one of the most obvious facts of our experience, and a radical difference in our modes of intuition would be a persuasive account of it. But as our own "inner world" is cognitively a composite of both types of intuition, the relationship between sensible and intellectual intuition becomes a problem. This is where Schelling enters. Our self-awareness is in the fullest sense *organic*. It is something that *grows*. The philosopher's view of it as founded in an intuition of a special kind is only the culminating phase of its perfect maturity. Ordinary consciousness seems, on the contrary, to have its *empirical* origin in sensation, the manifold which is somehow synthesized in sensible intuition. How is it then, that the intellectual intuition of the philosopher, the critic of pure reason, derives, or at any rate, emerges from sense-intuition? This was Schelling's problem in the *System of Transcendental Idealism*.

This problem of the transition in our self-knowledge leads on to a more general problem in the critical theory of our knowledge of nature as a whole. For if we are aware of *ourselves* as organisms of a very special kind, as conscious or rational organisms, how can we rest content with Kant's general theory of organism, and his account of organic teleology as a purely regulative ideal for our empirical knowledge? Once we have grasped the *constitutive* role of Reason in our own experience, and have successfully traced its evolution from the primitive spontaneity of sensory imagination to the conscious autonomy of moral freedom, we are in a position to assert that organic finality has more than a regulative function, that it is intuitively realized, or exemplified in our experience. But further, when we seek to define our own *Endzweck*, the constitutive purpose of the rational organism, we are driven by the organic conception of human experience that we have finally arrived at to face Spinoza's problem of man's place in nature, in Spinoza's terms. We must seek "the union of the mind with the whole of nature," because our empirically determinate goals, the finite purposes of our "animal" nature, can only become fully rational in that absolute perspective. Only by overcoming the opposition between intellectual and empirical intuition generally, can we mediate the contrast between our intellectual and empirical awareness of our own nature. Hence Kant's *Critique of Judgment*, especially the "Critique of Teleological Judgment," became the point of departure for a new era of genuinely *speculative* philosophy.

In this perspective, it is easy to see why Hegel's attitude to Fichte was so ambivalent. On the one hand, Fichte had laid the foundations for a new speculative philosophy upon critical foundations. But on the other, he had tried to complete his task by systematizing the very aspect of Kant's theory that was most objectionable, the sundering of human nature into reason and the senses, of human experience into the phenomenal and the noumenal, and of Reason itself into "pure reason" and "practical reason," or "reason" and "faith." Schelling's system, with its two philosophic sciences of transcendental idealism and natural philosophy might be, as yet, more a program than a reality, but it was at least an effort in the right direction and along the right lines. Hegel himself was never satisfied with Schelling's (or his own) execution of the program of the Identity Philosophy. He was, from the beginning, unhappy about Schelling's formulation of the theory of intuition. Eventually—at the cost of his break with Schelling— he arrived at a solution of that problem with which he was fairly content. He went on wrestling with the formulation of his philosophy of nature for most of his life. But at no time did he lose faith in the systematic ideal articulated in the original program.

On a cursory view, at least, Schelling's view of philosophical method in this period appears wavering and erratic. He was obsessed about, perhaps indeed possessed by, the moment of vision at the end of the road. Nevertheless it was not the consciousness of the goal, but a crucial starting point for the true method of philosophy that Hegel owed to Schelling. The abiding significance of the *Difference* essay emerges when we recognize that it is the first chapter of a "discourse on method" which Hegel carried on for the rest of his life. His views certainly evolved a great deal, and his way of articulating and expressing those views developed even more. But from this essay onwards he moved steadily forward, whereas previously he had known what his goal was, but had never been sure how to reach it. In this sense there is some justification—however slight—for the embittered conviction of the aged Schelling that Hegel's later fame and reputation all derived from what he, Schelling, had taught him.

4. AN ANALYSIS OF THE ARGUMENT:
(I) THE "GENERAL REFLECTIONS."

Let us try, now, to follow the argument of this first chapter of Hegel's lifelong "discourse on method." The occasion for it, as Hegel tells us in his preface, is Reinhold's misunderstanding of the new speculative philosophy, and specifically his failure to grasp what is new and original in the work of Schelling. Schelling, Fichte, Kant, Reinhold,[35] and Bardili[36] form in Hegel's mind a descending sequence of the possible degrees of consciousness with respect to speculation. Schelling knows what speculative philosophy is, and sees how it has to be done in the light of Kant's critical attack; Fichte knows what it must do, but not how to do it; Kant knows what it must do, and thinks he has proved that the task is impossible; Reinhold and Bardili do not even know what the real task of speculation is, and only aim to produce an imitation of it ("popular" or "formula" philosophy) which is more to the taste of the general public. The course of Hegel's argument rises from this popular level to the true pitch of speculative thought and then falls again to the bathos of "everything is what it is, and not another thing."

Hegel's project is to show what *is* original in Schelling's view, and how his view is superior to Fichte's.[37] Kant—who hardly gets into the essay by name at all, but whose continual implicit presence gives considerable significance to every explicit mention of him—made a new beginning of speculative philosophy possible, though he did not realize what he had done. Fichte saw how the new beginning could be used. The "deduction of the categories" must be replaced by a more organic derivation of the categories from the unity of apperception, and one which does not depend upon the problematic "thing-in-itself"; and the unity of apperception along with everything derived or deduced from it must be viewed not as formal structures but as *activities.*

Kant's failure to understand what he had done is all summed up, for Hegel, in his treatment of the categories of "modality." The other nine categories are genuine moments in the self-constitutive activity of human experience, but when we employ the categories of modality we presuppose "the non-identity of subject and object." We can see why Hegel says this if we look at § 76 and § 77 of the *Critique of Judgment.* Here Kant claims that:

> Human understanding cannot avoid the necessity of drawing
> a distinction between the possibility and the actuality of things.
> The reason for this lies in our own selves and the nature of our
> cognitive faculties. For were it not that two entirely hetero-
> geneous factors, understanding for conceptions and sensuous
> intuition for the corresponding Objects, are required for the exer-
> cise of these faculties, there would be no such distinction be-
> tween the possible and the actual. This means that if our under-

standing were intuitive it would have no objects but such as are
actual. Conceptions, which are merely directed to the possibility
of an object; and sensuous intuitions, which give us something
and yet do not thereby let us cognize it as an object, would both
cease to exist . . . the distinction of possible from actual things
is one that is merely valid subjectively for human understanding.
. . . For reason never withdraws its challenge to us to adopt
something or other existing with unconditioned necessity—a root
origin—in which there is no longer to be any difference between
possibility and actuality, and our understanding has absolutely
no conception to answer to this Idea. . . .[38]

Now since speculation is founded in intellectual intuition the truly
speculative intellect operates on what Kant calls the "standard of the
intuitive or archetypal understanding."[39] But Kant did not realize that
this was possible; and specifically he did not realize that he was himself operating on this standard, the standard of Reason itself, in carry-
ing out the critique of Reason. Speculation is Reason's own answer to
the challenge that it "never withdraws." Hence speculation must begin from "unconditioned necessity," not from the distinction of "the
actual" and "the possible." This "unconditioned necessity" is what
Fichte discovered in his principle of "pure thinking." But Hegel believes that Fichte was not faithful to the principle he has discovered
because he left the whole realm of natural phenomena, given in empirical intuition, quite unconnected with "pure thinking" and its necessary structures. In point of fact, as I have already suggested, Fichte
had no thought of doing what Schelling set out to do, because he was
quite satisfied with the architectonic structure of the Critical Philosophy. He did not have the standard of the intuitive intellect before his
eyes in quite the same way that Schelling did; and he certainly did
not have the driving urge to reform the whole relation between pure
and practical reason which Hegel had gained from his long struggle
with Kantian ethics. The "infinite progress" in morality which Fichte
accepted as the destiny of humanity, was for Hegel an endless tread-
mill of internalized slavery; it placed man in the situation of Sisyphus
or Tantalus, it deprived him even of the rational possibility of a real
self-fulfilment that could be known and enjoyed.

When we read Hegel's preface against this background, we can see
why the critique of Fichte has to be preceded by a series of general
reflections about the nature and task of speculative philosophy. If the
learned world is to understand the relation between Fichte and Schel-

ling properly they must first be made to see how different the real task of philosophy is from the image of it that is presented in the popular philosophy of a man like Reinhold. It is prototypical of Hegel's whole career as a professional philosopher that he should begin his first published essay with a discussion of the *history* of philosophy. The apparent confusion of tongues in the history of speculative philosophy was Kant's great argument in favor of his *dialectical* conception of pure reason. By reasserting the presence of a *philosophia perennis*, Hegel aimed to show that the dialectic of philosophical ideas is subordinate to, and instrumental for, the focal concern of rational speculation, which never varies. But at the same time he wanted to distinguish his notion of the *philosophia perennis* from the common-sense view of the philosophical tradition as a series of prior attempts to solve perennial problems which can be used by beginners as exercises or practice studies.

The lowest possible view of the history of philosophy is the merely historical approach, the approach which ignores the perennial character of philosophy altogether. Men's opinions about the world and about their place in it are one possible subject for a historian, and certainly not the least interesting one. But it is precisely the task of the philosopher in his relation to the public to make clear *why* this history is interesting. A historian of philosophy ought to have some general conception of his subject, in terms of which he can answer this question. Reinhold satisfies this condition; so he is not quite at the bottom of the ladder. But his image of previous philosophy as material for exercises is the perfect expression of an alienated consciousness, for it completely misrepresents the truth that in doing philosophy one is forming oneself, "founding and grounding" one's own being. Reinhold emphasizes the *eigentümlich* aspect of philosophical positions. This is an implicit acknowledgment of the self-founding character of philosophy; but since the only self that Reinhold can recognize is the private consciousness of the individual, he misunderstands what Fichte and Schelling grasped: that philosophy is the consciousness of the absolute self. He thinks of this insight as being their peculiar idiosyncrasy (178). But the recognition of the absolute self is just what philosophy is needed for; and it is also what is needed if there is to be philosophy.

Reinhold's view of philosophy as a progressive development in which personal idiosyncrasies manifest themselves is itself idiosyncratic. Equally idiosyncratic is the opposite view of Fichte, that philosophy really has *no* history, and cannot exhibit any personal idiosyncrasies. Fichte is certain that his science of knowledge is the one true philosophy; and Hegel agrees that it is *an* expression of truly speculative thought. But Fichte's inability to understand either the perennial or the personal character of philosophy leads him to suggest that Spinoza *could not* have believed his own philosophy, and that the Greeks did not even know what philosophy was (87). In Reinhold's conception there is no absolute knowledge at all; in Fichte's there is nothing else but absolute knowledge. The true conception of philosophy in its history is a synthesis of these opposites. On the one hand, one cannot enter upon the study of philosophy as a personal concern: one must set aside personal concerns entirely. But, on the other hand, in this absolute sacrifice of self, one becomes the mouthpiece of one's own time. The speculative philosopher speaks with the voice of universal Reason. But when he speaks from the past, his philosophical auditors in the new time will be those who can recognize "the organic shape that Reason has built for itself out of the material of a particular age" (88).

Philosophy arises only when it is needed. The need for it is felt precisely when what philosophy itself needs is not present. Philosophy is the overcoming of *Entzweiung,* of dichotomy in consciousness. In the history of philosophy the fundamental dichotomy is between God (the absolute self) and the world (the totality of objective reality). As long as the presence of God everywhere in the cultural world is directly apprehended and felt, philosophy does not arise at all. But when we begin to understand the world, and to manipulate it for our own ends, nature ceases to be "divine" and we have the sense of alienation from the power that creates and sustains it, and us within it. In our own culture the intellect has as its goal the grasping of the order of nature in its eternal, unchanging aspect, the formulation of its laws. Yet the more this intellectual endeavour appears to succeed, the more the sense of alienation increases. The reason for this is that our intellectual comprehension of nature as law excludes the spontaneity and freedom which belonged to the pre-philosophical awareness of the natural world as the expression of the divine life. But the intellect is, of course, always aware that all of the finite phenomena which are correlated in its system of laws require an infinite or absolute ground. So "when life as Reason steps away into the distance, the totality of limitations is at the same time nullified, and connected with the Absolute in this nullification, and hence conceived and posited as mere appearance" (90). This is exactly the result that Kant arrived at. The whole of our experience, which must be formulated by us in the categories of the understanding, is phenomenal, and hence it presupposes a noumenal foundation, the *Ding-an-sich*, of which it is the appearance. The phenomena are nothing *in themselves*. To call them phenomena is thus to nullify them, to deny that they have independent being. But it is also to concede that they arise from something else, they are appearances *of* something that does have being in its own account. And if we took away all possibility of finite appearance, the problematic thing-in-itself would be *nothing-in-itself* likewise. Hence "The split between the Absolute [the noumenal reality] and the totality of limitations [the phenomenal world] vanishes."

A world which has lost its soul in this way, however, will not for some time recognize what has happened to it. It will make do with a dualistic philosophy—an intellectual copy of the absolute positing of true speculation. The Absolute is intellectually fixed as a noumenal reality—to use the Kantian terminology—and absolute opposition is accepted in lieu of absolute identity. This is not surprising, because, as we shall see, absolute identity *involves* absolute opposition, and ordinary consciousness is full of oppositions—though it only remains healthy because of a secure *feeling* for "the might of union."

The need of philosophy arises, contingently, when the aesthetic and religious life of the time can no longer sustain the sense of living unity. "Far away and long ago" in classical Greece there was an immediate sense of the harmony of life. This was an aesthetic sense of the divine life—a paradise in which the apple of intellectual discord was still to be eaten. After the fall, the discords were eventually harmonized again in a long "age of faith" in which the "might of union" was sustained by the dominance of religion. The Reformation marked the beginning of the culture in which the need of philosophy became for the first time fully explicit. Descartes' dualism of thinking and extended substance was the philosophical expression of this need, and Hegel took the French Revolution to be the practical expression of it in social life.[40]

What Hegel says about art as the expression of the Absolute here is in full accord with Schelling's conception of aesthetic consciousness as the highest mode of experience. But the emphasis on religion is more distinctly his own. As we can see from *Faith and Knowledge* the underlying concern in his analysis of the disrupted cultural consciousness of his time was not just to make plain the need of philosophy but to prepare his audience for the proclamation of a new gospel. The proclamation will be made *by* the Identity Philosophy itself, but it will be embodied in a new religion, a new political and social culture, in short a new way of life.[41]

A dualism of the Cartesian type makes a peaceful division of cultural life between faith and intellect relatively easy. But in the realm of the intellect the dualism was fearlessly attacked by Spinoza. On the speculative level no one understood what he was doing; but within the context of the dichotomy the intellectual purport of his work was easy to appreciate and the reaction was violent. As Lessing remarked in his conversations with Jacobi, Spinoza was a "dead dog" in European philosophy for a hundred years. The dominant influence throughout this period was his exact contemporary John Locke, through whose conception of the philosopher as an underlaborer clearing away speculative rubbish one can fairly say that "the realm of the intellect rose to such power that it could regard itself as secure from Reason" (92). Thus modern culture entered the time of enlightenment.[42]

When the need for a speculative overcoming of the basic dichotomies of existence is felt in a culture in which all the dichotomies have been sharply formulated by the intellect, it naturally takes the *intellectual* form of a quest for the ultimate *foundation* of experience, the *principle* from which everything can be deduced or derived. The philosophical justification for the focal position that is allotted to Reinhold in the *Difference* essay—in spite of the low opinion of his philosophical achievement and his ultimate historical significance which Hegel so trenchantly expresses—is that no less an authority than Fichte had ascribed to him "the immortal merit of having made philosophical Reason aware . . . that the whole of philosophy must be led back to one unique basic principle";[43] and in his continuing quest for this *Grundsatz* Reinhold had at length fastened upon the formal logical principle of Identity. This is the emptiest possible formal expression for the lost "might of union"; and it is only one side of the intellectual presupposition of speculative philosophy. The other is the intellect itself—the consciousness that has "stepped out of the totality" and become an observing intellect which fixes the real in the context of an abstract range of possibilities. This polar conception of the real and the ideal is the basic error of the intellect. The *real* "might of union" now lies hid in the "night" of pre-reflective consciousness— and of the "dark ages."

Hegel does not choose, here, to consider the struggle between faith and reason, however. That study, which he pursues at length in the *Phenomenology*, begins in *Faith and Knowledge*. Here he looks rather at the *religious* expression of the triumph of the intellect, the dogma of Creation. The first article of the Creed in that earlier age of faith was that "in the *beginning*" God *created* the world "out of *nothing.*" The first created thing was light which shone in the primeval darkness. It is in this religious form that the speculative significance of reflection can best be appreciated. For the restoration of true speculation in a world that has now been completely enlightened by the intellect, will only be possible through a properly reflective understanding of the earlier religious tradition of which speculative philosophy is the true heir.

Hegel's doctrine of the Creation owes as much to the first chapter of John as to the first chapter of Genesis or to the Nicene Creed. The light that shines in the primeval darkness is the light of Reason—the Logos that was "begotten not made"; and it seems that the nothing *out* of which God the *Father* made the world is to be *identified* with the creative might of the Father himself. We should note that there are two sides to the speculative interpretation of all this religious language. On the side of the philosophy of nature, "light" refers both to the physical principle of light (and heat) and to the principle of life; and "night" means not only darkness but that which, being impervious to light, is shown up by it, the heavy matter which is always inwardly dark till the higher light of life itself shines within it. On the side of transcendental philosophy "light" stands for the reflective consciousness which discovers all the creative activity (of the Father?) that has already gone on in the "night" of unconscious nature; and "the nothing" means the mighty force of thought, the abyss out of which everything comes and into which it is hurled. God himself, when not identified with this abyss, which is both his creative power and his negative side, is identical with the life and order of the creative activity. Thus the night or the abyss is God the Father, while Reason in nature is God the Son, the Logos; and speculative Reason returning from the creation and reconciling it with its ground in the divine power will be God the Holy Spirit, "proceeding from the Father and the Son" or "positing being in non-being, as becoming [the Father], dichotomy in the Absolute as its appearance [the Logos], the finite in the infinite as life [the Spirit]" (93–4). The trinitarian dogma of the Christian faith is a proper religious expression of speculative truth; while on the other hand, the Judaic creation story (in Genesis) expresses the truth from the "standpoint of dichotomy."

If we approach the problem of philosophy in a reflective way—that is, as *observers* of a dichotomy in our own consciousness and our culture which *needs* to be overcome or healed—then we are bound to give both an analysis of the need and a prescription for the cure. But before we can think of doing this we are reflectively bound to examine first, in the same spirit of calm observation, the question of what capacity we have to deal with these philosophical problems at all. Thus, after Descartes expressed the divided condition of modern culture in clear intellectual terms, as a dualism of thinking and extended substance, we find that Spinoza's answer to the challenge thus posed by Reason to Reason was not properly heeded. The voice that was heard rather, was that of Locke, who asked whether we are in a position to say anything at all about the ultimate substance of things; and Locke's *Essay* was the beginning of a whole tradition which Hegel calls (in *Faith and Knowledge*) "the reflective philosophy of subjectivity."

It appears that, as far as the *speculative* purpose of philosophy is concerned, this reflective philosophy must remain eternally defeated, since it is self-defeating. The self-defeating character of reflection in philosophy is what Reinhold's endless multiplication of methodological prolegomena and preambles illustrates. But it is only for Reinhold and his like that defeat is inevitable, not for the principle of reflection itself. Reflection can *really* become "the instrument of philosophy." It can become Reason. This is the speculative significance of Kant's "Copernican Revolution."

In the *Critique of Pure Reason* reflection became the means for the reestablishment of speculative philosophy through a genuine conquest of the Cartesian dualism. In order to see how and why this is so, we must examine the structure of philosophical reflection. Whatever appears in reflective consciousness does so as an *object* of consciousness, as something *other* than, and opposed to, the thinking subject to whom it appears. But, *at the same time*—as we already find Locke saying—*nothing* can appear to the mind except its own products, its "ideas." Thus when we reflect *critically*—as Kant did—upon the process by which the mind *produces* all of its Lockean "furniture" we recognize that what initially appears to us as the passive reflection of a world of finite objects that *present themselves,* is actually an activity in which the mind *presents to itself* the results of its own synthesizing activity. Thus, what we do *consciously* in philosophical reflection, that is, make our own mental activity into an *object* for observation, is just what we are doing *unconsciously* in ordinary consciousness.

Thus philosophical reflection discovers that all consciousness is reflection. Our own activity is everywhere *reflected* back to us. It is only the structure of reflection itself—the process of dividing subject from object and opposing them—that disguises this from us. In the critical perspective, we can see that reflection is essentially antinomies. For consciousness *must have* an object, and the object must appear as *other* than the *receptive* activity of the intellect, which merely *observes* it. But when reflection is turned upon *itself*, when we become *consciously* reflective, we *observe* that what reflection *is*, is not what it *appears* to be (the *having* or *observing* of an object) but rather just the opposite (the *positing* or *constitution* of an object). At the same time, we must reflectively affirm that reflection *is* what it *appears* to be. It *is* the *having* of an object, and for this reason, we are only able to produce the critique of reflective reason by *observing* the process of conscious experience as the appearance of a thing-in-itself.

Until reflection "makes itself its own object" and so "becomes Reason" by "nullifying itself" in this discovery of its own antinomic character, the task that faces it is a hopeless one. It is forever involved in an infinite regress (theoretically) or an infinite progress (practically). The goal of philosophy is to comprehend the *unity* of all that is. In the world of the intellect the obvious hopelessness of ever achieving "a whole of the intellect's own kind" is the "force of the negative Absolute,"[44] just as Spinoza's *Ethics* is the presentation of "the force that posits the opposed objective and subjective totality" (95). But the reflective intellect remains stubbornly realistic, insisting on the independent *being* of the world that presents itself in consciousness, and ignoring the fact that nothing in finite consciousness ever really *is*. Every conscious datum refers beyond itself in one way or another; and the ultimate ground—Locke's Substance or Kant's thing-in-itself —must be "given up for lost" because it is "nothing" (i.e., nothing determinate).

Kant's Copernican revolution involved a recognition of the antinomic character of reflection. But Kant did not overcome the antinomy properly. Instead, he turned the opposite aspects of the antinomy into the phenomenal world of intellectual necessity and the noumenal world of rational freedom. The phenomenal world of Kant is the sphere where intellect remains supreme, and "does not become Reason" (96). But through its self-critical labours the intellect now knows that it is dealing only with phenomena which are nothing-in-themselves, because they are only the appearance of what truly is. The way forward from here lies in the recognition of the process of appearing as a *necessary* moment of what truly is. We have to comprehend experience as the presentation of the Absolute to itself, the self-knowledge of the Absolute. Hence when Reinhold complains that the basic fault of all past philosophy is "the habit . . . of regarding thinking as something merely subjective" (97), he would at least be right about all reflective philosophy, if he understood properly what non-subjective thinking was. But in fact he remains merely a philosopher of subjective reflection himself.

Just what Reinhold meant by his appeal to the learned world to conceive of thinking as an objective activity I have not discovered. But Schelling and Hegel had already taken up the challenge in the form in which Kant posed it. The noumenal world of freedom must be united with the phenomenal realm of necessity by something more powerful than an act of what Kant, in the introduction to the *Critique of Judgment* (cf. also §§ 69, 75) called "reflecting" judgment. Kant had declared that all teleological concepts were merely regulative (i.e., subjectively valid for the guidance of our reflections) not constitutive (i.e., objectively valid for the constitution of objects). This is the situation of Reason "operating as intellect" (97). Schelling and Hegel insisted that, on the contrary, all speculative thinking was *both* teleological *and* objective. Thus nothing could count as objective thinking for them if the thought had to be "applied" to the matter. The thinking must *constitute* the object, and it must use the standard of its own self-constitution in doing so.[45] When the whole range of our finite experience is consistently *organized* in this way we shall have the Absolute before us as "an objective totality, a whole of knowledge" (98). Instead of an endless chain we shall have a complete cycle of existence. Every proper part of this totality will be an organic system with the same cyclic structure as the totality. This community of structure is the "connection with the Absolute" that gives the part its standing. Nothing counts as real knowledge, or as an acceptable explanation, unless it places the *explanandum* in the context of an organic totality of this kind.

Having thus dealt, both negatively and positively, with the intellect as an instrument of philosophy, Hegel now turns to the question of the right relation between "healthy" intellect and speculative Reason. He has just laid down that speculative philosophy is the only real knowledge, and he has shown why isolated reflective cognitions are not knowledge. When reflection becomes philosophical and examines itself critically "its positing appears to Reason to be non-positing, its products to be negations" (95–6). But before Locke disturbed the naive realism of ordinary consciousness, and Kant imprisoned us in a world of appearances of which we are the unconscious stage-managers, we were all sure that we have quite a lot of real knowledge; and as soon as we leave the philosophy class-room we start living in a real world, praying to a real God and so on. The self-nullifying certainty of critical reason which tells us that we have no way of knowing this real world is forgotten. What is the relation of philosophic knowledge to this ordinary knowledge? What is the proper relation between philosophy and common sense? Can we reflectively develop a philosophy of common sense?

Hegel's answer to this last question is negative. Common sense is essentially unphilosophical, and as soon as it develops philosophical pretensions it becomes unhealthy. The man of sound sense has many principles to guide him in his life. In choosing and applying the one that is appropriate to his situation he is guided by his *feeling* for life as a whole. When a critical philosopher comes along—Socrates is the most notable example—he finds it easy enough to throw common sense into confusion by making it reflect upon itself. The proper defense against the Socratic elenchus was to refuse to argue. So far as it remains healthy, common sense is bound to regard philosophy with suspicion. In order to pass from the intuitive knowledge of feeling to the speculative knowledge of Reason, it is necessary to pass through the fire of philosophical reflection. But when he is asked to cast his naive reflection into the abyss of speculative reflection, the man of sense can only assume that he is in the presence of the evil one. Hence it comes about that intensely religious spirits—Socrates, Spinoza, Fichte—are held to be impious men or atheists.

The reflective form of common-sense—the way in which we naively deal with such dichotomies as actual/possible, real/ideal, and appearance/truth—is the form of *faith*. Healthy common sense has its feet on the ground, yet it walks in the sight of God. "The earth is the Lord's, and all that therein is" indicates a relation of reflection to the Absolute, for it preserves the "form of sundering"; yet "reflection is certainly Reason" because finite experience is here taken up into the infinite. But in this common sense faith it is the aspect of opposition— "all flesh is as grass" etc.—that is typically present to consciousness. So when speculation insists on the *redemption* of the finite world here and now—not at the Last Trump—it appears as the Antichrist.

Pre-critical speculation—any *monistic* form of what Kant called dogmatic metaphysics—is bound to be offensive to common sense because of its apparent one-sidedness. Thus Berkeley's idealism appears to Dr. Johnson very easy to refute. But when in the materialism of La Mettrie and D'Holbach the opposite is raised to the Absolute, the sense of absurdity turns to one of moral horror. The speculative reader, one who can recognize "flesh of his flesh," will not be deceived by any merely apparent one-sidedness. He will ask rather whether the

philosopher has *really* fallen victim to his time. Thus Hegel is prepared to defend D'Holbach (171); and his primary critical concern is
to show just where Fichte's speculation "succumbs to the fate of its
time" (101).

Thus common sense is normally enraged at speculation on two
counts. First, it does not understand the very project of suspending
the dichotomy—and so far as it comprehends the results it must find
them impious, because the salvation of the finite *here and now* is offensive to faith. Secondly, what it does perceive is the *one-sidedness*
of speculation—the apparent suppression of one of the poles of the
dichotomy. This may or may not appear impious—depending on what
is outwardly suppressed—but it is *bound* to appear absurd. A speculative theory that is completely successful—in Hegel's view—yet manages to offend common sense in every possible way is Spinoza's fatalism (to give it the name that shows what is outwardly suppressed).
D'Holbach's materialism plays rather the cultural role that Hegel
ascribes to a system that "strikes down with one stroke the whole
mass of finitudes that adheres to the opposite principle" (102).

Common sense, being rooted in "feeling," is an aspect of our social
nature. The society which because of its natural climatic environment
has produced Descartes, Newton and the Enlightenment, may take
some time to accept and come to a proper appreciation of the philosophical revolution which the advent of the Identity Philosophy represents. Hegel seems to think that common sense itself must be brought
to complete confusion and despair before the new philosophy can
triumph. Yet speculation has the principle of the *reality* of knowledge
in common with common sense. After all the intellectual oppositions
have been nullified in philosophical reflection, the mountains will once
more be known as mountains and the rivers as rivers—not as phenomenal appearances of a hidden power. The "night" of the enlightened intellect will be transformed into the "noonday" of Reason; and
the noonday of Reason is also the noonday of real life.

What distinguishes the knowledge of speculation from that of common sense is its *systematic* character. So far, we have advanced with
critical reflection to the *Kantian* conception of a philosophical system:
"the unity of the manifold modes of knowledge under one idea."[46]
And we have alluded to Reinhold's discovery of the principle of identity as the *Grundsatz* under which all modes of knowledge are to be
subsumed. But from our study of why common sense cannot understand speculation we have discovered that the speculative overcoming
of a dichotomy must at the same time *preserve* the dichotomy. It is no

surprise to find, therefore, that Hegel's next step is to show how the principle of Identity must comprehend its own "application" when it enters into the "thinking that is the absolute activity of Reason" (96). By so doing it becomes not a proposition, but an antinomy—a pair of contradictory propositions which describe the opposite aspects of conscious reflection.

In this connection Hegel needs to show us that the definition of substance from which Spinoza began was already a speculative antinomy of the same sort. He must do this because Schelling had chosen to expound the new philosophy of Identity on the model of Spinoza's geometric method. It is clear, too, that he means to demonstrate the superiority of Spinoza's procedure—however dogmatic and uncritical it may look—as compared with the essentially subjective procedure of analysing the foundations of consciousness that both Reinhold and Fichte practiced.[47]

But in spite of this polemical concern, the concession that "no philosophical beginning could *look* worse than Spinoza's" (105)—backed up as it is by the whole critique of the *Grundsatz* approach to systematic philosophy—contains a devastating implicit critique of Schelling's method. Nor should we forget the historical lesson of Spinoza's hundred years as a "dead dog." Hegel speaks in the Preface of the great millenium of Reason when "from begining to end it is philosophy itself whose voice will be heard" (83). When that day dawns no doubt all readers of philosophy will understand the foundations of speculative systems properly. What we are now bound to ask, however, is: what *need* will philosophy satisfy when the great day arrives? Speculation is the essential *self-mirroring* of the Absolute, the recognition of finite experience as the self-othering which is unavoidably necessary if the Absolute is to exist as *self*-knowledge. But how can this *absolute knowledge* come to birth except through the experience of reflective dichotomies? The philosophical millenium of the Preface will be the day when the Absolute can be "shot out of a pistol."[48] Hegel has already shown us why that day will never dawn. Schelling's procedure is that of one who expects it with tomorrow's sunrise.

It was Fichte, not Schelling, who set the pattern for Hegel's interpretation of the formal principle of identity in such a way as to make a *Gegensatz* out of it. In the first *Science of Knowledge* (1794), Fichte treated "A = A" as an abstraction from the self-positing of the Ego.[49] But his procedure was subjective only. Hegel proceeds objectively, that is, he treats the formal principle itself as the absolute activity of Reason. The object here is, as Hegel says, knowledge, for we know that the absolute activity of Reason must be a self-*knowing*. Seen in this perspective "A = A" becomes the formula of the semantic theory of truth. The first A stands for the truth in the mind of the subject, and the second A for the corresponding state of things in the world—Reinhold's "matter," to which the pure concept of reflective thought is to be "applied." As soon as we look at the proposition in this way we see that it is indeed a *Gegensatz*. For what "A = A" asserts is the Parmenidean identity of thought and being. But since the thought is evidently *different* from what is thought about, we cannot assert "A = A" without at the same time asserting "A ≠ A." "A" in the mind does *not* equal "A" in the world. So in order to make any effective *use* of the subjective principle of identity (which has perfect formal validity as a hypothesis of pure thought in isolation—"If anything is A, then it is A") we must say "A = B," the object of my thought is this real being. When we think *truly* we cannot just think hypothetically. Yet there is no more absolute and necessary *difference* than the difference between thought and being.[50]

In the world of finite experience, to which the formal logic of identity is supposed by its proponents to apply, the antinomy appears as the endlessness of the search for an ultimate ground. We want to think truly of "what is" and we are faced with the fact that nothing in our experience is self-subsistent: everything *is* the *effect* of some cause and becomes the cause of some further effect. Nothing is cause of itself, nothing abides, nothing remains equal to itself. Speaking more generally, nothing contains its own explanation within itself, nothing is its own *logos*. In order to *be what it is* ("everything is what it is and not another thing") everything requires that some other thing should equally be: and in order for the second thing to be, the first thing must cease to be (or be not yet). The causal relation is just the simplest illustration of this. For it shows us how the being of everything finite requires its own nonbeing, and the being of something else in its place, for the sake of its own finitude (which is just what gives it its identity as distinct from other things).

One can of course cling fast to the principle of identity, and move straight from the transitoriness of all finite existence to a sort of Parmenidean mysticism. Thus one accepts the nullification of all finite experience in the antinomy, and the intellect does not "grow into Reason," but is left unperturbed in ordinary life, because it is simply annihilated in the religious consciousness of the Absolute. As soon as one thinks of God, heaven and earth pass away; but from Sunday to Sunday one can live beneath the one and upon the other quite comfortably nevertheless. This is the position of Jacobi. Reinhold is more naive. He clings to the principle of identity without recognizing its antinomic character. He postulates the "matter" to which thinking, with its principle of identity, is "applied." Hegel calls this "a very inadequate synthesis." But inadequate as it is, it still involves the antinomy, for when the principle "A = A" is *applied* to some matter (i.e., to something other than thought itself) it is also asserted in the form "A = B." The "absolute stuff" which is the matter to which thought is applied has to "fit in" to the conceptual patterns in which thought strives to construct the self-identity of what truly *is*. In Hegel's view this doctrine of "fitting in" is the only original contribution of Bardili to the great programme for the "reduction of philosophy to logic." Reinhold had greeted Bardili's *Outline of Primary Logic* (1800) with great enthusiasm, declaring himself a follower of this new way. But Fichte was the first to say, and Hegel agreed, that Bardili's theory was only Reinhold's philosophy "warmed over" (188).

What is needed, if we are to transcend the standpoint of reflection and achieve a truly speculative grasp of the principle of identity is "transcendental intuition."[51] We have already seen that this claim refers to Kant's statement of what is required in order for us to comprehend the unity of mechanical and teleological explanation in the ultimate ground which Reason requires us to postulate. But now Hegel is ready to show us why Kant must be wrong in holding that what is required cannot be supplied by any means at our disposal. If Kant were right, then all cognition would come to grief, even the limited cognition that Kant believes we do have. All the relative identities (of concept and empirical intuition) must be connected with the Absolute if they are to have real cognitive status. But when they are connected they become antinomies. Thus, without transcendental intuition, philosophic knowledge can only lead us to the negative conclusion of Parmenides: "Being is, Not-Being is not." We can show, through the subordinate principle of causality or of sufficient reason, that the being of everything is *related* to (depends on) the being of something else; hence that its being as finite requires its own nonbeing; and since the chain of related grounds is an infinite regress theoretically, or an infinite progress practically, the whole that truly *is* becomes a contradiction and is really nothing. "Pure knowing," without intuition can have only an unknowable *Ding-an-sich* as its object. Intuition must therefore have a transcendental status if there is to be positive knowledge at all. We must be able to unite the *absoluteness* of pure being (or the *activity* of pure thinking) with the transitoriness of intuited existence (in the synthesis of finite thought). We can do this in the case of our own self-knowledge: the unity is the intuited *act* of "self-positing." But that self-positing is at the same time, and necessarily, the positing of a natural order in which we exist as mortal, finite, elements.[52] So what is intuited even in self-intuition is "an activity of both intelligence and nature" (110). The conceptual moment, the aspect of thought, is the moment of freedom; the intuitive moment, the aspect of nature, is the moment of necessity. We should notice that the self as concept, as a free activity of thinking, knows itself directly in philosophical reflection; but as a natural *being* it has to be "deduced as a link in the chain of necessity." That the self is an activity of both intelligence and nature is only intuited *properly* when the task of speculation is complete. But, at the same time, if we try to philosophize without the intuition of the whole, we shall be obliged to wander, as the Goddess tells Parmenides that all other mortals do, "ignorantly, with divided minds and scattered thoughts."[53]

Thus from the point of view of reflection, this intuition of the whole is the one thing that can and must be postulated as a condition of the possibility of philosophical knowledge. There can be no justification for postulating Ideas, no excuse for the celebrated postulates of God, and immortality; and no need to postulate freedom, if thinking itself is freedom. But how does the intuition of the whole differ as a postulate from God? When we raise this question we come back again to the influence of Spinoza on the philosophy of Identity. Kant postulates God as a moral Providence, a rational guarantee of the *summum bonum*.[54] He agrees that the archetypal intelligence is the only ground in which mechanism and finality can be satisfactorily united: but our theoretical need to appeal to final causes does not justify the postulate of God because "theism would first have to succeed in proving to the satisfaction of the determinant judgment that the unity of end in matter is an impossible result of the mere mechanism of nature. Otherwise it is not entitled definitely to locate its ground beyond and above nature."[55] "Postulating God" means, for Kant, positing something "über die Natur hinaus." This is the postulate that Hegel declares illegitimate.[56] From the (Kantian) standpoint of philosophical reflection we can best express what Hegel *is* prepared to permit as the postulate that "the unity of end in matter" is not "an impossible result of the mere mechanism of nature." He claims that for the sake of reflective cognition we are required to postulate that the finality of nature *coincides* with its mechanism, i.e., we must abandon the simple Kantian identification of nature with causal necessity. The Absolute is Fichte's

God as Absolute Subject, *and* Spinoza's God as Absolute Substance—or it is God as infinite *necessarily* comprehending Nature as finite.

Having thus far painfully constructed a ladder from reflection to speculation, by way of Kant's concept of Reason as dialectical—and particularly by a bold *generalization* of Kant's notion of antinomy—Hegel now begins to talk out of the other side of his mouth, and preach the gospel according to Schelling. Once we have climbed Hegel's ladder we must throw it away. For from the speculative point of view it is a mistake to regard transcendental intuition as a postulate at all: "this whole manner of postulating has its sole ground in the fact that the one-sidedness of reflection is accepted as a starting point" (112). When we rise to the standpoint of self-conscious Reason, we begin—as Spinoza did—from God as the essence that necessarily exists. This is really the *end* of our journey however. We can only speak of philosophy beginning here because the construction of the Absolute is not completed until we *return* to the point where we began "postulating" the Absolute.[57]

The last of Hegel's preliminary questions is: *must* philosophy be systematic? We have already noted that a mystical scepticism, which knows only the transitoriness of finite things is perfectly possible; and that in the absence of transcendental intuition this is the only form in which a genuinely speculative impulse can express itself (compare further 155–6). What Hegel now goes on to argue is that transcendental intuition can be imperfect in various ways and degrees so that the speculative impulse of the philosopher does not get completely articulated into his system. Fichte with his continual emphasis on "striving" is very much in Hegel's mind here (though the model of philosophy as a "constant flight from limitations" [113] is probably Jacobi). Fichte managed to produce a properly systematic theory of the self, but his theory of the world was all "postulation." The proper method, as sketched by Hegel, is to begin with the most immediate realities (objectively: "matter"; subjectively: "feeling") and show how they are necessarily related to other realities that are less immediate. Thus the totality is constructed in an organic order that corresponds to its natural genesis in experience. The *System of Ethical Life* which Hegel produced at the end of 1802[58] is an example of this progressive development. Being an essay in practical philosophy, it is subjective and begins with feeling.[59]

The history of speculative philosophy is "the history of the one eternal Reason" (114). But philosophies will have different contingent starting points according to the need of the culture in which they arise.

Thus the topic of systematization rounds out Hegel's general reflections by bringing us back to the problem of the use and abuse of the history of philosophy from which we began. Systems which appear to be most radically opposed to each other may equally be products of genuine speculation, that is, they may both be constructions that are validly founded in the transcendental intuition of the absolute whole that knows itself in the "history of the one, eternal Reason" (114). Thus both Fichte's idealism and D'Holbach's materialism are expressions of genuine speculation; and both of them also fall into dogmatism in so far as they are systematically imperfect. Hegel concedes that philosophical materialism typically involves a cruder kind of dogmatic failure (115). This is presumably because the primitive object of transcendental intuition is the thinking self.[60]

The mark of dogmatism is the substitution of the category of cause and effect for that of substantial relation in philosophical reflection about the relation of the Absolute to its appearance in the knowing consciousness of Reason. Kant regarded Descartes, Spinoza, and Leibniz as the paradigms of dogmatic metaphysics. In general, Hegel does not allow that Spinoza was guilty of dogmatism at all. Indeed, he cannot allow this without implicitly conceding that Schelling's philosophical procedure is misguided. All the same, the route to speculation that he has himself mapped out passes through the fire of Kant's Dialectic and for this reason his own conception of dogmatism comprehends Kant's view in a suspended form. Thus, what he refers to as "pure dogmatism" or as a "dogmatism of philosophy" seems to be characteristic of Descartes. For in Descartes we are presented with *two* substances which *interact*. "Consistent realism and idealism" are represented in the Kantian perspective by Spinoza and Berkeley. But since Hegel says that in the consistent forms of realism and idealism "the causal relation is essentially suspended" we probably ought to think rather of Spinoza and Fichte as the *speculative* proponents of these extremes. Certainly Fichte is the main example in Hegel's mind when he goes on to discuss the way in which transcendental philosophy (i.e., *speculative* idealism) passes over into dogmatism. So we can be sure that he has *Fichte's* distinction between "realism," "idealism," "dogmatism," and "critical philosophy" in his mind. Fichte usually *identifies* "realism" with "dogmatism" and "idealism" with "criticism," though he admits that *dogmatic* idealism is possible.[61]

Genuinely speculative philosophy always takes the substance/accident relation as basic. But just as causality is thought of as *reciprocal* in *pure* dogmatism, so the substance/accident relation is shown to be reciprocal in pure speculation. Thus in the philosophy of nature self-positing is the *abstract schema* of the real world, and in transcendental philosophy nature is only the abstract schema of self-conscious Reason (110). Fichte starts out among the speculative lambs, but since he does not attempt to *construct* nature on the model of the self, but rather regards it as an *endless* practical problem to reconstruct it in accordance with the moral law (causality through freedom), he ends up among the dogmatic goats. For his *moral* idealism requires "a relation of the Absolute to appearance *other* than that of nullification." But in Fichte only the nullification ever *appears*; the identity of the Ego and its world remains a subjective intuition.

The exposition of Fichte, to which Hegel now proceeds, is designed to establish this thesis in detail, but we should never forget that Hegel is only spelling out the *cost* of a conclusion which Fichte himself proclaims as necessary from the outset. There is no question of Hegel's accusing Fichte of failing to do something that Fichte had originally proposed to do.

5. ANALYSIS (II) : FICHTE

About the fairly lengthy exposition of Fichte which makes up the central section of the essay we can here afford to be much briefer. The argument is more straightforward, and Hegel himself has provided another version of most of it in his discussion of Fichte in the *History of Philosophy*.[62] We shall here confine ourselves to the briefest outline possible, along with the identification and discussion of a few cruces.

The general line of Hegel's criticism of Fichte has already been indicated. Fichte's science of knowledge is a genuinely speculative theory of the self which shows us how the self produces the world, but not how the world is the real world of the self. It is natural therefore that Hegel should concentrate on Fichte's deduction of nature in its various aspects. We should notice at once, however, that he ignores what was at that moment Fichte's most recent (and accessible) statement of his views in the *Vocation of Man* (1800). The reason for this, which is not explicitly stated in the essay, was made plain the following year, in *Faith and Knowledge*, and we have already referred to it. Fichte's decline from speculative philosophy to dogmatism becomes complete in that work. It is therefore excluded from the *Difference* essay as unworthy of treatment. Hegel is here concerned only with Fichte's system as an expression of genuine speculation.[63]

In his lecture course on the *History of Philosophy*, Hegel lays it down that among Fichte's works only the *Science of Knowledge* is genuinely speculative. Fichte's *Science of Rights* and his *System of Ethics* "contain nothing speculative, but demand the presence of the speculative element."[64] This contention follows quite naturally from the argument of the *Difference* essay taken together with *Faith and Knowledge*. The completion of his critical survey of Fichte in *Faith and Knowledge* caused Hegel to be rather more trenchant from the outset in the lecture course, than he is in the *Difference* essay. In the lectures he complains straight away that "the form in which Fichte's philosophy is presented has . . . the real drawback of bringing the empirical ego ever before one's eyes, which is absurd."[65] But it seems to me that the *Vocation of Man* and the "non-speculative" parts of Fichte's system have improperly influenced this verdict, and that Hegel's initial stance in the *Difference* essay was sounder.

Here he begins by contrasting pure thinking with ordinary consciousness and saying that the task of Fichte's speculative philosophy is to explain this antithesis, that is, to show the *positive* relation of ordinary finite consciousness to the pure act of self-positing. The negative aspect of the relation is already given by a simple consideration of what it means to be finite. This is what we have in the religious consciousness that "all flesh is as grass." The desired positive relation would be an *explanation* of this transitory existence. The *opposition* between the infinite and the finite self must be suspended or overcome, in other words there must be no recourse to the Kantian thing-in-itself as the ultimate origin of sensuous data. The opposition must be suspended because the world of empirical consciousness is what we are primarily aware of. Philosophical consciousness comes later, and reflects on, looks back upon, ordinary consciousness. If this pure consciousness is indeed the real origin of empirical consciousness we must be able to deduce empirical consciousness from pure consciousness. Otherwise we shall not have shown that pure consciousness *is* pure, that is, a priori. It is only by this deduction, by showing how every aspect of empirical consciousness is adequately grounded in pure consciousness, that we can transform the empty *concept* of pure consciousness into an intuition. Empirical consciousness, i.e., the world as we experience it, must be shown to be a self-actualization of the pure self-positing Ego.

Fichte fails to solve this problem. Pure consciousness does not "become objective to itself," does not become an intuition. First he disguises the antinomy of consciousness by separating it into two seemingly independent propositions: "the Ego posits itself" and "the Ego posits a non-Ego opposed to itself." Then his reconciliation "the Ego posits within itself a divisible Ego and a divisible non-Ego" is never shown to be identical with the original absolute positing. The original self-positing ought not to have been divided into a sequence of distinct acts like this. This is how the reflective intellect is bound to proceed; but once Fichte has taken the activity of the Ego to pieces like this he is never able to put it together again.

The Ego and the non-Ego fall apart just as, in Kant, transcendental apperception and the thing-in-itself fall apart. The self-positing and the oppositing remain quite independent and opposed, so that the self within which the two activities are supposedly united remains unknown and transcendent like the traditional God of theism. The third principle ought to be the only one. We have to comprehend the way in which the activity which Kant called "productive imagination" establishes both self and world in one fell swoop. What Fichte establishes instead is a finite self enveloped in a mystery which it struggles endlessly and hopelessly to dissolve. The easy interpretation of Fichte's theory, the one that a formalist like Reinhold naturally seizes on, is the dogmatic idealist one. But Fichte is too honest and too clearheaded to solve his problem by the *fiat* of dogmatic idealism; so his idealism remains simply problematic.[66] Empirical consciousness is explained equally well either in terms of the self-positing or in terms of the oppositing: "it offers no more and no less warrant for pure consciousness than for the thing-in-itself" (127).

In the theoretical activity of the Ego the mystery appears in the form of the incomprehensible "impact" which the Ego meets. This is just Kant's *Ding-an-sich*; and transferring it, by hypothesis, into the Ego itself does not make it any more comprehensible than it was before. Here we are face to face with the absolute oppositing that is not resolved in the synthesis. Nature is deduced from this primordial defectiveness of the Ego—from the fact that it meets an impact. "As Fichte put it, the advance to empirical consciousness is made because pure consciousness is not a complete consciousness" (129–30). I have not been able to find any passage in which Fichte does put it quite like this. But he does say that intellectual intuition "never occurs in isolation, as a complete act of consciousness."[67] And in the *Science of Knowledge* itself, he asserts several times that pure self-positing cannot constitute what we mean by consciousness *at all*. Here is what he says, for example, in the section on which the rest of Hegel's outline appears at this point to be based: "A self that posits itself *as* self-positing, or a *subject*, is impossible without an object brought forth in the manner described."[68] The expression that I cannot trace probably occurs in some exposition of 1797 or later—or perhaps Hegel's memory is slightly at fault here.

Because of his admission of the impact Fichte's system falls short of being a system of perfect freedom. The impact is obviously a boundary for productive imagination in theoretical cognition; but Fichte seeks to maintain his idealism by proving that it must arise from the practical activity of the Ego. On that side, however, it turns out to be a necessary presupposition for the existence of freedom as an endless striving. The conquest of the non-Ego, the establishment of equivalence between the first principle "Ego = Ego" and the third "Ego = (Ego + non-Ego)" is a moral requirement. But the existence of the self as an agent presupposes that this requirement cannot finally be met. So in the end "Ego = Ego" turns into "Ego *ought* to be equal to Ego." Pure consciousness has flown up into the noumenal realm of the moral law; empirical consciousness remains sundered between what ought to be and what is. And, in Fichte's view, it is only *what ought to be* that is intellectually intuited. What is real, on the contrary, is always the lived antithesis between this intellectually intuited ideal, and the empirically intuited situation. Human rational existence is simply moral striving. The Absolute is thus a "bad" infinity of moral progress in perpetuity.

All the concrete applications of Fichte's philosophy to human life are reflective rather than speculative because they rest on this foundation. Hegel now comes to his main topic, which is the conception of nature in Fichte's system. The most immediate form of nature in rational consciousness is a "drive" (*Trieb*); while the finite manifestation of rational freedom is a "concept of purpose." Synthesized as a mode of consciousness these two elements make up a *feeling*. We should note that Hegel accepts this synthesis himself, just as he accepts the theoretical synthesis of self-positing and opposing. For "feeling" is one of the primitive notions that he mentions as appropriate starting points for speculative development (113). But he does not agree with the analytical, compositive method by which Fichte arrives at it. The whole context into which Fichte's synthesis is inserted is wrong, for "feeling is finite only from the point of view of reflection" (136). In the *System of Ethical Life* Hegel himself begins with the intuition of a "feeling"—but he allows the context of relations that are involved in it to develop from it.[69]

According to the principle of self-positing, freedom and drive should coincide. They are just different ways of looking at the same basic drive (*Urtrieb*). But since drive or impulse is thought of as completely determinate it can only be identified with freedom by coming under the *control* of the practical concept which decides whether or not it is to be gratified or suppressed. This is the moral tyranny that Hegel had already condemned in Kant. The unity is merely formal, and the form conceals an inner disruption. What makes things still worse is that so far as the disruption is overcome, the union involves the corruption of pure freedom. It is always some impulse of nature that is gratified in an action; the final purpose of absolute rational freedom is endlessly postponed. The best that we can do is make progress towards it.

The weakness of this view is that Nature is regarded as mechanically determined and lifeless. Schelling and Hegel must have spent hours poring over the "Critique of Teleological Judgment"; but it seems safe to say that Fichte did not. The simple antithesis of mechanical necessity and freedom was sufficient for him, and for that reason he declines into a reflective philosopher as soon as he reaches the problems of practical philosophy. For it is just this antithesis of freedom and necessity that is the final shipwreck of reflection; this is the abyss from which speculation begins. Reflective thought is aware of itself as a free, spontaneous activity, since it operates in the infinite realm of possibilities; yet the ideal that it strives after is to comprehend the actual world as a system of perfect determinism. This is the impasse that Fichte avoids by the device of absolute postponement.

But if the establishment of nature, of the non-Ego, really is an aspect of the free self-positing of the Ego, this simple antithesis of freedom and mechanism is an illusion of the intellect. Nature as a whole must be conceived as a self-determining system, an organic living whole, Spinoza's *natura naturans*. Fichte acknowledges this in his *System of Ethics* but he maintains the rigid opposition between nature and freedom nonetheless.[70] The organic view of nature does not confer any standing on it in the face of the law of Reason. We can see this with particular clarity in the *Science of Rights*. The whole deduction proceeds as if nature were simply dead matter, varying only in its degree of plasticity to the imposed rational purpose. Kant preserved a certain independence for the organic aspect of nature by insisting that we are obliged to conceive of the purpose of a "natural end" (i.e., an organism) as if it were determined by and for another intelligence (though we are not thereby entitled to postulate the existence of that other intelligence). Fichte "does not need this detour" (143). But it is highly questionable whether he is really better off than Kant in Hegel's eyes.[71]

In Fichte's theory "nature is determined immediately by and for intelligence" (143). So we do not have to concern ourselves with the pur - pose for which it was designed by an intelligence *other* than ours. But we still have to take a "detour through the dominion of the concept" (144). The "rational being," or finite intelligence, is a composite of soul and body, the combination of pure rational freedom with a limited set of physical possibilities. There is the freedom that man *is,* and the freedom that *a* man *has.* Nature is the sphere of the freedom that we *have,* and because we *all* have it, we necessarily impinge on one another. So for the sake of rational freedom, the spontaneous capacity of the individual to act for its own ends must be surrendered. Only the freedom of obedience to the law of Reason matters. The individual must be absolutely *at the disposal* of that law. *His* freedom is to be measured as the degree of his plasticity, his indeterminateness, the range of possibilities that stands at the disposal of Reason in his person. Thus if *my* spontaneous impulses are interfered with and curbed for the sake of the community, this is not really an *infringement* of my freedom but the *realization* of it. Fichte could not speak, as Rousseau did, of "being forced to be free," but this is exactly how the moral compulsion exercised by Fichte's rational will appears to Hegel. The moral freedom of Fichte is quite different from voluntary commitment to a social purpose that one understands and identifies with. Self-commitment and identification of this sort is the "free limitation of one's freedom" that is characteristic of natural organic community. Natural needs only become compulsive in the way that Fichte's moral requirements are, when they rise to the pitch of what Hegel calls *Not* in his Frankfurt manuscripts. Thus Fichte's image of human society can be called a *Notstaat.*[72] Everything in society must be regulated by Reason (embodied in an external authority). The ordinary societies which are less ambitious on behalf of Reason are actually more concordant with Reason.

Thus Fichte's theory of law involves a universal *external* tyranny of Reason. His theory of ethics involves an even more effective internalized tyranny. The external tyranny seems more objectionable, but it can be evaded; whereas the rational man will not even *wish* to evade his own conscience. Furthermore, because of the empirical component in any drive, ethical volitions are bound to conflict; so there are "conflicts of duty"—for any ethical volition will be defensible at the bar of Reason, that is, it can be presented as a duty. Kant recognized the necessity for casuistry in order to resolve moral difficulties of this sort. But because Fichte aims to be systematic, his doctrine of moral duty needs to be as completely determinate as his theory of legal right.

The "indifference point" which Fichte cannot reach is an *aesthetic* ideal. Now Fichte, too, has read Kant's *Critique of Judgment* and Schiller's *Aesthetic Letters*. So he can write eloquent pages about the aesthetic harmony of human nature, and he appreciates the *instrumental* role which Schiller assigns to aesthetic education. Even the role of beauty as a regulative ideal (which is also in Schiller) is one that Fichte can verbally appropriate. Hegel approves of what Fichte wrote on this topic, but finds it to be inconsistent with his basic position. He claims that Fichte's *Ethics* is condemned out of his own mouth when the criteria of beauty, harmony and spontaneity are applied to it. This judgment is unfair. For Fichte's position clearly is that we must "relate to the moral law like a slave" only if we can do no better. The only valid complaint is that Fichte never explains *how* we can do better. "Striving" is all that he explains; and although striving can be noble, it can certainly also be ugly.

Thus in spite of its genuinely speculative impulse, Fichte's system is ultimately an exercise of mere intellect. This was evident at the beginning from the way in which Fichte analytically separated the "acts" of the Ego. And in the end the aspects of identity and difference (of pure and empirical consciousness) go apart into a causal relationship. Causality is the model case of a relative identity; and Fichte's practical philosophy, where all the problems of the theoretical philosophy are supposed to be resolved, turns out to be just a matter of the causal efficacy of Reason, or of the dominance of the concept over impulse.

6. ANALYSIS (III): SCHELLING

Schelling's *system*, by contrast, is completely speculative; it is an organic expression of his basic philosophical insight. Pure consciousness (insight) and empirical consciousness (system) coincide. He shows us both how the self becomes a world—the "subjective Subject-Object," and how the world becomes a self—the "objective Subject-Object." The "point of indifference" from which this double task starts is the transcendental intuition of the self positing itself as other in order to achieve self-consciousness. Earlier Hegel spoke of this moment positively as the "infinite focus which irradiates the radii (i.e., finite cognitions] at the same time that it is formed by them" (111). This language comes from the tradition of Augustinian theology. It was used by the theologians to describe God's relation to the created world. In the context of the Identity theory it only becomes meaningful when speculation has arrived at its goal. Hegel generally prefers to describe the indifference point as a vanishing-point. It is the moment where finite consciousness *annihilates* itself by recognizing its own antinomic character. Thus transcendental intuition is the intuition of nothingness. Only a religious enthusiast could be satisfied with "this intuition of colorless light" (156) which is merely the birth-pang of speculative philosophy, the point of "absolute contraction."

Philosophy must *justify* finite experience, it must "give the separation into subject and object its due" (156). Finite experience is appearance (both of the *being* of a "thing-in-itself" on the objective side, and of the *activity* of human imagination and intellect on the subjective side). But neither the *being* nor the *activity* can exist without manifesting themselves. Both for the subject and for the object it is essential that they should appear. Thus an intuition of the ultimate identity of subject and object is not enough: "the Absolute itself is the identity of [noumenal] identity [of subject and object] and [phenomenal] non-identity" (156). Absolute *knowledge* is the identity of being and appearance, or the comprehending of the finite as a mirror (*speculum*) of the infinite. Unless we admit "the claims of separation" we cannot reach the absolute identity at all. Both subject and object are equally finite and equally contingent in ordinary experience. The contingency is overcome when the finite phenomena are comprehended under laws. But to put the legislation of freedom on the noumenal side and that of nature on the phenomenal side is not good enough, if all that there is on the noumenal side for reflection and knowledge is "nothing." Moral freedom will only become *comprehensible* when the programme of the Identity philosophy is carried out, or when Nature, the realm of the finite phenomena of ordinary cognition is exhibited as self-determining. The antinomy of necessary and free causality, which was so fundamental in Kant's view that one must be ascribed to phenomenal nature exclusively and the other to the noumenal self exclusively, must be shown up as an *ideal* opposition, a matter of intellectual perspective: while the difference between conscious and unconscious activity, which is reduced to an *ideal* difference, a matter of perspective, in Fichte's idealism, must be given its proper status as a *real* opposition. For it is the conscious/unconscious opposition (not the necessary/free opposition) that genuinely characterizes the realms of nature and culture into which experience is *really* divided.

The indifference point from which speculative philosophy starts is the self that intuits its own spontaneity. This is the philosophical common ground shared by the two systems. For reasons of neutrality (as between natural and transcendental philosophy) Hegel refers to it as the "point of contraction." It will be helpful here, therefore to consider *generally* the relation of the poles of contraction and expansion to the two forms of the indifference point that are spoken of in the Identity Philosophy. The indifference point as unity is the rationally self-conscious individual. When philosophic reflection turns in upon itself and seeks the pure activity which is the point of origin of all consciousness it discovers the pole of contraction—Fichte's self-positing Ego or the spark of divine life which is the basis of our existence as rational individuals. This moment of pure consciousness, so called, whether it be pure thinking or pure intuition, is not consciousness in any ordinary sense at all. It is the fount of feeling and thought—or of "life" and of "light" in the language of the first chapter of *John*—and the starting point of transcendental philosophy. It is also the *goal* of natural philosophy which moves from the infinite extent of nature at the opposite extreme of expansion to the absolute source of life in the self-conscious living organism. The "indifference point as totality" is only really reached when *both* sciences are completed. In the same way, the indifference point of the magnet (upon which the whole analogy is founded) is only really known for what it is, when the field of force between the two poles of which it is the center are plotted and shown in relation to it. The natural philosopher's journey from the boundaries of physical existence to its center must be complemented and fulfilled by the transcendental philosopher's journey from the origin of consciousness to the conscious union of the mind with the whole of nature. This is the expansion of the *self* from unity to totality. But we cannot unpack all the riches of the spirit practically, unless we know theoretically what is packed up in its nature. Thus he journey from the immensity of space *to* the *external center*—the human organism—is just as necessary to philosophical comprehension as the journey *from* the *internal center*—the human mind, and specifically the productive imagination which is its point of origin—to God. Fichte rightly believed that he could find the secret of existence in the depths of the self. But it was still a secret when he found it. All of his constructive account of human life rests on an *intellectual* (i.e., mechanical) concept of nature. If we really want to formulate the purpose of human life in the world, we must comprehend *adequately* our own place in the order of *living* nature.

We can go this far with the identity theory without any great strain. For, ambitious though it may be, it surely makes sense to set up the organic comprehension of the world as the goal of philosophical endeavor; and it makes sense to insist that the task must be conceived in an organic or teleological frame, since the enterprise of comprehension itself, as a goal set by a conscious, goal-seeking organism, is to be comprehended within that frame. But why do the proponents of this programme insist *a priori*, that every part of the organic totality must itself be organic? We surely cannot assert *a priori* that "every speck of dust is an organization?" (157).

This is probably the gravest crux in the identity theory. What appears to be a quite dogmatic assumption that *everything* is organic, contrasts very sharply with the careful and critical concern of Kant to do justice to the organic world *along with* the inorganic. And it is undeniable that the identity theorists were over-confident. Nothing can save them from the reproach of over-simplification and wild generalization. They were even conscious of it themselves. Both Schelling and Hegel continually reformulated their philosophy of Nature, struggling to find the *right* application of the concept of organism to it and in it. Hegel later accused Schelling of using a few general analogies everywhere and calling the result "science." But even to a sympathetic Hegelian critic like Croce, it was not clear what gave Hegel the right to condemn Schelling. For—to Croce at least—Hegel's own mature philosophy of Nature appeared to be liable to the same criticism.[73] We shall have to re-examine later the question whether Hegel's critique of Schelling really was a matter of pot calling kettle black.

For the present, the fact that neither Hegel nor Schelling was *philosophically* troubled by difficulties which were almost as obvious to them as they are to us, suggests that we may not have understood properly what the *philosophical* enterprise was. The Identity Theory in its primitive form is quite evidently a latter-day version of the traditional conception of the "great chain of being." But it is indeed a latter-day version—or in other words it is meant to have a critical interpretation. Interpreted *critically* the proposition that "every speck of dust is an organization" is a thesis about what can count as a satisfactory explanation of any phenomenon. The claim is that the model of theoretical explanation is an *organic system*. The "speck of dust" is plainly a metaphor for the "smallest part." The microscope had, of

course, revealed that there *were* living specks; and Leibniz had gener-
alized and extrapolated from that discovery with a boldness that still
inspires awe. But that is not the crucial point: indeed it will only mislead us, if it causes us to think that the Identity theory is a direct
return to Leibniz. The claim of the Identity theorists is rather that
explanation in terms of *causal chains* does not satisfactorily explain
anything. A proper *explanation* must place the explanandum in a pattern that is self-subsistent and self-sufficient; and a philosophical system must be an all-inclusive pattern of this same type. Just how phenomena can be arranged in organic patterns is a matter for empirical
investigation. In this respect the original formulation was certainly at
fault, being both too dogmatic in the old style, and too little attentive
to the actual state of empirical science.

The thesis about what can count as a satisfactory explanation, is
what is locked up in the claim that the object itself is a Subject-Object.
All knowledge, it is claimed, must be modelled on, must have the
structure of, our self-knowledge. Fichte's right to be considered an important speculative philosopher rests on the fact that he was the one
who had analysed that structure. But he fell short of the goal because
he analysed *only* self-knowledge. He could not provide any ground
for the knowledge of objects which would give the objective (or natural) sciences an independent, self-subsistent status. The natural
world was for him simply the stage for moral activity, the place where
the Ego *ought* to be equal to itself, but *cannot* be, because it needs the
tension of the *ought* in order to go on existing at all.

That nature has no *independent* status, no subsistence on its own
account, is what the claim that there is only an ideal opposition of
subject and object in Fichte means. Hegel showed earlier that Fichte
is in trouble about the opposition of the first two acts of the Ego, its
self-positing and the positing of the opposite. If they are just ideal
factors, and only the third synthetic proposition is real knowledge,
then Fichte's system becomes a form of dogmatic theism since only
God can know things as they are: the absolute self-positing is quite
outside of our finite experience. But if the absolute positing and oppositing are real, then they are not properly united in the synthesis of
our finite experience; and then Fichte's system which rests on the self-
positing and suppresses the positing of the object by fiat, is a dogmatic idealism.

Whether we adopt the theistic or the idealistic interpretation, Nature has in Fichte the status of an absolute object; it never achieves
the status of something which *posits itself* like a subject. Even if God

knows it as it is *in itself*, it exists *for us* only as a moment in the synthesis of conscious reflection. But then the synthesis becomes merely formal, that is, the thing-in-itself remains independent of it, and so does the real subject. These reflective forms—the thing-in-it-self and the I think—are just what have to be nullified in the antinomy of self-conscious reflection. Then speculative thought can proceed to construct the Subject-Object in metaphysical intuition. This "construction" of Nature as a Subject-Object is a matter of interpreting our experience of nature in the categoreal pattern provided by the transcendental theory of the self. We can only claim to have philosophically comprehended our own position in Nature, when all of our empirical knowledge has been organized conceptually with the emergence of the self as its *telos*. This is "the work of Reason which posits the opposites identity and non-identity, as identical, not just in the form of cognition, but in the form of being as well."

It is only if Nature is a mirror of the Self in this way that there can be true self-knowledge. Fichte speaks in one place of the difference between God's point of view and ours, that is, he speaks as if the *theistic* interpretation of his system were correct. But he immediately makes clear that we cannot even *think* what God's consciousness would be like, because pure self-positing of the Ego cannot constitute consciousness for us.[74] Thus the only consistent way to avoid the demands of the Philosophy of Identity is Kant's critical conception of all knowledge as phenomenal. This is the "legislation of reflection" (159); and no matter how much Fichte may insist on the life and activity of the Ego he cannot escape Kant's net.

From the Kantian viewpoint only limited things can be known. So Hegel describes the *a priori* synthesis of cognition itself in terms of the categories of quantity and quality:

> The identity, insofar as it synthesizes the opposites [i.e., intuition and concept], is itself just a quantum [a *particular* cognition] and the difference [between subject and object generally] is qualitative [i.e., it is a *real* difference between separate beings, the *Ding-an-sich* and the noumenal Self behind the "I think"] in the manner of the categories where the first, for example reality [compare the *Ding-an-sich*] is posited in the third [limitation— compare the formal synthesis of intuition and concept] and so is the second [negation—compare the noumenal self] but only quantitatively [compare the use of *quantum* earlier]. (159–60)

Speculation, on the other hand, requires a *real* synthesis of these real opposites (whose reality remains entirely *problematic* in the doctrine of *formal* synthesis). There must be an actual not a formal identity of being and nothing, reality and negation, and it must be *known* to appear in our limited experience. This *knowledge* is the "identity of identity and non-identity."

There are, therefore, two absolute sciences or types of science: transcendental philosophy and natural philosophy, or the science of intelligence and the science of life. The structure of consciousness becomes both the activity and the content of absolute knowledge when both the pure subject and the pure object are taken as opposed aspects of the original self-manifesting Subject-Object. The *reality* of the opposition appears here as a *reversal* of categoreal values. From the point of view of transcendental philosophy the objective aspects of experience are empirical or accidental facts; but from the point of view of natural philosophy the subjective aspects are epiphenomenal or accidental forms.

The independence of the two standpoints is something that we are quite naturally, and commonsensically, aware of. But common sense is never comfortable with the strict opposition. Descartes postulated two substances and then struggled to find the point of union between them. Others, who are less clearheaded, just take criteria and problems that belong to one perspective and import them into the other. Thus we can ask, "What are the physical causes of truth?" and we then arrive at a "transcendental hypothesis" like the "membrane theory" of J. C. Lossius.[75] Or we can ask "What is the rational purpose of the cork tree?" and make Wolff's eternally amusing discovery that it was intended by nature for the plugging of wine bottles.[76]

The typical *philosophical* mistake is to fall into an aggressive dogmatism that denies the validity either of the transcendental or of the natural point of view. Dualism gets along comfortably enough by ignoring the fundamental requirement that the dualism must be explained. Aggressive dogmatism takes the task more seriously. Hegel now presents the idealism of Kant and Fichte as the final sophistication of dogmatism. He has to include Kant along with Fichte here, because Kant was a notable philosopher of Nature, whereas Fichte contributed nothing in this area. We should be glad of this accident because it is only at this point that his own debt to Kant's *Critique of Judgment* (of which I have already made so much) comes right to the surface in the essay.

First he sums up the doctrine of a "natural end" in the "Critique of Teleological Judgment." Here we have only to notice the translation rules. Kant's insistence that the category of natural end has a regulative not a constitutive function for our understanding becomes "This *human* perspective is not supposed to affirm anything concerning the *reality* of nature" (163). Kant would have been surprised to learn that he had left the reality of nature in doubt. But he was philosophically obliged to leave the reality of the *Ding-an-sich* in doubt; and so, according to Hegel, "nature remains something merely thought." To be *real*, nature must exist "for itself," it must have its own essence and purpose, and not just be the result or product of our constructive efforts with our categories. Kant rises to the idea of a "natural end," and even to the idea of a "sensuous intellect" (again he would be surprised, and when he recognized his *intellectus archetypus* or "intuitive understanding" under this strange name he would not be very pleased). But Kant does not comprehend the necessary *reality* of either of them. So he is, like Newton, ultimately a sceptic about human science. His *Metaphysical Foundations of Natural Science* is an exposition of Newtonian metaphysics—and Kant himself said that we must not hope for the Newton of a blade of grass.[77]

But, alas for Kant, not even Newtonian mechanics can be consistently derived in accordance with the dictates of Newtonian epistemology. The attractive and repulsive forces that have to be united in the concept of matter already constitute an organic whole. Kant may protest, like Newton, that we have "no insight into the possibility of basic forces" but he knows what he means by a force, and he knows that matter, according to his concept of it, is composed out of opposite forces. Kant's matter thus prefigures the Fichtean Ego, and not even the most elementary phenomena of dynamics fall within the constitutive purview of the understanding. Whether this contention of Hegel's is justified or not, would require a lengthy inquiry, and one that is beyond my competence. But at least, we can see clearly at this point why Schelling and Hegel thought they *must* assert that "every speck of dust is an organization."

On the basis of this universal mechanism of Newton and Kant, Fichte erected a moral teleology that is indistinguishable in principle from that of Wolff. Since his starting point is supplied by his own existence as a finite rational being, Fichte, like Wolff before him, is doomed to fall prey to the immense variety of nature and the still greater variety of its practical possibilities for use. "The only way in which this dispersion could be avoided at all, would be for the deduction to draw its various points into a circle" (165). But before one can draw a circle one must fix the center.

Here at last Hegel arrives at the stage of positive statement. The true method of philosophy should be modelled on the pattern of organic growth. Both transcendental and natural philosophy should trace the evolution (of self-consciousness and of nature) from germ to ripeness, or from unity to totality. There will thus be a parallel like that which Spinoza asserted between the "order of ideas" and the "order of things." The ideas and things that are ordered will themselves be organic patterns; so no matter how finite they are, they will be "internally unlimited." The most ephemeral of organizations can be viewed *sub specie aeternitatis*. The important claim of the identity theory, as against Spinoza or any mechanistic theory, is that it is not just the whole but every naturally produced organic cycle or pattern that can be comprehended in its eternal aspect. If every moment of experience, philosophically interpreted, were not in this way a mirror of the Absolute—like one of the monads of Leibniz—if only the infinite whole were eternal, then Kant would be right, and Reason would be dialectical in a self-destructive sense. But if Kant were right, Jacobi would be right in his turn: all the finite science that Kant wanted to defend would be no more than the organization of our ignorance. In fact, however, finite cognition becomes knowledge by being "organized"—and the Identity Philosophy shows us how this miracle can come about in spite of our human limitations.

Each of the two philosophical sciences reaches its limit where the other begins. The pole of expansion belongs peculiarly to natural philosophy, and the pole of contraction to transcendental philosophy. Natural philosophy falls short of the contraction of all extended organization into the temporal point of self-consciousness. Self-consciousness is engulfed in the immensity of physical space. Natural philosophy moves from the immensity of space to the unity of the most complex and highly developed physical organism—man, the "outer center." Transcendental philosophy moves from the most primitive sensational consciousness (the "inner center") to the religious experience of the most civilized community. It would seem that the two sciences *cannot* directly touch one another because the medium of the one is physical reality while that of the other is conscious ideality. But natural philosophy is *theoretical*, i.e., it is concerned with the conceptualization of physical reality; and transcendental philosophy is practical, i.e., it is concerned with the realization of consciousness. So an ultimate suspension of the opposition between them is not inconceivable, and as we shall soon see, Hegel has some important things to say about it.

Another note is needed here, however, about the "indifference points" in natural philosophy. We indicated earlier that natural philosophy goes from the pole of expansion to that of contraction and we characterized the indifference points only as they appear in transcendental philosophy. But the Spinozistic doctrine of a parallel between the two orders requires Hegel to say, and he does say, that both sciences move from unity to totality. What then is the unity from which natural philosophy begins? What is the indifference point that somehow *unifies* the bad infinite of space? It appears that the answer is "a *spatial* point regarded as a center of force." For we know that "the identity that is least dichotomous" is "at the objective pole, matter" (113); and we can infer something of the theory of matter from Hegel's critical comments about Kant's mechanics (163–5). Every point of space is a center from which force radiates out over the whole universe and also a center on which the force of the universe is focussed. Viewed in this way the physical point is an intuition of the primitive structure of the Ego according to Fichte. This center of cohesion is the minimal form of physical organization. The maximum or totality of physical organization is represented by the living body which is, in Spinoza's terminology, "the object of the idea that constitutes the human mind."[78]

Each of the sciences is a system of freedom *and* of necessity. Thus freedom and necessity are not *real* opposites—as Kant thought when he assigned each to its own world—but ideal moments or aspects of the one absolute reality. Freedom is the inner aspect of the organic whole, whether we view it in nature or in spirit; and necessity is its external aspect even if it is a link in an intelligible, not a physical, chain. This assimilation of physical to logical necessity which Hegel inherited from Spinoza, has been one of the great curses of his philosophy, perhaps the greatest impediment to understanding that derives from its origins in the Identity theory of Schelling.[79] The naturalization of freedom, on the other hand, must be accounted one of the great advances of post-Kantian speculation.[80]

But even if natural development is spontaneous, and the evolution of self-consciousness is conditioned, still the development of freedom is impossible in nature, and the natural conditioning of consciousness is not a matter of "physical causes of truth." Nature is the realm where necessity is predominant; and nothing spiritual is physically necessitated in a mechanical way. Hence the philosophy of Nature is the *theoretical* part of philosophy (where we contemplate necessity) and transcendental philosophy is the *practical* part (where we enjoy the consciousness of our own productive activity). But since this opposition is only an ideal one, and each of the two sciences is a conscious expression of the whole, each of them must strive away from its own ideal pole (necessity or freedom) towards the opposite one. Thus *within* the theoretical philosophy of nature there is a tension between the theoretical "construction" of inorganic nature and the practical "re-construction" of the organism. Biology is in a difficult position as an empirical science, not because, as Kant thought, our minds are not properly equipped for it, but because its subject matter is the *anticipation* in nature of what only consciousness is properly fitted to achieve. Similarly within the practical philosophy of consciousness there is a theoretical part which deals with the "construction" of consciousness itself as the capacity for theoretical cognition, as well as a fully practical part which deals with the transformation of the natural world through the realization of consciousness. All of nature-philosophy is really constructive, that is to say it involves the *projection* (in metaphysical intuition) of the structure of consciousness at the unconscious level. Construction is thus the instantiation of the absolute concept in intuition, the *externalization* of the divine Logos. But within the construction of the eternal order of nature, we can distinguish two phases, a spatial one and a temporal one, and the temporal phase is a reconstruction of the spatial order at a higher level. What I have called the spatial phase already involves time, for the *organic* motion of inorganic nature in space—the *solar system*—is the foundation of the temporal order, it gives us our standing measures for time. But this original construction is an image of life without change in the elements—the stars continue for ever in their courses. The reconstructive phase of natural philosophy is the internalization of the organic cycle within the cycling elements; the elements must now grow and decay, and hence they must produce their own successors. The *years* succeed one another, even though "heaven and earth do not pass away"; and with the passing of the years, the *generations* succeed one another, though life itself does not pass away. Thus, even within the unchanging natural order, "the Logos is begotten, not made."

But all of this *happens*, and it happens *all the time*. Consciousness does not make it so, and consciousness is not necessary to it. Consciousness itself, on the other hand, is the true reconstruction of the Absolute, the resumption into unity of the totality spread out in space and time, the synthesis of absolute intuition and absolute concept. The first phase of this reconstruction is self-*discovery*. From this point of view it resembles the constructive phase in the observation of nature; but at this level the activity of consciousness *is* essential. We only come to *be* what we really are, when we *know* what we really are. The conscious observer of nature is the "center" of an *external* world which he organizes in his empirical knowledge. But as he does transcendental philosophy he discovers himself to be the *internal* center, to be the focus of the life that animates the world. This is the *true* "begetting of the Logos," the discovery of our identity with the eternal Reason. It is a discovery which is throughout a self-*making*; and when the self-making is recognized as fundamental we pass from the *theory* of the self, to *practical* philosophy in the higher or stricter sense. This is the theory of the conscious *community*; that is, practical philosophy is economic and social thought, political and legal theory rather than ethics and moral philosophy as they have been traditionally understood in what Hegel calls subjective reflection.

When the goal of transcendental philosophy is reached, when man knows himself as the Logos, the culminating phase of the Identity philosophy opens. This is the suspension of the real opposition between the two philosophical sciences in the consciousness of the absolute indifference of knowing and being, discovering and making, construction and reconstruction. Philosophy as pure speculation is concerned with this suspension of the opposition between the two philosophic sciences (of nature and the self). The account that Hegel gives of the absolute point of indifference is an indication of the general content of this phase, at least. It should certainly be recognized as a third distinct phase of systematic philosophy. For otherwise we should have to regard the philosophy of art as part of *natural* philosophy (which does not seem to be possible). Art, which Schelling had declared to be the "organon of philosophy,"[81] is said by Hegel to be the grasping of the point of absolute indifference from the side of nature; speculation grasps the indifference point from the other side, the side of transcendental activity. But art is creative activity, and speculation is the contemplation of what is; so there is a perfect balance of subjective activity and objective being in both of them. As moments in the consciousness of absolute being (the culminating phase of science or absolute knowledge) they are both aspects of religion, which is the communal experience of the Absolute.

Hegel does not explicitly say that the theory of the absolute indifference point is a distinct phase of systematic philosophy, and not part of transcendental philosophy in the strict sense. But I think that this is the view that he actually holds, and that his failure to be explicit only reflects the difficulty of discussing a system which for the most part remains still to be expounded, and one whose exposition more properly belongs to someone else. He has to project an image of what Schelling's system will look like when Schelling has completed it. But he could not expound the system fully in the *Difference* essay, because in this period Schelling's activity was concentrated exclusively on the side of natural philosophy. Transcendental philosophy was to be *Hegel's* sphere. All the lecture courses that he was to give before Schelling left Jena, were conceived either as transcendental philosophy or as a critical propaedeutic to philosophy (like the general reflections with which the *Difference* essay opens). Since both Schelling and Hegel were by temperament and by express declaration systematic philosophers it was very comfortable to have a systematic conception which enabled them to divide the field while still continuing, each of them, to expound the Absolute Identity completely.

It is not surprising therefore, that in his account of Schelling's system in the *Difference* essay Hegel concentrates on the theory of organic nature. This is, in any case, what the comparison with Fichte requires, when that comparison is seen as an integration of Fichte's inadequacies, in line with the general project of showing that Schelling's system is not only different but also superior. And this was just where Schelling's own "Exposition of My System" broke off, so that as Hegel said in his preface even Schelling himself had never made the difference clear (79).

Hegel's condensed exposition does not clarify the problem very much, however. For help in understanding it we had best turn to the summaries of his system that Schelling himself produced during the next year or two. Schematically the main "levels" (*Potenzen*) of his Philosophy of Nature in this period were as follows:[82]

First *Potenz*: (of Nature or finitude, as opposed to God or infinity)
Reflection, or reception of the infinite in the finite:
1. World-structure (in the whole)
2. Body, material forms (in singulars)
3. Spatialization

Second *Potenz*: *Subsumption*,[83] or the reception of the finite into the infinite:
1. Light (the universal principle)
2. Dynamic series of bodies (in three *Potenzen*):
    a) Magnetism—one dimensional or linear
    b) Electricity—two dimensional or square
    c) Chemical process—three dimensional or cubic

3. Divine Light and Gravity
   Universal Mechanism and Necessity

Third *Potenz*: *Reason*, or the absolute equality of finite and infinite Organism (identity of form and matter):
1. *Bildungstrieb* (reproductive power, analogous to magnetism and cohesion)
2. Irritability (analogous to electricty or relative cohesion)
3. Sensibility (analogous to chemical process)

Indifference Point: The organism is "Objective Reason" or "Truth" as the real side of "Absolute Indifference." It corresponds to "imagination" or "Beauty" as the ideal side.[84]

I shall not try to expound this scheme but a few words about the basic concept of *Potenz* are needed. This is a term which Schelling always continued to use from about 1797 onwards—when his friend Eschenmayer was the first to use it in print.[85] It was borrowed from the theory of powers in mathematics (x, x^2, x^3, etc.), and together with *plus* and *minus* signs (for "positive" and "negative" or "A" and "non-A") it provided Schelling with all the formal equipment he needed for a conceptual algebra of the Identity theory. Hegel does not use this algebra in the *Difference* essay, though he began to employ it in *Faith and Knowledge*. But he does employ the term *Potenz*. It is the general name for an organic pattern of the kind which the Identity theory requires as the unit of existence or of explanation. According to Schelling's "Exposition": "The Absolute Identity only exists under the form of all *Potenzen*."[86] His fullest and least technical account of the concept—which I can scarcely hope to improve on—is in the introduction to his lectures on the *Philosophy of Art* (first delivered October 1802):

> There is only One philosophy and One science of philosophy; what are called distinct philosophical sciences, are either quite perverse or these sciences are just expositions of the One and undivided whole of philosophy in distinct *Potenzen* or under distinct ideal determinations.
> . . . this expression . . . is connected with the general doctrine of philosophy about the essential and inward identity of all things and of everything which we distinguish at all. There is truly and in itself only One essential being, One absolute real, and this being an absolute is indivisible, so that it cannot pass

over into distinct beings through division or separation; since the one being is indivisible, diversity of things is only possible at all, in so far as it is posited as the undivided whole under distinct determinations. These determinations I call *Potenzen*. They change nothing whatsoever in the essential being, which remains always and necessarily the same, which is why they are called *ideal* determinations. For example, what we cognize in history or in art, is essentially the same as what also exists in nature; in each of them the whole absoluteness is innate, but this absoluteness stands at distinct levels [*Potenzen*] in nature, history, and art. If one could take the *Potenz* away, so as to see the *pure essence* naked so to speak, One being would truly be in all of them.

But *Philosophy* in its complete appearance, emerges only in the totality of all *Potenzen*. For it ought to be a true image [*Bild*] of the Universe—and this equals the *Absolute set forth in the totality of all ideal determinations*. God and the Universe are one, or they are only different aspects of One and the same being; God is the universe regarded from the side of identity; he is *All* since he is the only real being, and hence there is nothing outside of him, while the *Universe* is God grasped from the side of totality. But in the absolute idea which is the principle of philosophy, both identity and totality are once again one. Now the complete appearance of philosophy, as I say, emerges only in the totality of all *Potenzen*. In the Absolute as such, and therefore also in the principle of philosophy there is no *Potenz* precisely because it comprehends all *Potenzen*, and conversely just in virtue of the fact that there is no *Potenz* in it, all *Potenzen* are contained in it. I call this principle the *absolute point of identity* of philosophy precisely for this reason, that it is not equal to any particular *Potenz*, and yet it comprehends all of them.

Now this indifference point, just because it is the point of indifference, and it is strictly unique, indiscernible and indivisible, necessarily exists again in every *particular* unity (another name for a *Potenz*); and this is not possible unless in each of these *particular* unities all unities, hence all *Potenzen*, return once again. Thus there is in philosophy overall nothing but the Absolute, or we meet with nothing in philosophy but the Absolute—always just strictly the One, and just this unique One in particular forms.[87]

The illustration that Hegel offers us is mainly a development of the analogy between the third *Potenz* of Nature and the second. The basic concept is the theological one of the "divine light" (of John 1) which shone (outwardly) in the primeval darkness at the moment of Creation, but which was also (inwardly) "the life of men" (and of lower organisms). On the other side of the antinomy, the darkness is not only the uncreated (or infinite) nothing out of which the finite world was made but also the inward darkness of the created (i.e., finite) solid bodies which are impervious to the light of their central sun. Just how the power of light is supposed to split and integrate the general force of gravity into the differentiated "specific gravity" of the "cohesive series" we need not enquire. There was never anything to be said in support of this hypothesis except that the Sun is, after all, the general centre of gravity for our cosmos (the solar *system*). This stage corresponds to the production of objective intuitions by the imaginative intelligence. We can agree, at least, that the work of the productive imagination is equally mysterious. The self-positing of Reason is unconscious, and the self-positing of nature (as light and gravity) is a simple compresence of the different forces. The infinite source is the Sun, but all the sundered aspects of the finite dynamic series are united in the reflective, (and finite) form of the crystal. This is the theoretical parallel of our thinking activity.

The practical parallel is between man's conscious remaking both of his physical environment and of himself in his culture, and the internalization of the divine light as the life of an organism. The organism has as its focus a kind of "organic crystal" (in higher animals, the brain) which is a higher *Potenz* of contraction because it has an *inner* side; the animal feels, it is aware of itself (though not yet as a self, for that is the extreme of contraction which Nature points to but cannot reach). But this higher contraction is accompanied by sexual differentiation.[88] Sexual attraction, which is specific to animals is *electric* (rather than cohesive or magnetic) in character because it involves the linking of two sundered poles.

Thus it is transmitted by voice which is the first seed of that uttering of the inner consciousness which distinguishes (and constitutes) *spiritual* being. The inwardness of natural organisms is not self-uttered, however, except at this limit, and in this absolutely limited way. In general, it has to be reconstructed, by the introjection of the organic patterns that lie open to view in the inorganic world. Thus, in the two axes of a planetary ellipse, nature already presents us with the poles of a magnet without a joining bar.[89] This "line of cohesion" is some-how internalized in the organization of the animate body (Hegel does not say how). The internalized electricity of sex is easy enough to rec-ognize[90] and needs no further comment. Voice is analogous to the electric *current* that passes between the poles of a Voltaic pile in the "chemical process."[91]

Here we must reconsider the problem of the place of *analogy* in the philosophy of nature. Hegel never quite gave up using inorganic anal-ogies based on magnetism and electricity in his philosophy of the or-ganism. But he did later see the error of this wholesale introjection of inorganic patterns into the interpretation of organic phenomena. This is the "capricious exercise of the imagination and the most common-place way of reasoning by superficial analogy," the "crude empiricism" that he later condemned.[92] His own approach even in these earliest days was more dependent on the projection outwards and downwards of patterns discovered in self-conscious life. We have an example of this in the remark that even an animal cry "posits itself as cognizing and to be recognized" (168). The "struggle for recognition" is a He-gelian motif (not found at all in Schelling) which makes its first ap-pearance here. It plays a prominent role in the *System of Ethical Life*.

The two philosophic sciences are *really* opposed because each is an integrated unity of being and cognition. But in natural philosophy, the moment of objectivity, of external being is predominant (the algebraic formula for it is $A \overset{+}{=} B$); whereas in transcendental philosophy the moment of subjectivity, of cognition is dominant. It has *being* because its self-knowing is also a self-making (and the formula for it is $\overset{+}{A} = B$). Cognition and being, the dialectical elements for which A and B stand, are only *ideal* opposites, not real ones. And because of their real oppo-sition, their independence, the two sciences cannot simply exist side by side in parallel (that is their "ideal" relation). They must be or-dered in relation to one another as existences; and their order is already apparent. Transcendental philosophy is *higher* than natural philosophy which leads up to it. Each is complete and closed in itself, but only in a relative way, that is, a way that points to its completion in the other. They each culminate in the same point of indifference but they express it from opposed aspects (objective and subjective). They form a *line* (which Schelling called the "constructed line") through the point of indifference. Schelling drew it thus:

Ideal Pole $\overset{+}{A} = B$ $\qquad\qquad$ (0) $\qquad\qquad$ $A = \overset{+}{B}$ Real Pole
$$A = A$$

Zero is the negative expression for the point of indifference or the Absolute Identity. "$A = A$" is the positive expression. Schelling prefers the positive expression, but Hegel adopts the negative one (as a formula for *nullification*). We have already seen (pp. 21–4 above) how Hegel's preference arises from his conception of the birth of speculation from the antinomic character of reflection. Schelling's choice arises from his Spinozist conviction that speculative philosophy can be expounded directly from the absolute standpoint of God. Hegel's eventual condemnation of Schelling's Absolute as "the dark night in which all cows are black" is already implicit in his use of zero; and Schelling's sense of outrage at this verdict is easy to understand since he did *not* take an antinomic view of "$A = A$."

The constructed line is the formula which expresses the opposition of the two sciences in parallel or as mutually balancing one another. But the "midpoint is doubled" in each of them because each is a line in itself. They must join one another not just at the center but at the extremes. This is the "self construction of identity into totality" which is best represented as the circle produced by the spinning of the whole line upon its center point through 180° so that the ends change places and the line itself is inverted:

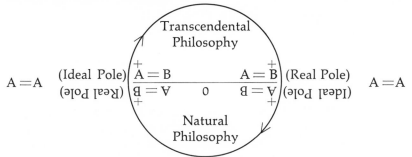

I hope it will be clear why I have preferred to use Hegel's zero for the indifference point as "identity." The center of the circle is the negative Absolute, the nothing out of which the world is created, and the abyss in which all finitude is engulfed. The starting point of the "infinite movement" is indicated above the line and the finishing point below. With a clockwise motion this enables us to place transcendental philosophy "above," which is where it belongs. The circle that is produced by the motion is the "indifference point as totality," which is what is properly expressed by the formula A = A. The "relative totalities" are the closed half-circles.[93]

The point of transition which is now represented by the constructed line (as the diameter that divides the realm of nature from that of intelligence) is man himself as the crowning achievement of natural creation, and the maker of the cognitive circle. For human consciousness is the incarnation of the Logos, the "lightning stroke of the ideal upon the real" (170). This is the dividing line between unconscious production and conscious self-production.

Hegel's final remarks about the polarity of intellectual intuition itself cannot be interpreted on the circumference of the circle at all; for they concern the relation of Art, Speculation, and Religion, to the absolute indifference point in the center. As we have suggested, this final phase of philosophy should be thought of as distinct from the two philosophical sciences. Art is the resumption of human *life* in the Absolute, and Speculation is the resumption of human *thought* in the Absolute. To express this on our diagram we should probably return to the radial line and think of a movement toward the center from each end. But Hegel's doctrine that Art is *natural* and Speculation *transcendental* is not at all the same as Schelling's; and the identification of both of them as forms of "divine Service," so that they are aspects of Religion which is the "resumption of the whole into one," is also Hegel's own (though of course Schelling identified the totality with God). Art and Speculation are uniquely individualized creative activities (in which feeling and conception are respectively dominant). But Religion is a communal activity. Because he begins from the contrast of aesthetic and religious intuition, Hegel speaks at first as if religion was simply emotional, not conceptual. But since he regards Speculation as a form of divine service it is evident that Religion is really the ultimate point of union, and hence that it is not vitiated by any one-sidedness of this kind.[94]

Speculation becomes divine service when it transcends its own onesided intellectual character. This certainly implies that one cannot be a philosopher without having a kind of aesthetic awareness. But this sober criticism of reflective thought is far removed from Schelling's enthusiastic pronouncement that "Art is the organon of Philosophy." It is clear that for Hegel, Speculation is higher than Art, and also that, at this stage in the development of his thought, Religion is higher than either of them.

I have thus far sought to interpret what Hegel says about Schelling's System in the light of Schelling's own contemporary statements about it. But already I have ventured to propose a circular diagram which goes beyond anything in Schelling. I will try finally to sketch the outline of the System that seems to be implicit in the text of the *Difference* essay as I have interpreted it. This outline is by no means independent of the tabular presentation of Schelling's view that I have already given, but it departs from it in a few places, and in many respects it falls short because I have only included points for which there is evidence in Hegel's own texts in this period. Hence, this outline should be thought of as no more than a fragment of the whole, and as no more than a probable conjecture at best:

I. *The theoretical Science of Nature* (the unconscious self-production of the Absolute *observed or contemplated* by Reason)

A. *Theoretical Part:* Inorganic Nature
   (1) Magnetism: the level of connected poles—theory of universal and specific gravity, and of cohesion
   (2) Electricity: level of separated poles
   (3) Chemical process: self-resolution of the poles into neutrality

   Point of Union for the inorganic: Crystallization (a self-determined form)

B. *Practical Part:* Organic Nature (the active reconstruction of the inorganic process from an inner center)
   (1) Living magnetism (organic cohesion)
   (2) Living electricity (sexual attraction and reproduction)
   (3) Living chemical process (voice—communication)
   Point of Union for the organic: the brain (this is the highest product of organic cohesion)

II. *The practical Science of Intelligence* (the conscious self-reproduction of the Absolute by and as Reason)

A. *Theoretical Part:* Knowledge (here Reason produces itself as the *outer center*, the observer)
   (1) Sense intuition and imagination
   (2) Reflection and intellect
   (3) Reason

Point of Union: Transcendental intuition (the "outer" center becomes "inner")

B. *Practical Part:* Ethical Life (here Reason as the "inner center" produces its own world)
    (1) Individual and family (spiritual cohesion)
    (2) Conflict and War (opposition)
    (3) Ethical life (substantial existence)
Point of Union: Religion (this leads to III below)

III. *Theory of the Indifference of Nature and Intelligence*
    (1) Theory of art
    (2) Speculative theology
    (3) Religion

Sections IA and IB in this scheme are based on the *example* that Hegel gives in the *Difference* essay (168–9). As the reader will see by examining the tabular summary of Schelling's theory given above, this example corresponds fairly closely to the second moment of Schelling's Second *Potenz*, and it *can* be viewed as an expansion of the second moment of Schelling's Third *Potenz* (which is what the parallelism obviously requires). This gives us some measure of how much is omitted in the present schema. The structure of the Science of Intelligence can scarcely be inferred from the text of the *Difference* essay at all, but the correspondence between the structure of Schelling's *System of Transcendental Idealism* and Hegel's constructive analysis of Kant in *Faith and Knowledge* makes me fairly confident in claiming that the critical remarks about reflective philosophy in the *Difference* essay presuppose a speculative structure of the type suggested. I have filled in the practical part by inserting the skeleton of the subsequent *System of Ethical Life*. This is much more conjectural. But it is supported on one side by the parallel with Schelling's Third *Potenz* and on the other side by the natural transition that it provides to the theory of the absolute indifference point which is outlined in he *Difference* essay.

Hegel's own discussion of Schelling's system ends by returning to the comparison with Fichte. If speculative Reason does not transcend its own limits, but simply comprehends the Absolute formally as an absolute activity, instead of comprehending the antinomic identity of this Absolute with its appearance—the "identity of identity and non-idenity"—then an opposition between the noumenal and the phenomenal world is set up, and the only integration that is possible is through the dominance of the noumenal reality as moral law. The boundary between the two worlds (of Reason and sense) is an incomprehensible one; this is what follows directly from the fact that speculative Reason remains pure and does not "suspend itself." Because transcendental philosophy *is* an independent science of the Absolute, this "great refusal" is *possible*. One cannot hope to stir Fichte out of his "entire Science of Knowledge" therefore, because it is formally complete; it is unsatisfactory because it is only formal, but that limitation is formally necessary. The only way that Fichte could be moved would be through a re-examination of his conception of intellectual intuition. The primary activity of thought as *reflection* is the abstraction of the pure form from the manifold of empirical consciousness. So if we take this reflective activity as the intuited *object* of our *philosophical* reflection—which is what Fichte does—we are beginning with something that is *conditioned*. We need to take the *further* step of abstraction, to remove the subjectivity and grasp the identity of being (the *condition* of reflection) and thinking (the activity that reflects). We may well feel that in this "negation of negation" we do indeed have "the dark night in which all cows are black." But although he said this later himself about Schelling's theory of the absolute indifference point, Hegel continued to tell his students that the beginning of philosophy was the comprehension of "the nothing." He only objected when this beginning was set us as the final *goal*. The intuition when it is thus absolutely comprehended, has two sides: it is both subject and object, both thinking and being, both Ego and nature. The adequate development of the side of self-consciousness *requires* the development *pari passu* of the philosophical comprehension of nature. Fichte tried to ignore this requirement.

We know and understand ouselves, exactly as well, and to the degree, and in the respects, that we know our world. This is the fundamental thesis of the Identity Philosophy, and it stands unshaken in Hegel's mind throughout his later development. Whatever follies we may find in the Philosophy of Nature that Schelling or Hegel formulated, the only question that we can properly raise is whether it expresses a "thinking comprehension" of the world of that time, and of its experience of Nature as systematized in its science. Hegel subsequently asked this question about Schelling's philosophy of nature and answered in the negative. Everyone agrees with him. But no one, as far as I know, has properly studied whether the same verdict really holds about Hegel's Philosophy of Nature; the general assumption has been that it does. Perhaps it does indeed; there are reasons for thinking that it may. Hegel's intense aversion for Newtonian *meta-physics* may have distorted his understanding of Newtonian physics, for example; and he certainly espoused several lost causes in chemistry, in optics, and in physiology. But even at the worst, even if his effort was not notably more successful than Schelling's, it would be rank dogmatism to conclude without further study that his *project* was mistaken because the *execution* failed. A systematic philosophy of human knowledge and human experience must involve some account of man's place in nature; and the more "formal" it is in this respect, even if the formalism can be intellectually justified and defended (which seems more questionable in our non-Euclidean, post-Newtonian, evolutionary culture than it did in the scientifically secure century that followed Kant's death), the less valuable it will be for our human purposes. Certainly no modern attempt to construct the Identity Principle into a system could be the unaided work of one mind. But then Hegel did not really claim that that was possible even in the heyday of romanticism. The Philosophy that speaks through his mouth is no respecter of persons—his own included.

7. THE CODA: REINHOLD.

At this point our analysis ceases, for Hegel's argument is now complete. The essay ends with a discussion of Reinhold (and Bardili). But for the most part this is easy enough to follow. We have already appealed to it for aid several times in our study of the "general reflections" at the beginning. Hardly anything in it requires further explanation until the very end when it returns to the topic of "the need of philosophy."

Hegel did not dignify this section with a heading; and the chief question to be asked about it is why he wrote it at all. "It still remains," he says blandly, "for us to say something about *Reinhold's view of Fichte's and Schelling's philosophy* and about his own philosophy" (174). But *why* does it remain? The topic which Hegel italicized is germane to the project of the essay because Reinhold's misunderstanding of Schelling's system is the external occasion, the historical stimulus for the writing of it. This fact is recorded on the title page of the essay itself; a discussion of Reinhold's criticism of Schelling in the first fascicle of his *Contributions* had been promised to the reader and must be supplied. But Hegel dispatches this topic in a few pages, and then devotes three times as much space to a discussion of "Reinhold's own philosophy." This is not merely gratuitous; it is almost directly contrary to his explicit declaration at the outset that his essay will *not* be concerned with Reinhold's "revolution of bringing philosophy back to logic" (79).

Why then does Hegel discuss it after all? Walter Kaufmann, ignoring the Preface and everything on the title page *except* the reference to Reinhold's *Contributions*, says that the essay is "an extended review of a work by Reinhold."[95] If ever there was a case of the tail being made to wag the dog this is one. Kaufmann's comment is not even an accurate characterization of the tailpiece, for the works "reviewed" here are not the ones mentioned on the title page at all, but rather Reinhold's old *Versuch* and Bardili's new *Grundriss der Ersten Logik*. Nevertheless, Kaufmann's view contains, in a distorted way, the clue that we need. For while Hegel was writing this essay, Schelling was excitedly pursuing the project of a *Critical Journal of Philosophy* which would survey the whole range of the contemporary philosophical literature and sift out what was worthy of note from the point of view of the new speculative idealism. When his other hoped-for collaborators failed him, he turned to Hegel for help.[96] The critical appraisal of the "logical reduction of philosophy" with which Hegel's essay ends is a foretaste of what he could and would do to the popular philosophy of the time in his contributions to the new *Journal*.

The discussion is witty; it shows us a lighter, though not a gentler, side of Hegel. But the outcome is entirely negative, and the polemical tone and stance is ultimately rather repellent. As with the many pages of the *Critical Journal* that was devoted to the strenuous campaign against "non-philosophy," it is wisest to read these final pages of the *Difference* essay for their amusement value and then to forget them. What we have here is, for the most part, the spectacle of the Young Turks of Academe railing against the old fogies who have all the best jobs.

A very different view has, of course, been defended, and it is easy to see why. Whatever we may think about Bardili, Reinhold is not a contemptible figure in the history of philosophy. He is not unworthy of attention; and in the *Critical Journal*, Hegel generally gives serious attention to those who deserve it, however hostile and negative he may be. But the results of serious critical attention on Hegel's part are never simply negative, as any careful student of *Faith and Knowl-*

edge or of Hegel's review of G. E. Schulze's *Critique of Theoretical Philosophy*[97] can testify. Now Reinhold certainly was not a philosopher of the stature of Kant or Fichte; perhaps he should not even be ranked with Jacobi. But surely he was the equal of Schulze? And if we look again with this in mind, do we not see that just as the critical evaluation of scepticism was important for the *Phenomenology*, so the "reduction of philosophy to Logic" is the watchword of Hegel's mature system?

Several scholars—the French translator Méry among them[98]—have tried to argue this way on behalf of Reinhold, and more especially on behalf of Bardili. But I think they are mistaken, or at least they are mistaken in so far as they seem to hold that the stimulus and example of Reinhold and Bardili were important. What *is* true is that the focal importance which was ascribed to the principle of Identity in their programme makes Hegel's critical exercise into a useful foil for the exposition of the *speculative* philosophy of Identity. This connection and contrast was his *excuse* for concluding his comparison of Fichte and Schelling, who had constructed different systems on a common philosophical base, with a critique of two thinkers who did not have that philosophical base at all.[99]

The reduction of philosophy to logic, in the sense in which Hegel took it up, was the project of Kant in the three Critiques. Hegel did not intend to address the general topic of the relation of logic to philosophy in the *Difference* essay. That is why he says in the "Preface" that he does *not* propose to deal with this latest revolution in Reinhold's thought. Careful examination of the "Kant" section of *Faith and Knowledge* will show that Hegel's *Logic* grew out of the "critical philosophy," which Bardili regarded as a mental sickness that needed his logical "medicine." In the *Difference* essay there is still no sign of a speculative conception of Logic as such. I hope that my analysis of the argument has shown that "speculative logic" is almost ready to be born. But there is external evidence to show that the birth has not yet happened. Hegel began teaching "logic and metaphysics" shortly after he penned these closing pages on Reinhold and Bardili. He taught this subject regularly for several terms, and he began at once to write a textbook for it. We have some bits of evidence to show that in all of his early lecture courses his conception of logic remained *critical*, rather than speculative. He did not have the project of a speculative logic that would stand in the same relation to the logic of Reinhold and Bardili as his *speculative* principle of Identity stands to their formal principle in the *Difference* essay. Rather he held that the study of logic must prepare the way for philosophy by confronting all forms of finite thought with the Absolute, and casting them "into the abyss of their own perfection," to borrow a phrase from the *Difference* essay (140). This critical conception of logic is expressed in the introductory lecture for a winter course—a lecture that was probably given in September/October 1802.[100] Hegel had then completed, and was about to publish, a complete survey of the "forms of finite thought" in *Faith and Knowledge.* All the manuscripts from the earliest courses on logic are lost, but I think *Faith and Knowledge* is the conscious precipitate of everything valuable produced by this critical conception of logic, made at the moment when Hegel was almost ready to advance to the speculative conception of the subject—a conception which was publicly announced in the Summer of 1803, and first formulated around the previous Christmas. If this hypothesis is right, then Jacobi was a far more immediate stimulus than Reinhold or Bardili for the thought-revolution that was involved. For it was Jacobi who emphasized the *self-destructive* character of philosophical reflection.

But, finally, was it not Reinhold who proclaimed the need for an *objective* conception of thinking? Indeed it was, and Hegel waxes very ironic about what Reinhold produced in answer to his own challenge. It is clear from the *Difference* essay that Hegel and Schelling did not need Reinhold to deliver any such challenge. Again, they had already found their challenge in Kant's declaration that teleological concepts could only be employed *regulatively* in our thinking. Reinhold's demand did not even have the irritant power of the one made by the egregious W. T. Krug who asked whether the Identity Philosophers could "deduce his pen."[101] It was obviously quite useless to respond to that challenge as far as Krug himself was concerned, for the way in which he framed it showed that he was quite incapable of understanding any response that was possible within the Identity System. Among the things that he demanded a deduction for, there were some (e.g., the Moon) for which the deduction had already been given. But Krug struck a nerve; for the sake of the "identity of identity and non-identity" Hegel went on struggling to decide what *ought* to be said about "Krug's pen," and in consequence, a complete nonentity has crept for ever into a place among the necessary footnotes of the history of philosophy.

Reinhold did not have that luck; but he did not, and does not, need it. Hegel had never been much interested in him.[102] In the *Difference* essay he brings him tumbling in upon the stage, along with his latest mentor Bardili, like the clowns bowing and taking the curtain calls for that daring young man on the flying trapeze, Schelling. This is certainly not fair treatment. But the unfairness itself is part of the life of Reason. For there are philosophical enterprises other than the one in which the Identity philosophers were engaged; and philosophers engaged in different enterprises are bound to appear ridiculous to one another when they seem to be talking about the same questions. If it really is the case (whatever that means) that the history of Philosophy is "the story of the one eternal Reason" (114), it is certainly also the case that that story will never be told with perfect balance and adequacy in one book, or from a single point of view. We can admit this without doubting that Hegel's conception of the history of philosophy is an immense advance over Reinhold's. And we can assert that in turn, without denying that Hegel is unjust to Reinhold. The fact is that he is consistently unjust to the whole tradition of philosophy that stems from Locke. But not more unjust, certainly, than the heirs of that tradition have been to him. An understanding of how philosophical prejudice arises from the "need" of the time is one of the things that Hegel sought to bring about. His own is not the least important case where his insight needs to be applied.

H. S. HARRIS

NOTES

1. He had previously published (at Frankfurt in 1798) an anonymous translation with introduction and notes of the *Confidential Letters* of J. J. Cart, a political pamphlet against the administration of the Vaud by the Canton of Berne. A facsimile reprint was recently issued by Vandenhoek and Rupprecht (Göttingen, 1970).

2. Schelling told Fichte that it had appeared "in the last few days" on 3 October 1801 (Nicolin, report 42). Hegel's birthday was on 26 August.

3. The whole career outlined in the following paragraphs is fully discussed and documented in Harris, *Toward the Sunlight*.

4. This was first published in 1794. There is an English translation by Fritz Marti in *Metaphilosophy* VI, 1, 1975.

5. It was Schiller, not Goethe, who pressed for Schelling's appointment in the first instance. Goethe was unimpressed by Schelling's first essay on the philosophy of nature: he feared that Schelling was only Fichte in disguise, and would prove to be even more of a political radical than Fichte. But he changed his mind after his first long conversation with Schelling; and his reception of Schelling's next essay of the philosophy of nature (*On the World–Soul*, 1798) was enthusiastic. (See Fuhrmans, I, 131–5).

6. The first continuous draft of the essay which later editors have called

"The Constitution of Germany" was written in this period. (An English translation—the first half of which is based on the unfinished second draft—is in Knox and Pelczynski, pp. 143–242).

7. As we shall see later, there is some evidence that even in the *Difference* essay Hegel has modified what he calls "Schelling's System" to accord with his own beliefs. See pp. 51–2 above.

8. Letter 167 (to Sinclair [October 1810]), Hoffmeister, I, 332. (For Hölderlin's position at this stage see Hannelore Hegel, *Isaak von Sinclair*).

9. See Kant's "Open Letter" of 7 August 1799, *Akad.* XII, 370–1; the crucial passage is translated in Zweig, pp. 253–4.

10. An anonymous reviewer (actually Karl August Böttinger) who surveyed the Michaelmas publication lists in the *Allgemeine Zeitung* of Stuttgart (Hegel's home city) at the beginning of November, informed his readers that "Schelling has now fetched a stout warrior to Jena from his fatherland Württemberg, through whom he gives notice to the astonished public, that even Fichte stands far below his own viewpoint." Someone passed on a garbled version of this report to Fichte, and Fichte was naturally upset. The only signed statement in the whole of the *Critical Journal* (edited by Schelling and Hegel together) was a footnote near the end of the first issue in which Hegel flatly called the author of this report "a liar" (*N.K.A.* IV, 190 n.).

After receiving Schelling's explanations Fichte affected to be perfectly at ease about the whole matter (see Letter 483, Schulz II, 345). But if *he* read the essay he can hardly have been happy about it. Probably he did no more than glance at it. At any rate it was no lie to say that Hegel clearly

declares that Schelling's viewpoint stands far above Fichte's. Schelling would probably have preferred *not* to see the declaration made quite so plainly. But since it was *not* true that Hegel was merely Schelling's mouthpiece, the most that Schelling could do was to deny responsibility for what Hegel had written. He did this very explicitly when he wrote to Fichte shortly after the essay appeared (3 October 1801; see Nicolin, report 42, or Schulz, II, 340).

11. Nohl, pp. 356–61; translated by R. Kroner under the title "Fragment of a System" in Knox and Kroner, pp. 309–19.

12. See Knox and Kroner, p. 318. The quotation which Kroner detects but cannot identify in this passage is from Fichte's "Appeal to the Public" of 1799 (*Werke* V, 237); the same echo occurs twice in *Faith and Knowledge,* pp. 174, 177.

13. *Science of Knowledge* (translated by P. Heath and J. Lachs), pp. 117–119, 146, 226, 101, 81. It will be helpful to examine the passages in this order. We should notice the shift in the meaning of "dogmatism," for which Fichte was primarily responsible. Kant called any metaphysics dogmatic if it failed to inquire into the foundation of its truth claims. In Fichte dogmatism is the only alternative to idealism—and hence virtually a synonym for realism. The Identity Philosophy was in part an attempt to overcome *this* dogmatic opposition. Hegel regards Fichte's supposedly critical idealism as dogmatic in its moral opposition to all realism. All of these later pejorative uses of 'dogmatic' spring from Kant's. But what is qualified as dogmatic depends on what is accepted as being fully critical by the author concerned. (For further discussion, illustrations and references see notes 60 and 61 below.)

14. The parenthetic numbers in the text refer to the relevant page of the translation below.

15. Schelling himself says "As far as the exposition is concerned I have taken Spinoza as my model." (*Werke* IV, 113.)

16. *Doktor der Weltweisheit* was a quite common form for "Doctor of Philosophy" employed by scholars who were averse to Latin terms and Latinate borrowing. But Hegel probably adopted it because he was not, in point of fact, a "Doctor" at all. He was a *Magister* of Tübingen. At Tübingen this dignity was considered equal to the doctorate of other institutions, but it was not widely recognized as such. If Hegel had called himself *Philosophiae doctor* the question "from what institution?" would have arisen. The German periphrasis enabled Hegel to avoid this problem, and in order to make this advantage visible we have translated the vernacular phrase literally.

17. There is even some evidence which suggests that there were people who genuinely believed at the time that Hegel was faking. Heinrich Laube in his *Moderne Charakteristiken* (published in 1838) gives the following report about Hegel at Jena thirty-five years before: "He paid for his *Habilitation* comically enough with bad *Louis d'or* that Fichte had given him, his philosophy was always counterfeit coin, but he was bold as brass to defy the Faculty with a leg-pull. Hegel was a real good fellow, full of good fun" (Nicolin, report 116).

One of Schelling's best students, I. P. Troxler, remarked in a letter of 1854 that Laube had "sketched the Jena period very well" (Nicolin, report 50). So although Laube's story can hardly have gone the rounds in quite this form when the *Difference* essay first appeared, the view that Laube

suggests may well be a genuine echo of that time. Of course, Hegel did not really "pay" for his *Habilitation* with the *Difference* essay: he had to produce a Latin dissertation *On the Orbits of the Planets* for that (as well as some honest money!). But at the moment when he applied for his license to lecture both he and everyone else certainly regarded the *Difference* essay as the principal basis for his claim to an academic career.

18. See especially Klaus Düsing, "Spekulation und Reflexion," *Hegel–Studien* 5 (1969): 95–128.

19. Haldane and Simson, III, 513. This comment probably goes back to 1805.

20. A useful survey of the different "system outlines" that Schelling gave in his various works between 1801 and 1806 will be found in Xavier Tilliette, I, 417–21. The best conspectus I can arrive at for 1801–2 is given and discussed on pp. 52–3 above.

21. Haldane and Simson, III, 515. I do not know whether Tilliette was consciously influenced by this comment. But, if not, his own title (*Schelling: une philosophie en devenir*) is an independent confirmation of its accuracy.

22. Because of the distinction between "spirit" and "letter" even this philosophy common to Fichte and Schelling did not "lie before the public" of 1801 so very plainly. Hegel castigates Reinhold for seeming not to know that "there has been a philosophy other than pure transcendental idealism before the public for years" (174). By "a philosophy other than pure transcendental idealism" he probably means "the *speculative* philosophy of both Fichte and Schelling." Fichte's *Science of Knowledge* was published in 1794 and Schelling's *System of Transcendental Idealism* in 1800.

23. *Critique of Pure Reason*, B135.

24. *Werke* I, 91 (Heath and Lachs, p. 93).

25. Haldane and Simson, III, 481.

26. Werke I, 100–2; Heath and Lachs, pp. 100–2.

27. *Ibid.*, p. 102 (Heath and Lachs, p. 102).

28. *Akad.* V, 401 (Meredith, *Teleological Judgment*, p. 55).

29. *Akad.* V, 412 (Meredith, *Teleological Judgment*, p. 70–1). The emphasis in the first sentence of the quotation is mine.

30. *Critique of Pure Reason*, B, xxx.

31. Hegel deals with Fichte as a theorist of "faith" in *Faith and Knowledge*. In the *Difference* essay he is treated strictly as a theorist of knowledge. This is the key to an understanding of the enormous contrast in the way Fichte is treated in the two essays.

32. "Second Introduction to the Science of Knowledge," *Werke* I, 466 (Heath and Lachs, p. 41). Kant uses the expression "*intellektuelle Anschauung*" only in the second edition of the *Critique of Pure Reason*; and the very first time he does so he flatly contradicts the interpretation Fichte later adopted (B35n). In the *Critique of Judgment* he speaks rather of an "*intuitive Verstand*"; and just once, in the same connection, of "*eine andere als sinnliche Anschauung*" (*Akad.* V, 418; all the relevant passages can be found under "intuition" in the indices of Kemp Smith and Meredith). The possibility of "intuitions different from ours" is mentioned three or four times in the first edition of the *Critique of Pure Reason*, as is the impossibility of "representing to ourselves the possibility of an understanding which should know itself, not discursively through categories, but intuitively in a non-sensible intuition" (A256/B311–2).

The "intuitive understanding" is also discussed in the second version of the Transcendental Deduction. It was unfortunate that Kant's successors generally adopted the expression which Kant used *only* in the *Critique of Pure Reason*, since it was the doctrine of the *Critique of Judgment* that impressed them. The expression "transcendental intuition" which Hegel sometimes uses is in some ways preferable (see n. 51 and pp. 109–11). But Hegel's one reference to the "intuitive understanding" in the *Difference* essay is very paradoxically phrased, for he speaks of a "sensuous understanding" (163), an expression which neither Kant nor anyone else ever used.

33. *Werke* I, 467 (Heath and Lachs, pp. 41–2). "Construct" is one of Schelling's trademarks. I was delighted to find my hypothesis that it was Schelling who led Fichte to begin thinking in this way, supported—and to my mind conclusively confirmed—by W. C. Zimmerli, pp. 177 ff.

34. The most forceful statement of Hegel's earlier critique of Kant (based on a detailed study of the *Metaphysics of Ethics*—for which his notes no longer survive) is in "The Spirit of Christianity and its Fate" (Knox and Kroner, pp. 209–15, 244).

35. Reinhold was a "fashionable" author among the bright students at Tübingen when Hegel was there, but Hegel never found him very interesting: his work was "of more relevance just for theoretical reason [rather] than of greater applicability to concepts that are generally useful." (Letter 8, to Schelling, January 1795, *Briefe* I, 16.) He did admit at that time that Reinhold was an important philosopher. In his first letter to Schelling he remarked that it would take the appointment of "someone like Reinhold or Fichte" to make a real difference in the academic situation at Tübingen

(Letter 6, Christmas Eve 1794, *Briefe* I, 12).

36. The reader should note that C. G. Bardili (1761–1808) was one of Hegel's first teachers at the Tübingen seminary. He was a *Repentent* (a "graduate assistant") during Hegel's first two years at Tübingen (1788–90); and Hegel took Bardili's course on "the use of profane authors in theology" in 1789. At that time Bardili was more interested in poetry and literature than in logic (see *Toward the Sunlight*, pp. 81, 84–5).

37. In the *curriculum vitae* that he wrote in 1804 Hegel gave the title as "Difference of the Systems of Fichte and Schelling and the inadequacy of the former" (Hoffmeister, *Briefe* IV, 92).

38. *Akad.* V, 401–2 (Meredith, *Teleological Judgment*, pp. 56-7).

39. *Akad.* V, 407 (Meredith, p. 64).

40. This is an interpretation of the enigmatic paragraph on p. 92 below. which depends heavily on what Hegel says about the Cartesian philosophy in the "Introduction" to the *Critical Journal* (*N.K.A.* IV, 126–7) and partly on the first section of *Faith and Knowledge* (pp. 57–9).

41. For the evidence in support of this claim see *Toward the Sunlight* chapter V, and the summary of Hegel's Jena lectures on "ethical life" given by Rosenkranz (*Hegels Leben*, pp. 133–41). Within the *Difference* essay itself, a partial confirmation of the position here adopted is provided by the account which Hegel gives of the "absolute indifference point" (169–72).

42. I do not think there can be any doubt that this period of "intellectual security against Reason" must be identified with the Enlightenment. Hence I take my reference to Locke to be justified. My reference to Spinoza is, of course, only a conjecture; and the conjecture depends on the assumption

that when Hegel writes *die Versuche . . . können eher verstanden werden* he means . . . *eher verstanden werden* [*als begriffen*], "more easily understood intellectually [than comprehended philosophically]."

43. This remark occurs in his review (1794) of the attack on Reinhold's "Elementary Philosophy" by Aenesidemus (G. E. Schulze). See Fichte, *Werke* I, 20. Of course Fichte was not satisfied with Reinhold's "ultimate fact of consciousness" (ibid., p. 8) or with the "principle of identity." But his own procedure in the first *Science of Knowledge* (likewise 1794) shows the influence of Reinhold.

44. In *Faith and Knowledge* (83) Hegel says that Kant's "*mathematical antinomies* deal with the application of Reason as mere negativity to something reflection has fixed." These are the antinomies of temporal beginning/ perpetuity and spatial atom/infinite divisibility. Compare also *Critique of Pure Reason*, B536–7.

45. It is not clear, and it does not become clear later (at least to me), just what—if anything—the "self-constitution" of the different "potencies" of nature in speculative thought means over and above the adoption of this standard. Perhaps that is all it *does* mean. In *that* case this must be what Hegel means when he says that "only the connection with the Absolute persists, and it is the sole reality of the cognition" (97).

46. *Critique of Pure Reason*, A832/ B860. I believe it is helpful to place the discussion in this Kantian context because Hegel intends to show that the principle of Identity is *dialectical*, as a Kantian "Idea of Pure Reason" should be.

47. Spinoza's definition of substance was a truly speculative antinomy because that which is "cause of itself" must at the same time be effect of it-

self. But his procedure was misleading, because an antinomy of this sort is not a basic proposition from which consequences can be drawn by simple linear inference. Hegel himself used Spinoza's *principium* in a properly speculative way when he enounced his celebrated dictum that "the Absolute is not merely substance, it is also subject" in the Preface to the *Phenomenology* (Hoffmeister, p. 19; Baillie, p. 80). But in the end he did not choose to begin philosophy either with Spinoza's "substance" or with "the principle of identity"; instead he turned "the positing of being in nonbeing as becoming" around into "the positing of non-being in being." "Identity" becomes (virtually) the beginning of the "logic of essence" and Spinoza's concept of Substance is (again virtually) its culmination.

48. In the *Phenomenology* Hegel accuses *Fichte* of trying to do this: see Hoffmeister, p. 26 (Baillie, p. 89).

49. *Science of Knowledge, Werke* I, 91–102 (Heath and Lachs, pp. 93–102). This passage is well analysed from the Hegelian point of view by S. Rosen in his *G. W. F. Hegel* (pp. 95–104). Schelling is so far from Hegel's *antinomic* interpretation of the formal principle of Identity in his own "Exposition" that he writes: "16. Between the A that is posited as subject in the proposition 'A=A,' and that which is posited as predicate, no *Gegensatz* is in principle possible" (*Werke* IV, 17). As his explanation there shows, Schelling does not want to use the formula to express the identity of essence and existence. He does not want us to conceive the Absolute from the side of this reflective dichotomy at all. As Hegel would put it, Schelling wants us to "reflect on connectedness" only: every *Potenz* expresses the Absolute Identity—and so on.

50. When Hegel uses "difference" as a technical term in his speculative vocabulary in this period he generally means to refer to the "difference" between essence and existence on which Kant relied in his Critique of the Ontological Argument. But this is *also* the Platonic difference between the One (concept) and the Many (particulars).

51. There can be no doubt that this is what Hegel also calls intellectual intuition elsewhere. By calling it transcendental Hegel opposes it to sensuous or empirical intuition. Thus he does claim, against Kant, that we have "an intuition different from our sensuous intuition" (*Critique of Judgment* § 80, *Akad.* V, 418, Meredith, *Teleological Judgment*, p. 77) but he is not committed to the position that this transcendental intuition satisfies exactly the requirements laid down by Kant for intellectual intuition (compare note 32 above and pp. 109–14 below.

52. To *show* this is the task of the Identity Philosophy as a whole. Thus "transcendental intuition" is a "postulate" by means of which the *totality* of experience is to be "constructed." Just as the mathematician *constructs* mathematics—especially geometry—in the a priori "form of outer intuition," so the metaphysician *constructs* nature and the self in the a priori form of inner intuition—which is Fichte's original self-positing. The *construction*, when completed, validates the initial "postulate." This is because the construction is not *complete* until it returns to its starting point.

53. Diels-Kranz, *Fragmente der Vorsokratiker*, 18 B6.

54. *Critique of Practical Reason*, Part I, Book II, Section 2, Subsection V. (*Akad.* V, 124–32).

55. *Critique of Judgment*, Section 73 (*Akad.* V, 395; Meredith, *Teleological Judgment*, p. 47).

56. Compare his comment that

"Fichte does not need this detour" (143).

57. Although I accuse Hegel of shifting from his own dialectical position to Schelling's visionary one here, it should be noted that in *one* important respect he is being faithful to his own critical ideal. That ideal does require the elimination of *all* postulation: "this whole manner of postulating" does indeed "have its whole ground in the acceptance of a one-sided starting point." But the leap that Hegel makes here in order to escape from the "one-sidedness of reflection" is exactly what he will eventually write the *Phenomenology* to avoid. The reflective consciousness must be *shown* how to escape from its own one-sidedness, not prophesied to from the other side of the abyss.

58. First published by Lasson in 1913; now reprinted separately (Hamburg: Meiner, 1967).

59. In the *System of Ethical Life* the role of the negative is constructive: it stimulates growth. In the *Phenomenology* we find ourselves on a "highway of despair" (Hoffmeister, p. 67; Baillie, p. 135), since every constructive step involves destruction, every significant advance involves the recognition of failure. The method of the *Encyclopaedia* is again positive. Thus the *progressive* dialectic described in the *Difference essay* (113–4) for the first time, remains for Hegel the dialectic of speculative philosophy as such. The dialectic of failure (in the *Phenomenology*) is the dialectic of phenomenal experience.

60. Reinhold applied the word *Geistesverirrung* both to D'Holbach's *Système de la Nature* and to Schelling's *System of Transcendental Idealism* (177). It might seem that if he was wrong about one of them he had to be right about the other. But Hegel turns aside for a moment in his de-

fense of Schelling, to show that Reinhold was just as badly mistaken about D'Holbach. The *Système de la Nature* begins from "matter"; but both speculative idealism and speculative materialism begin from "the absolute identity" of mind and nature. Matter and feeling are literally poles apart as appearances of the Absolute; and a system (D'Holbach's for instance) will be defective if it suspends the opposition transcendentally or *an sich*. This is the typical defect of a dogmatic philosophy. Fichte's system suspends the opposition of mind and nature in a similar way, so that, in spite of his protestations, Fichte's idealism is almost as dogmatic as D'Holbach's materialism.

61. See for instance the "First Introduction to the Science of Knowledge," Sections 3–6 (*Werke* I, 425–40; Heath-Lachs, pp. 8–20). Fichte there opposes dogmatism to idealism. But in the *Science of Knowledge* itself he had distinguished dogmatic from critical idealism. See for instance, *Werke* I, 156, 172–3 (Heath and Lachs, pp. 147–8, 160) and compare *Difference* pp. 126–9 below. When Fichte draws this distinction he also formulates the ontological contrast in terms of idealism and realism.

62. Haldane and Simson, III, 479–505.

63. Hegel's decision to chop Fichte in two, which is not clearly *explained* in either essay, gave rise to some critical misunderstandings of *Faith and Knowledge*; but we need not concern ourselves with that here (see the introduction to that work, pp. 5–6). Even the *History of Philosophy* lectures which did make the distinction between the two Fichtes clear (Haldane and Simson, III, 480–1, 505–6) did not point out the relation of Hegel's two critical essays; for in his lectures Hegel discussed the *Way to the Blessed*

Life as a specimen of the "popular" Fichte. He again ignored the *Vocation of Man* altogether at that stage.

64. Haldane and Simson, III, 504.

65. *Ibid.*, III, 481–2.

66. See the references given in note 61 above.

67. "Second Introduction," *Werke* I, 463; Heath and Lachs, p. 38.

68. *Werke* I, 218 (Heath and Lachs, p. 195). The "wavering of imagination" is discussed ibid., pp. 216–7 (Heath and Lachs, p. 194); and Hegel's assertion that "pure and empirical consciousness condition one another mutually" seems to be based on Fichte's account of the reciprocal determination of "the activity" (of the Ego) and "the interplay" (with the non-Ego)—ibid., p. 212 (Heath and Lachs, p. 190).

69. See Lasson (1967), pp. 9–24.

70. *System der Sittenlehre, Werke* IV, 114–5 (Kroeger, *Ethics*, p. 119).

71. In the *Vocation of Man* Fichte develops a "postulational" version of the older external teleology; Nature is prophetically presumed to keep pace with the moral advance of man (compare *Faith and Knowledge*, pp. 177–79). This certainly represents a degeneration rather than an improvement upon Kant's position.

72. In the *German Constitution* essay Hegel calls Fichte's rational community "the machine-state." (Knox and Pelczynski, pp. 159, 163–4); as early as 1796 (in the "System-Programme of German Idealism") he had insisted that this conception of the state, which he first found in Moses Mendelssohn, must be transcended: see *Toward the Sunlight*, pp. 510, 250–2; also Hegel's essay on *Natural Law* (Knox and Acton, pp. 85–7, 124–6).

73. Hegel, *Philosophy of Nature*, Introduction (Miller, p. 1); Croce, p. 164.

74. "For the deity, that is, for a consciousness in which everything

would be posited by the mere fact of the Ego having been posited (though for us the concept of such a consciousness is unthinkable) our Science of Knowledge would have no content . . . but even for God the Science would have formal correctness" (*Werke* I, 253; Heath and Lachs, p. 224).

75. The title of Lossius' book, *Physische Ursache der Wahrheit*, seems to me a powerful argument in favor of the view that Hegel has him in mind here (161–2).

76. Credit for this discovery should actually go to F. L. von Stolberg; and it was Goethe who let the world in on the joke (see Petry, I, 293–4). But Beck gives some examples from Wolff's discussion of the purpose of the sun and the earth that would have amused Hegel even more (*Early German Philosophy*, pp. 273–4).

77. *Critique of Judgment*, Section 75 (*Akad.* V. 400; Meredith, *Teleological Judgment*, p. 54).

78. *Ethics*, part II, prop. 13.

79. One of the most important achievements of Hegel's *Logic* is his account of the different types of *necessity*. But that came later (and it is doubtful whether it has ever been understood properly). The monochrome character of the Identity theory (which Hegel himself attacked within a few years) was much easier to grasp—and to draw mistaken conclusions from.

80. Arbitrariness, and its natural counterpart chance, are quite different from the natural spontaneity, or conscious acting in and for the whole, which are what Hegel means by "freedom." All the same, the derogatory way in which he speaks of them is unfortunate, because although their place in the scheme of things is subordinate, they do have a *necessary* place, and Hegel was fully aware of this, as

the *System of Ethical Life* demonstrates. But there is nothing arbitrary or casual about the organic structure in which arbitrariness and chance play their necessary role. One could not, for instance, produce an explanation of the world order that would satisfy Hegel upon the principles of the ancient atomists. For to assert that everything is *basically* a matter of chance is to assert precisely that there *is* no satisfactory explanation of things. This is the hypothesis that philosophical speculation is essentially impossible—a hypothesis which makes no sense for man as the natural consciousness of Reason; Hegel is confident therefore that it will never be accepted as final. Whether the hypothesis really does make no sense, or whether Hegel's confidence was misplaced, is a much more open question for us, because our view of nature and of our place in it has been transformed since his time. But we must, in any case, acknowledge the importance of his philosophical justification of chance. Because of it his system can retain its validity (as Spinoza's, for example, cannot) even for someone whose philosophy of nature is fundamentally evolutionary.

81. *System of Transcendental Idealism, Werke* III, 627.

82. My scheme is based mainly on the *Fernere Darstellungen* of 1802 (*Werke* IV, 213–23); a few details come from the second edition of the *Ideen* (1803).

83. Schelling's distinction of the levels of "reflection" and "subsumption" should be seen as a metamorphosis of Kant's distinction between "determining" and "reflecting" judgment—first made in the Introduction to the *Critique of Judgment*, section IV, *Akad.* V, 179–80 (Meredith, *Aesthetic Judgment*, p. 18–9).

84. I have added this note about the final terms of the "real series" and the "ideal series" in order to underline the fact that Hegel's placing of "Art" and "Speculation" (or "beauty" and "truth") in relation to the "point of difference" is the opposite of Schelling's own. There is *no* scheme of Schelling's in this period, in which Art is placed at the apex of the real series. (See Tilliette, *Schelling* I, 417–21 for a convenient conspectus of all of Schelling's efforts to arrange the "real series" and the parallel "ideal series." Note how often the latter series is completely ignored.)

85. In a work called *Propositions from Nature—Metaphysics.* See Schelling's dialogue "On the Absolute Identity System" in the *Critical Journal* (Hegel, *N.K.A.* IV, 162 n.).

86. Schelling, *Werke* IV, 31.

87. Schelling, *Werke* V, 365–7.

88. Hegel regarded sex-differentiation as specific to the animal kingdom and as merely accidental and symbolic in its vegetable forms. This can be gathered already from his Frankfurt essays (see Knox and Kroner, p. 261) and is confirmed in the *System of Ethical Life* (Lasson [1967], p. 15). But in the present context (168) Hegel speaks of the sexual differentiation of plants, without qualification. So presumably Schelling was inclined to emphasize the continuity of organic forms, and Hegel has here accepted this emphasis. But sexual *attraction*, at least, is a form of animal *irritability*, which Schelling gives as the second *Potenz* in the *Ideen* of 1803. See the table in the text.

89. This was one of the main topics of Hegel's Latin dissertation *On the Orbits of the Planets* (1801), which was already drafted (in German) when he wrote the *Difference* essay.

90. It becomes even easier when we realize that where electricity is referred to, it is static electricity that is meant.

The charge is released when the two differently charged bodies come sufficiently close to each other. What *we* generally call electricity belongs to what Hegel calls the chemical process because it is generated in that process.

91. Subsequently Hegel's theory of the chemical process came to embrace more of what we recognize as chemistry. But it always included and began from galvanism. To the very end of his life Hegel stoutly resisted the assimilation of the different types of electrical phenomena under one category.

92. *Philosophy of Nature*, trans. A. V. Miller, p. 1.

93. The "constructed line" is Schelling's (see *Werke* IV, 137). But this circle is my own.

94. The remarks about religious intuition here show the influence of Schleiermacher's *On Religion*, to which Hegel makes a laudatory reference in his preface (83). By the time he wrote *Faith and Knowledge* his enthusiasm had cooled somewhat. He still rated Schleiermacher's achievement highly, but insisted that it was one-sided; it was the height of subjectivity only.

95. *Hegel* (Anchor), p. 47.

96. A few further details will be found in the introduction to *Faith and Knowledge*. (See pp. 1–3.)

97. "Verhältniss des Scepticismus zur Philosophie," *N.K.A.* IV, 197–238. (There is a French translation by B. Fauquet.) It deserves to be noted that just as Hegel's critique of Reinhold and Bardili is only a foil for his appreciation of the *speculative* philosophy of Identity, so the critique of Schulze's formal scepticism is only a foil for his appreciation of the truly *speculative* scepticism of the Ancients—and especially for his appreciation of Plato's *Parmenides*.

98. Méry, p. 189, note U. He cites Glockner as the great champion of this view. His careless syntax also creates the impression that Rosenkranz belongs to his party—but Rosenkranz was actually one of its most trenchant critics. See *Hegel's Leben*, pp. 150–1.

99. It is much more correct to say as Zimmerli does (pp. 8–9) that the discussion of Reinhold was regarded by Hegel as part of the "Comparison of Schelling's Principle with Fichte's," than to regard the whole essay as a review of Reinhold (as Kaufmann suggests). But Zimmerli ignores the conflict between Hegel's programme as announced in the "Preface" and the discussion of Reinhold's philosophy in the closing pages. There is thus more excuse for Lasson's *fourfold* division of the essay than Zimmerli allows.

100. See Rosenkranz, pp. 190–2. The only *possible* times for this course were Winter 1801 (Hegel's first term) or Winter 1802 (his third). All the internal and external indications support the later date, but none of them is very decisive.

101. See Hegel's review in *N.K.A.* IV, 178–9. Also the note in the *Philosophy of Nature* (*Encyclopedia*, section 250; Miller, p. 23).

102. See note 35 above.

The Difference Between
Fichte's and Schelling's
System of Philosophy
in connection with
the first fascicle of
Reinhold's *Contributions*
to a more convenient
survey of the state of
philosophy at the beginning
of the nineteenth century
published in Jena, 1801.

Preface

In those few public utterances in which a feeling for the difference between Fichte's and Schelling's systems of philosophy can be recognized, the aim seems to be more to hide their distinctness or to get round it than to gain a clear awareness of it. Neither the systems as they lie before the public for direct inspection, nor among other things, Schelling's answer to Eschenmayer's idealistic objections against the philosophy of nature have brought the distinctness of the two systems out into open discussion.[1] On the contrary, *Reinhold*, for example, is so far from an inkling of it that he takes the complete identity of both systems for granted.[2] So his view of Schelling's system is distorted in this way too [as well as in other ways]. The occasion for the following treatise is this confusion of Reinhold's, rather than his revolution of bringing philosophy back to logic—a revolution that he has not merely threatened us with, but has proclaimed as already accomplished.[3]

The Kantian philosophy needed to have its spirit distinguished from its letter, and to have its purely speculative principle lifted out of the remainder that belonged to, or could be used for, the arguments of reflection. In the principle of the deduction of the categories Kant's philosophy is authentic idealism; and it is this principle that Fichte extracted in a purer, stricter form and called the spirit of Kantian philosophy.[4] The things in themselves—which are nothing but an

1. K. A. Eschenmayer, "Spontaneität = Weltseele oder das höchste Prinzip der Naturphilosophie," and F. W. J. Schelling, "Anhang zu dem Aufsatz des Herrn Eschenmayer," in *Zeitschrift für spekulative Physik* II, 1–68 and 109–46; see Schelling, *Werke* (1856–63) IV, 79–103.

2. See K. L. Reinhold, *Beyträge* I (Hamburg, 1801), especially pp. 85–89 and 135–54.

3. Reinhold believed the revolution was accomplished in the work of C. G. Bardili, *Grundriss der Ersten Logik* (Stuttgart, 1800). The full title of this work was: "*Outline of Primary Logic* purified from the errors of previous Logics generally, and of the Kantian logic in particular; not a Critique but a *medicina mentis*, to be employed mainly for Germany's Critical Philosophy."

4. Compare Fichte: "That our proposition [—The Ego originally and absolutely posits its own being—] is the absolutely basic principle of all knowledge was

objective expression of the empty form of opposition—had been hy-
postasized anew by Kant, and posited as absolute objectivity like the
things of the dogmatic philosophers. On the one hand, he made the
categories into static, dead pigeonholes of the intellect; and on the
other hand he made them into the supreme principles capable of nullifying the language that expresses the Absolute itself—e.g., "substance" in Spinoza. Thus he allowed argumentation to go on replacing
philosophy, as before, only more pretentiously than ever under the
name of critical philosophy. But all this springs at best from the form
of the Kantian deduction of the categories, not from its principle or
spirit. Indeed, if we had no part of Kant's philosophy but the deduction, the transformation of his philosophy [from speculation into re-
flection] would [6] be almost incomprehensible. The principle of speculation is the identity of subject and object, and this principle is most
definitely articulated in the deduction of the forms of the intellect
(*Verstand*). It was Reason (*Vernunft*) itself that baptized this theory
of the intellect.

However, Kant turns this identity itself, which is Reason, into an
object of philosophical reflection, and thus this identity vanishes from
its home ground. Whereas intellect had previously been handled by
Reason, it is now, by contrast, Reason that is handled by the intellect.
This makes clear what a subordinate stage the identity of subject and
object was grasped at. The identity of subject and object is limited to
twelve acts of pure thought—or rather to nine only, for modality
really determines nothing objectively; the nonidentity of subject and
object essentially pertains to it.[5] Outside what is objectively determined by the categories there remained an enormous empirical realm

---

pointed out by *Kant* in his deduction of the categories; but he never laid it down
specifically *as* the basic principle." (*Foundation of the Science of Knowledge*
[1794], *Werke* [1845] I, 99; Heath and Lachs, p. 100.) For the claim that this
principle is the "spirit of Kantian philosophy" see Fichte, *Werke* I, 186 n., 479
(Heath and Lachs, pp. 171 n., 52). This last passage, in the "Second Introduction
to the Science of Knowledge" (1797), occurs in the context of a discussion
(*Werke* I, 468–91; Heath and Lachs, pp. 42–62) that is very important for the
understanding of what "intellectual intuition" means to Schelling and Hegel.

5. For Kant's table of categories see *Critique of Pure Reason* B 106. The triad
of modality is: 1. Possibility/Impossibility; 2. Existence/Non-existence; 3. Neces-
sity/Contingency. As to the peculiarity of modality compare A 74 (B 100) and A
219 (B 266).

of sensibility and perception, an absolute *a posteriori* realm. For this realm the only a priori principle discovered is a merely subjective maxim of the faculty of reflecting judgment.[6] That is to say, nonidentity is raised to an absolute principle. Nothing else was to be expected, once the identity, i.e, the rational, had been removed from the Idea, which is the product of Reason, and the Idea had been posited in absolute opposition to being. Reason as a practical faculty had been presented as it must be conceived by finite thought, i.e., by the intellect: not as absolute identity, but in infinite opposition, as a faculty of the pure unity [typical] of the intellect. Hence there arises this contrast: there are no absolute objective determinations for the intellect [i.e., in critical philosophy], but they are present for Reason [i.e., in speculative philosophy].

The principle of Fichte's system is the pure thinking that thinks itself, the identity of subject and object, in the form Ego = Ego.[7] If one holds solely and directly to this principle and to the transcendental principle at the basis of Kant's deduction of the categories, one has the authentic principle of speculation boldly expressed. However, as soon as [Fichte's] speculation steps outside of the concept that it establishes of itself and evolves into a system, it abandons itself and its principle and does not come back to it again. It surrenders Reason to the intellect and passes over into the chain of finite [acts and objects] of consciousness from which it never reconstructs itself again as identity and true infinity. Transcendental intuition, the very principle [of speculation], thereby assumes the awkward posture of something that is in opposition to the manifold deduced from it. The Absolute of the system shows itself as apprehended only in the form in which it appears to philosophical reflection. This determinacy which is given to the Absolute by reflection is not removed—so finitude and opposition are not removed. The principle, the Subject-Object, turns out to be a subjective [7] Subject-Object. What is deduced from it thereby gets the form of a conditioning of pure consciousness, of the Ego = Ego; and pure consciousness itself takes on the form of something conditioned by an objective infinity, namely the temporal progression *ad infinitum*. Transcendental intuition loses itself in this infinite progression and the Ego fails to constitute itself as absolute self-intuition.

6. For the maxim of reflecting judgment see *Critique of Judgment*, Introduction section IV, and sections 75–76 (*Akad.* V, 179–80, 397–404).

7. See especially the first section of the *Science of Knowledge* (Fichte, *Werke* I, 95–100; Heath and Lachs, pp. 97–101).

Hence, Ego $=$ Ego is transformed into the principle 'Ego *ought* to be equal to Ego.' Reason is placed in absolute opposition, i.e., it is degraded to the level of intellect, and it is this degraded Reason that becomes the principle of the shapes that the Absolute must give itself, and of the Sciences of these shapes.[8]

These are the two sides of Fichte's system. On the one hand it has established the pure concept of Reason and of speculation and so made philosophy possible. On the other hand, it has equated Reason with pure consciousness and raised Reason as apprehended in a finite shape to the status of principle. That these two sides should be distinguished must be shown to be an inner necessity of the problem itself (*die Sache selbst*), even though the external occasion for making the distinctions is a need of the time and is now provided by a bit of contemporary flotsam in time's stream, namely Reinhold's *Contributions* to a Survey of the State of Philosophy at the Beginning of the New Century. In these *Contributions* the aspect of authentic speculation and hence of philosophy in Fichte's system is overlooked;[9] and so is the aspect of Schelling's system that distinguishes it from Fichte's —the distinction being that in the philosophy of nature Schelling sets the objective Subject-Object beside the subjective Subject-Object and presents both as united in something higher than the subject.

As to the need of the times, Fichte's philosophy has caused so much of a stir and has made an epoch to the extent that even those who declare themselves against it and strain themselves to get speculative systems of their own on the road, still cling to its principle, though in a more turbid and impure way, and are incapable of resisting it. The most obvious symptoms of an epoch-making system are the misunderstandings and the awkward conduct of its adversaries. However, when one can say of a system that fortune has smiled on it, it is because some widespread philosophical need, itself unable to give birth to philosophy—for otherwise it would have achieved fulfilment through the creation of a system—turns to it with an instinct-like propensity. The acceptance of the system seems to be passive but this is only because what it articulates is already present in the time's inner core and everyone will soon be proclaiming it in his sphere of science or life.

8. *Ihrer Wissenschaften*: *ihrer* may refer either to the "shapes" or to "this degraded Reason."

9. Hegel plays on Reinhold's use of *Übersicht*. In his "Contributions to an *Overview*" Reinhold manages to *overlook* the most important points.

In this sense one cannot say of Fichte's system that fortune has smiled on it.[10] While this is partly due to the unphilosophical [8] tendencies of the age, there is something else that should also be taken into account. The greater the influence that intellect and utility succeed in acquiring, and the wider the currency of limited aims, the more powerful will the urge of the better spirit be, particularly in the more openminded world of youth. A phenomenon such as the *Speeches on Religion*[11] may not immediately concern the speculative need. Yet they and their reception—and even more so the dignity that is beginning to be accorded, more or less clearly or obscurely, to poetry and art in general in all their true scope—indicate the need for a philosophy that will recompense nature for the mishandling that it suffered in Kant and Fichte's systems, and set Reason itself in harmony with nature, not by having Reason renounce itself or become an insipid imitator of nature, but by Reason recasting itself into nature out of its own inner strength.

This essay begins with general reflections about the need, presupposition, basic principles, etc. of philosophy. It is a fault in them that they are general reflections, but they are occasioned by the fact that presupposition, [9] principles, and such like forms still adorn the entrance to philosophy with their cobwebs. So, up to a point it is still necessary to deal with them until the day comes when from beginning to end it is philosophy itself whose voice will be heard. Some of the more interesting of these topics will be more extensively treated elsewhere.[12]

Jena, July 1801.

10. Compare Fichte, "Ueber den Begriff der Wissenschaftslehre" (1794), *Werke* I, 34–36.

11. [Friedrich Schleiermacher], *On Religion: Speeches to its Cultured Despisers* (Berlin, 1799).

12. This promise suggests that Hegel was already looking forward to his work as a contributor to the *Critical Journal*. The most obvious and important publication in which it was fulfilled is *Faith and Knowledge* (trans. Cerf and Harris [Albany: State University of New York Press, 1976]).

Various Forms Occurring
in Contemporary Philosophy

An age which has so many philosopical systems lying behind it in its past must apparently arrive at the same indifference which life acquires after it has tried all forms. The urge toward totality continues to express itself, but only as an urge toward completeness of information. Individuality becomes fossilized and no longer ventures out into life. Through the variety of what he has, the individual tries to procure the illusion of being what he is not. He refuses the living participation demanded by science,[1] transforming it into mere information, keeping it at a distance and in purely objective shape. Deaf to all demands that he should raise himself to universality, he maintains himself imperturbably in his self-willed particularity. If indifference of this sort escalates into curiosity, it may believe nothing to be more vital than giving a name to a newly developed philosophy, expressing dominion over it by finding a name for it, just as Adam showed his dominance over the animals by giving names to them.[2] In this way philosophy is transposed to the plane of information. Information is concerned with alien objects. In the philosophical knowledge that is only erudition, the inward totality does not bestir itself, and neutrality retains its perfect freedom [from commitment].

No philosophical system can escape the possibility of this sort of reception; every philosophical system can be treated historically. As every living form belongs at the same time to the realm of appearance, so too does philosophy. As appearance, philosophy surrenders

---

1. *Wissenschaft.* It is characteristic of Schelling and Hegel (largely as a result of Fichte's *Wissenschaftslehre*) that they do not merely regard speculative philosophy as *a* "Science," but as the *only* "Science" worthy of the name. Hence "Science" and "philosophy" become synonymous.

2. In his first "Philosophy of Spirit" (Winter 1803) Hegel makes the following remark about this: "The first act by which Adam constituted his dominion over the animals is that he gave them names, i.e., he nullified them as beings and made them into essentially ideal things *(für sich Ideellen)*" (N.K.A., VI, 288). Similarly then, the historian turns the living spirit of a philosophy into a definite "idea" in his own mind.

to the power capable of transforming it into dead opinion and into something that belonged to the past from the very beginning. The living spirit that dwells in a philosophy demands to be born of a kindred spirit if it is to unveil itself. It brushes past the historical concern which is moved by some interest, to [collect] information about opinions. For this concern it is an alien phenomenon and does not reveal its own inwardness. It matters little to the spirit that it is forced to augment the extant collection of mummies and the general heap of contingent oddities; for the spirit itself slipped away between the fingers of the curious collector of information. The collector stands firm in his [10] neutral attitude towards truth; he preserves his independence whether he accepts opinions, rejects them, or abstains from decision. He can give philosophical systems only one relation to himself: they are opinions—and such incidental things as opinions can do him no harm. He has not learned that there is truth to be had.[3]

The history of philosophy [seems to] acquire a more useful aspect, however, when the impulse to enlarge science takes hold of it, for according to Reinhold, the history of philosophy should serve as a means "to penetrate more profoundly than ever into the spirit of philosophy, and to develop the idiosyncratic views of one's predecessors about the grounding of the reality of human cognition further in new views of one's own."[4] Only if this sort of information concerning previous attempts to solve the problem of philosophy were available could the attempt actually succeed in the end—if mankind is fated to succeed in it at all.

As can be seen, the project of such an investigation presupposes an image of philosophy as a kind of handicraft, something that can be improved by newly invented turns of skill. Each new invention presupposes acquaintance with the turns already in use and with the purposes they serve; but after all the improvements made so far, the principal task remains. Reinhold evidently seems to think of this task as the finding of a universally valid and ultimate turn of skill such that the work completes itself automatically for anyone who can get acquainted with it. If the aim were such an invention, and if science were a lifeless product of alien ingenuity, science would indeed have

---

3. In his *Lectures on the History of Philosophy* (first given in 1805) Hegel criticized Dietrich Tiedmann as a collector of this kind. See Haldane and Simson, I, 112–3; or Gray, pp. 314–5.

4. *Beyträge* I, 5–6.

the perfectibility of which mechanical arts are capable. The preceding philosophical systems would at all times be nothing but practice studies for the big brains. But if the Absolute, like Reason which is its appearance, is eternally one and the same—as indeed it is—then every Reason that is directed toward itself and comes to recognize itself, produces a true philosophy and solves for itself the problem which, like its solution, is at all times the same. In philosophy, Reason comes to know itself and deals only with itself so that its whole work and activity are grounded in itself, and with respect to the inner essence of philosophy there are neither predecessors nor successors.

Nor is it any more correct to speak of *personal views* entertained in philosophy than of its steady improvement. How could the rational be a personal idiosyncrasy? Whatever is thus peculiar in a philosophy must *ipso facto* belong to the form of the system and not to the essence of the philosophy. If something idiosyncratic actually constituted the essence of a philosophy, it would not be a philosophy, though even where the system itself [11] declared its essence to be something idiosyncratic it could nevertheless have sprung from authentic speculation which suffered shipwreck when it tried to express itself in the form of science. One who is caught up in his own idiosyncrasy can see in others only their idiosyncrasies. If one allows personal views to have a place in essential philosophy, and if Reinhold regards what he has recently turned to as a philosophy peculiar to himself, then it is indeed possible generally to regard all preceding ways of presenting and solving the problem of philosophy as merely personal idiosyncrasies and mental exercises. But the exercises are still supposed to prepare the way for the attempt that finally succeeds —for though we see that the shores of those philosophical Islands of the Blest that we yearn for are only littered with the hulks of wrecked ships, and there is no vessel safe at anchor in their bays, yet we must not let go of the teleological perspective.

Fichte dared to assert that Spinoza could not possibly have believed in his philosophy, that he could not possibly have had a full inner living conviction; and he said of the ancients that it is even doubtful that they had a clear conception of the task of philosophy.[5] This, too, must be explained in terms of the idiosyncratic form in which his philosophy expressed itself.

5. See the "Second Introduction to the Science of Knowledge" (Fichte, *Werke* I, 513; Heath and Lachs, pp. 81–2).

In Fichte, the peculiar form of his own system, the vigor that characterizes[6] it as a whole produces utterances of this sort. The peculiarity of Reinhold's philosophy, on the other hand, consists in its founding and grounding concern with different philosophical views, making a great to-do about the historical investigation of their idiosyncrasies. His love of, and faith in, truth have risen to an elevation so pure and so sickening that in order to found and ground the step into the temple properly, Reinhold has built a spacious vestibule in which philosophy keeps itself so busy with analysis, with methodology and with storytelling, that it saves itself from taking the step altogether; and in the end, as a consolation for his incapacity to do philosophy, Reinhold persuades himself that the bold steps others have taken had been nothing but preparatory exercises or mental confusions.

The essence of philosophy, on the contrary, is a bottomless abyss for personal idiosyncrasy. In order to reach philosophy it is necessary to throw oneself into it *à corps perdu*—meaning by 'body' here, the sum of one's idiosyncrasies. For Reason, finding consciousness caught in particularities, only becomes philosophical speculation by raising itself to itself, putting its trust only in itself and the Absolute which at that moment becomes its object. In this process Reason stakes nothing but finitudes of consciousness. In order to overcome these finitudes and construct the Absolute in consciousness, Reason lifts itself into speculation, and in [12] the groundlessness of the limitations and personal pecularities it grasps its own grounding within itself. Speculation is the activity of the one universal Reason directed upon itself. Reason, therefore, does not view the philosophical systems of different epochs and different heads merely as different modes [of doing philosophy] and purely idiosyncratic views. Once it has liberated its own view from contingencies and limitations, Reason necessarily finds itself throughout all the particular forms—or else a mere manifold of the concepts and opinions of the intellect; and such a manifold is no philosophy. The true peculiarity of a philosophy lies in the interesting individuality which is the organic shape that Reason has built for itself out of the material of a particular age. The particular speculative Reason [of a later time] finds in it spirit of its spirit, flesh of its flesh, it intuits itself in it as one and the same and yet as another living

---

6. *Sthenische Beschaffenheit*: the term is borrowed from the physiological theory of Dr. John Brown (1735–88), which influenced Schelling and Hegel greatly in this early period. Reinhold is, by contrast, an "asthenic" philosopher, but Hegel leaves it to us to supply this Brownian complement.

being. Every philosophy is complete in itself, and like an authentic work of art, carries the totality within itself. Just as the works of Apelles or Sophocles would not have appeared to Raphael and Shakespeare—had they known them—as mere preparatory studies, but as a kindred force of the spirit, so Reason cannot regard its former shapes as merely useful preludes to itself. Virgil, to be sure, regarded Homer to be such a prelude to himself and his refined era, and for this reason Virgil's work remains a mere postlude.

THE NEED OF PHILOSOPHY[7]

If we look more closely at the particular form worn by a philosophy we see that it arises, on the one hand, from the living originality of the spirit whose work and spontaneity have reestablished and shaped the harmony that has been rent; and on the other hand, from the particular form of the dichotomy from which the system emerges. Dichotomy is the source of *the need of philosophy*; and as the culture of the era, it is the unfree and given aspect of the whole configuration. In [any] culture, the appearance of the Absolute has become isolated from the Absolute and fixated into independence. But at the same time the appearance cannot disown its origin, and must aim to constitute the manifold of its limitations into one whole. The intellect, as the capacity to set limits, erects a building and places it beween man and the Absolute, linking everything that [13] man thinks worthy and holy to this building, fortifying it through all the powers of nature and talent and expanding it *ad infinitum*. The entire totality of limitations is to be found in it, but not the Absolute itself. [The Absolute is] lost in the parts, where it drives the intellect in its ceaseless development of manifoldness. But in its striving to enlarge itself into the Absolute, the intellect only reproduces itself *ad infinitum* and so mocks itself.[8] Reason reaches the Absolute only in stepping out of

7. As is often the case in Hegel, the genitive here fulfils more than one function. "The need of philosophy" means *both* the need (at this time) for philosophy, *and* what philosophy needs (at this time).

8. There is perhaps an echo here of Goethe's *Faust: Ein Fragment* (1790), lines 415–20. These lines of Mephistopheles were reproduced without change in *Faust Part I* (1808). Walter Kaufmann's translation is as follows: "Who would study and describe the living starts / By driving the spirit out of its parts: / In the palm of his hands he holds all the sections, / Lacks nothing except the spirit's

this manifold of parts. The more stable and splendid the edifice of the intellect is, the more restless becomes the striving of the life that is caught up in it as a part to get out of it, and raise itself to freedom. When life as Reason steps away into the distance, the totality of limitations is at the same time nullified, and connected with the Absolute in this nullification, and hence conceived and posited as mere appearance. The split between the Absolute and the totality of limitations vanishes.

The intellect copies Reason's absolute positing and through the form [of absolute positing] it gives itself the semblance of Reason even though the posits are in themselves opposites, and hence finite. The semblance grows that much stronger when intellect transforms and fixes Reason's negating activity [as distinct from its positing activity] into a product. The infinite, insofar as it gets opposed to the finite, is a thing of this kind, i.e., it is something rational as posited by the intellect. Taken by itself, as something rational, it merely expresses the negating of the finite. By fixing it, the intellect sets it up in absolute opposition to the finite; and reflection which had risen to the plane of Reason when it suspended the finite, now lowers itself again to being intellect because it has fixed Reason's activity into [an activity of] opposition. Moreover, reflection still pretends to be rational even in its relapse.

The cultures of various times have established opposites of this kind, which were supposed to be products of Reason and absolutes, in various ways, and the intellect has labored over them as such. Antitheses such as spirit and matter, soul and body, faith and intellect, freedom and necessity, etc. used to be important; and in more limited spheres they appeared in a variety of other guises. The whole weight of human interests hung upon them. With the progress of culture they have passed over into such forms as the antithesis of Reason and sensibility, intelligence and nature and, with respect to the universal concept, of absolute subjectivity and absolute objectivity.

The sole interest of Reason is to suspend such rigid antitheses. But this does not mean that Reason is altogether opposed to opposition

---

connections, / *Encheiresis naturae* the chemists baptize it / Mock themselves and don't realize it" (*Goethe's "Faust"* [Garden City, N.Y.: Doubleday, Anchor Books, 1961], p. 199, lines 1936–41). (We know that this passage impressed Hegel, and stuck in his mind. For he quoted it, from memory, in his Berlin lectures on *Logic* and again in his course on the *Philosophy of Nature*. See *Encyclopaedia*, Sections 38 Addn. and 246 Addn.)

and limitation. For the necessary dichotomy is One factor in life.[9] Life eternally forms itself by setting up oppositions, and totality at the highest pitch of living energy (*in der höchsten Lebendigkeit*) is only possible through its own re-establishment out of the deepest fission. [14] What Reason opposes, rather, is just the absolute fixity which the intellect gives to the dichotomy; and it does so all the more if the absolute opposites themselves originated in Reason.

When the might of union vanishes from the life of men and the antitheses lose their living connection and reciprocity and gain independence, the need of philosophy arises. From this point of view the need is contingent. But with respect to the given dichotomy the need is the necessary attempt to suspend the rigidified opposition between subjectivity and objectivity; to comprehend the achieved existence (*das Gewordensein*) of the intellectual and real world as a becoming. Its being as a product must be comprehended as a producing. In the infinite activity of becoming and producing, Reason has united what was sundered and it has reduced the absolute dichotomy to a relative one, cne that is conditioned by the original identity. When, where and in what forms such self-reproductions of Reason occur as philosophies is contingent. This contingency must be comprehended on the basis of the Absolute positing itself as an objective totality. The contingency is temporal insofar as the objectivity of the Absolute is intuited as a going forth in time. But insofar as it makes its appearance as spatial compresence, the dichotomy is a matter of regional climate. In the form of fixed reflection, as a world of thinking and thought essence in antithesis to a world of actuality, this dichotomy falls into the Northwest.[10]

9. Hegel capitalized *Ein*. The "Other" factor is "union" or "identity" (with the Absolute).

10. *Als eine Welt von denkendem und gedachtem Wesen, in Gegensatz gegen eine Welt von Wirklichkeit fällt diese Entzweiung in den westlichen Norden.* The reference here is to Descartes. This is not quite as plain as the French translator, Méry, thinks (p. 175, note F), but it is rendered certain by what Hegel says about the Cartesian philosophy in the "Introduction" to the *Critical Journal* (which he drafted only a few months later): "Against the Cartesian philosophy, which has expressed in philosophical form the all-encompassing dualism in the culture of the modern period in our northwestern world . . . philosophy, like every aspect of living nature must seek means of salvation . . ." (*N.K.A.* IV, 126). From the context of this latter passage it emerges clearly that Hegel regarded the Reformation as the religious expression, and the French Revolution as the political expression, of the dualism to which Descartes gave philosophical form. The "old life" of which these revolutions, together with the Cartesian philosophy were the

As culture grows and spreads, and the development of those outward expressions of life into which dichotomy can entwine itself becomes more manifold, the power of dichotomy becomes greater, its
regional sanctity is more firmly established and the strivings of life
to give birth once more to its harmony become more meaningless,
more alien to the cultural whole. Such few attempts as there have
been on behalf of the cultural whole against more recent culture, like
the more significant beautiful embodiments of far away or long ago,
have only been able to arouse that modicum of attention which remains possible when the more profound, serious connection of living
art [to culture as a living whole] can no longer be understood. The
entire system of relations constituting life has become detached from
art, and thus the concept of art's all-embracing coherence has been
lost, and transformed into the concept either of superstition or of en-
tertainment. The highest aesthetic perfection, as it evolves in a determinate religion in which man lifts himself above all dichotomy and
sees both the freedom of the subject and the necessity of the object
vanish in the kingdom of grace, could only be energized up to a certain stage of culture, and within general or mob barbarism. As it [15]
progressed, civilization has split away from it [i.e., this aesthetic religious perfection], and juxtaposed it to itself or vice-versa. Because
the intellect has grown sure of itself, both [intellect and the aesthetic
religious perfection] have come to enjoy a measure of mutual peace
by separating into realms that are completely set apart from one another. What happens in one has no significance in the other.

However, the intellect can also be directly attacked by Reason in
its own realm. These attempts to nullify the dichotomy, and hence the
absoluteness of intellect, through reflection itself are easier to understand. Dichotomy felt itself attacked, and so turned with hate and
fury against Reason, until the realm of the intellect rose to such power that it could regard itself as secure from Reason. —But just as we
often say of virtue that the greatest witness for its reality is the semblance that hypocrisy borrows from it, so intellect cannot keep Reason off. It seeks to protect itself against the feeling of its inner empti-

---

downfall, was that of *Roman* Catholic feudalism. But Christian culture was infected with this dualism from the beginning. The new life of which the "saved"
philosophy (of Identity) will be the scientific expression must unite the North
Western pole of dualism with the South-Eastern pole of "Union" found in classical Greece "far away and long ago." Hegel and Schelling presumably regarded
their native Swabia as the geographical "point of indifference" on this axis.

ness, and from the secret fear that plagues anything limited, by whitewashing its particularities with a semblance of Reason. The contempt for Reason shows itself most strongly, not in Reason's being freely scorned and abused, but by the boasting of the limited that it has mastered philosophy and lives in amity with it. Philosophy must refuse friendship with these false attempts that boast insincerely of having nullified the particularities, but which issue from limitation, and use philosophy as a means to save and secure these limitations.

In the struggle of the intellect with Reason the intellect has strength only to the degree that Reason forsakes itself. Its success in the struggle therefore depends upon Reason itself, and upon the authenticity of the need for the reconstitution of totality, the need from which Reason emerges.

The need of philosophy can be called the *presupposition* of philosophy if philosophy, which begins with itself, has to be furnished with some sort of vestibule; and there has been much talk nowadays about an absolute presupposition.[11] What is called the presupposition of philosophy is nothing else but the need that has come to utterance. Once uttered, the need is posited for reflection, so that [because of the very nature of reflection] there must be two presuppositions.

One is the Absolute itself. It is the goal that is being sought; but it is already present, or how otherwise could it be sought?[12] Reason produces it, merely by freeing consciousness from its limitations. This suspension of the limitations is conditioned by the presupposed unlimitedness.

The other presupposition may be taken to be that consciousness has stepped out of the totality, that is, it may be taken to be the split into being and not-being, concept and being, finitude and infinity. From the standpoint of the dichotomy, the absolute synthesis is a beyond, it is the undetermined and the shapeless as opposed [16] to the determinacies of the dichotomy. The Absolute is the night, and the light is younger than it; and the distinction between them, like the emergence of the light out of the night, is an absolute difference—the nothing is the first out of which all being, all the mainfoldness of the finite has emerged. But the task of philosophy consists in uniting these presuppositions: to posit being in non-being, as becoming; to

11. Hegel is principally thinking of Reinhold with his "founding and grounding" and his "arch-truth" (compare pp. 179–86 below).

12. There may perhaps be an echo of Pascal here: "Tu ne me chercherais pas, si tu ne m'avais trouvé" (*Pensées*, VII, 553).

posit dichotomy in the Absolute, as its appearance; to posit the finite in the infinite, as life.

Still, it is clumsy to express the need of philosophy as a presupposition of philosophy, for the need acquires in this way a reflective form. This reflective form appears as contradictory propositions, which we shall discuss below.[13] One may require of propositions that they be justified. But the justification of these propositions as presuppositions is still not supposed to be philosophy itself, so that the founding and grounding gets going before, and outside of, philosophy.

REFLECTION AS INSTRUMENT OF PHILOSOPHIZING

The form that the need of philosophy would assume, if it were to be expressed as a presupposition, allows for a transition from the need of philosophy to the *instrument of philosophizing*, to *reflection* as Reason. The task of philosophy is to construct the Absolute for consciousness. But since the productive activity of reflection is, like its products, mere limitation, this task involves a contradiction. The Absolute is to be posited in reflection. But then it is not posited, but cancelled; for in having been posited it was limited [by its opposite]. Philosophical reflection is the mediation of this contradiction. What must be shown above all is how far reflection is capable of grasping the Absolute, and how far in its speculative activity it carries with it the necessity and possibility of being synthesized with absolute intuition. To what extent can reflection be as complete for itself, subjectively, as its product must be, which is constructed in consciousness as the Absolute that is both conscious and non-conscious at the same time?

Reflection in isolation is the positing of opposites, and this would be a suspension of the Absolute, reflection being the faculty of being and limitation. But reflection [17] as Reason has connection with the Absolute, and it is Reason only because of this connection. In this respect, reflection nullifies itself and all being and everything limited, because it connects them with the Absolute. But at the same time the limited gains standing precisely on account of its connection with the Absolute.

Reason presents itself as the force of the negative Absolute, and

13. See pp. 103–9.

hence as a negating that is absolute; and at the same time, it presents itself as the force that posits the opposed objective and subjective totality. Reason raises the intellect above itself, driving it toward a whole of the intellect's own kind.[14] Reason seduces the intellect into producing an objective totality. Every being, because it is posited, is an opposite, it is conditioned and conditioning. The intellect completes these its limitations by positing the opposite limitations as conditions. These need to be completed in the same way, so the intellect's task expands *ad infinitum*. In all this, reflection appears to be merely intellect, but this guidance toward the totality of necessity is the contribution and secret efficacy of Reason. Reason makes the intellect boundless, and in this infinite wealth the intellect and its objective world meet their downfall. For every being that the intellect produces is something determinate, and the determinate has an indeterminate before it and after it. The manifoldness of being lies between two nights, without support. It rests on nothing—for the indeterminate is nothing to the intellect—and it ends in nothing. The determinate and the indeterminate, finitude and the infinite that is to be given up for lost,[15] are not united. The intellect stubbornly allows them to subsist side by side in their opposition. And stubbornly it holds fast to being as against not-being; yet being and not-being are equally necessary to it. The intellect essentially aims at thoroughgoing determination. But what is determinate for it is at once bounded by an indeterminate. Thus its positings and determinings never accomplish the task; in the very positing and determining that have occurred there lies a non-positing and something indeterminate, and hence the task of positing and determining recurs perpetually.

If the intellect fixes these opposites, the finite and the infinite, so that both are supposed to subsist together as opposed to each other, then it destroys itself. For the opposition of finite and infinite means that to posit the one is to cancel the other. When Reason recognizes this, it has suspended the intellect itself. Its positing then appears to

14. We have omitted the *einmal* at the beginning of this sentence, because Hegel seems to have forgotten it himself. But it should be noticed that in the present paragraph Hegel seeks to show that "Reason makes the intellect boundless," and in the next that "Reason suspends itself."

15. *Aufgegeben* may means either "given up" or "set as task." It is likely that Hegel is employing it in both meanings here. To the intellect, totality is something that is only present as infinite regress (or progress). Hence the totality is for it a *task* that is for ever set anew. But this "bad" concept of the infinite is the same as "giving it up" altogether.

Reason to be non-positing, its products to be negations. If Reason is placed in opposition to the objective infinite, this nullification of the intellect or Reason's pure positing without oppositing is subjective infinity: the realm of freedom as opposed to the objective world. But in this form, the realm of freedom is itself something opposite and conditioned. In order to suspend opposition absolutely, Reason must also [18] nullify the independence of this realm. It nullifies both of the opposed realms by uniting them; for they only are in virtue of their not being united. Within the union, however, they subsist together; for what is opposite and therefore limited is, in this union, connected with the Absolute. But it does not have standing on its own account, but only insofar as it is posited in the Absolute, that is, as identity. The limited is either necessary or free, according to whether it belongs to one or the other of the mutually opposed and therefore relative totalities. Insofar as the limited belongs to the synthesis of both totalities, its limitation ceases: it is free and necessary at the same time, conscious and nonconscious. This conscious identity of the finite and infinite, the union of both worlds, the sensuous and the intelligible, the necessary and the free, in consciousness, is *knowledge*. Reflection, the faculty of the finite, and the infinite opposed to it are synthesized in Reason whose infinity embraces the finite within it.

So far as reflection makes itself its own object, its supreme law, given to it by Reason and moving it to become Reason, is to nullify itself. Like everything else, reflection has standing only in the Absolute; but as reflection it stands in opposition to it. In order to gain standing, therefore, reflection must give itself the law of self-destruction. The immanent law, the law through which reflection by its own power would constitute itself as absolute, would be the law of contradiction: namely that, being posited, reflection shall be and remain posited. Reflection would thus fix its products as absolutely opposed to the Absolute. It would have as its eternal law to remain intellect and not to become Reason and to hold fast to its own work, which, as limited, is opposed to the Absolute and as opposed to the Absolute, is nothing.

When placed in an opposition, Reason operates as intellect and its infinity becomes subjective. Similarly, the form which expresses the activity of reflecting as an activity of thinking, is capable of this very same ambiguity and misuse. Thinking is the absolute activity of Reason itself and there simply cannot be anything opposite to it. But if it is not so posited, if it is taken to be nothing but reflection of a purer kind, that is, a reflection in which one merely abstracts from the opposition, then thinking of this abstracting kind cannot advance beyond the intellect, not even to a Logic supposed capable of comprehending Reason within itself, still less to philosophy. Reinhold sets up identity as "the essence or inward character of thinking as such": "the infinite repeatability of one and the same as one and the same, in and through one and the same."[16] One might be tempted by this semblance of identity into regarding this thinking as Reason. But because this thinking has its antithesis (a) in an application of thinking and (b) in absolute materiality (*Stoffheit*),[17] it is clear that this is not the absolute identity, the identity of subject and object which suspends both in their opposition and grasps them within itself, but a *pure* identity, that is, an identity [19] originating through abstraction and conditioned by opposition, the abstract intellectual concept of unity, one of a pair of fixed opposites.

Reinhold sees the fault of all past philosophy in "the habit, so deeply rooted and widespread among contemporary philosophers, of regarding thinking both in general and in its application as something merely subjective."[18] If Reinhold were truly serious about the identity and non-subjectivity of this thinking, he could not make any distinction between thinking and its application. If thinking is true identity, and not something subjective, where could this application that is so distinct from it come from, let alone the stuff that is postulated for the sake of the application? To the analytic method an activity must appear to be synthetic precisely because it is to be analysed. The elements that originate in the analysis are unity and a manifold opposed to it. What analysis presents as unity is called subjective; and thinking is characterized as a unity of this sort opposed to the manifold, that is, it is an abstract identity. In this way thinking has become something purely limited, and its activity is an application [of the identity] to some independently extant material, an application which conforms to a law and is directed by a rule, but which cannot pierce through to knowledge.

Only so far as reflection has connection with the Absolute is it Reason and its deed a knowing. Through this connection with the Absolute, however, reflection's work passes away; only the connection persists, and it is the sole reality of the cognition. There is therefore no truth in isolated reflection, in pure thinking, save the truth of

16. *Beyträge* I, 106.
17. Compare *ibid.*, pp. 108–12.
18. *Ibid.*, p. 96.

its nullification. But because in philosophizing the Absolute gets produced by reflection for consciousness, it becomes thereby an objective totality, a whole of knowledge, an organization of cognitions. Within this organization, every part is at the same time the whole; for its standing is its connection with the Absolute. As a part that has other parts outside of it, it is something limited, and is only through the others. Isolated in its limitation the part is defective; meaning and significance it has solely through its coherence with the whole. Hence single concepts by themselves and singular cognitions (*Erkenntnisse*) must not be called knowledge. There can be plenty of singular empirical known items (*Kenntnisse*).[19] As known from experience they exhibit their justification in experience, that is, in the identity of concept and being, of subject and object. Precisely for this reason, they are not scientific knowledge: they find their justification only in a limited, relative identity. They do not justify themselves as necessary parts of a totality of cognitions organized in consciousness, nor has speculation recognized the absolute identity in them, i.e., their connection with the Absolute.

RELATION OF SPECULATION TO COMMON SENSE[20]

What the so-called common sense takes to be the rational, consists similarly of single items drawn out of the Absolute into consciousness.

19. The "singular empirical known items" would here include—and indeed largely consist of—generic classifications and laws or law-like statements. The "limited, relative identity" in which they find their justification would be a basic assumption or general explanatory hypothesis of some kind.

20. *Der gesunde Menschenverstand* is very much what "common sense" is in English (and "le bon sens" in French). We have therefore followed the general practice of Hegel translators in rendering it thus. However, in its Hegelian context the German phrase has two advantages over its English and French counterparts. It carries in its "*Menschen* Verstand" an opposition to the *divine* intellect, and in its "Menschen *Verstand*" an opposition to *Vernunft*. These contrasts are lost in "common sense" and "bon sens." They could only be preserved by a literal rendering ("healthy human intellect") which would mislead the reader because of its seemingly technical character. Hegel's attitude to the boasted "soundness" or "health" of "common sense" when it is exploited in support of a philosophical position is highly ironic. For this reason, although he has nothing against "common sense" in its proper sphere (the making of practical decisions in ordinary life) he sometimes switches from the honorific "*gesunde* Menschenverstand" to "*gemeine* Menschenverstand" which has a slightly pejorative ring.

They are points of light that rise out of the night of totality and aid men to get through life in an intelligent way. They serve as correct standpoints from which one takes off and to which one returns.

In fact, however, men only have this confidence in the truth of these points of light because they have a feeling of the Absolute attending these points; and it is this feeling alone that gives them their significance. As soon as one takes these truths of common sense by themselves and isolates them as cognitions of the intellect, they look odd and turn into half-truths. Reflection can confound common sense. When common sense permits itself to reflect, the proposition it states for the benefit of reflection claims to be by itself knowledge and valid cognition. Thus sound sense has given up its strength, the strength of supporting its pronouncements and counteracting unsteady reflection solely by the obscure totality which is present as feeling. Although common sense expresses itself for reflection, its dicta do not contain the consciousness of their connection with the absolute totality. The totality remains inward and unexpressed.

For this reason, speculation understands sound intellect well enough, but the sound intellect cannot understand what speculation is doing. Speculation acknowledges as the reality of cognition only the being of cognition in the totality. For speculation everything determinate has reality and truth only in the cognition of its connection with the Absolute. So it recognizes the Absolute in what lies at the basis of the pronouncements of sound sense too. But since, for speculation, cognition has reality only within the Absolute, what is cognized and known in the reflective mode of expression and therefore has a determinate form, becomes nothing in the presence of speculation. The relative identities of common sense which pretend to absoluteness in the limited form in which they appear, become contingencies for philosophical reflection. Common sense cannot grasp how what has immediate certainty for it, can at the same time be nothing to philosophy. For in its immediate truths it only feels their connection with the Absolute, and it does not separate this feeling from their appearance, wherein they are limitations, and yet they are supposed as such to have standing and absolute being. But in the face of speculation they vanish.

Common sense cannot understand speculation; and what is more, it must come to hate speculation when it has experience of it; and, un-

---

Where he does this, we have used "ordinary common sense." We have also used "sound sense" and "sound intellect" occasionally—to remind the reader of *gesund.*

less it is in the state of perfect indifference that security confers, it is bound to detest and persecute it.[21] For common sense, the essential and the contingent in its utterances are identical and this identity is absolute; and, just as it cannot separate the limits of appearance from the Absolute, so what it does separate in its consciousness, becomes absolutely opposed, and what it cognizes as limited it cannot in consciousness unite with the unlimited. Limited and unlimited are, to be sure, identical for common sense, but this identity is and remains something internal, a feeling, something unknown and unexpressed. Whenever it calls the limited to mind, and the limited is raised into consciousness, the unlimited is for consciousness absolutely opposed to the limited.

In this relation or connection of the limited with the Absolute there is consciousness of their opposition only; there is no consciousness at all of their identity. This relation is called *faith*.[22] Faith does not express the synthesis inherent in feeling or intuition. It is, rather, a relation of reflection to the Absolute, and one in which reflection is certainly Reason. But though it nullifies itself as something that sunders and is sundered, and also nullifies its product too—an individual consciousness—it still preserves the form of sundering. The immediate certitude of faith, which has been much talked of as the ultimate and highest consciousness, is nothing but the identity itself, Reason, which, however does not recognize itself, and is accompanied by the consciousness of opposition. Speculation, however, lifts the identity of which sound sense is not conscious into consciousness. In other words, speculation constructs conscious identity out of what, in the consciousness of the ordinary intellect, are necessarily opposites; and this synthesis of what is sundered in faith is an abomination to faith. In its consciousness the holy and the divine only have standing as ob-

---

21. Speculative philosophers had, of course, hosts of critics who attacked speculation in the name of common sense. Among the so-called *Popular Philosophers* of the Enlightenment F. Nicolai (1733–1811) comes to mind, and among the followers of Kant and Fichte perhaps W. T. Krug (1770–1842). It is more probable, though, that Hegel's reference, if it is to any particular person or event at all, is to the *Atheismusstreit* through which Fichte had lost his chair at Jena in 1799.

22. Just as, in the preceding pages, the target of Hegel's attack is not so much common sense as the role that certain philosophers give to it, so here he is not so much arguing against faith as such, as against certain philosophic conceptions of faith. He is probably thinking mainly of Jacobi, but Kant, Fichte and Schleiermacher—besides a host of lesser figures—may be in his mind too. Compare *Faith and Knowledge*, passim.

jects. So the healthy intellect sees only destruction of the divine in the suspended opposition, in the identity brought into consciousness.

In particular, ordinary common sense is bound to see nothing but nullification in those philosophical systems that satisfy the demand for conscious identity by suspending dichotomy in such a way that one of the opposites is raised to be the absolute and the other nullified. This is particularly offensive if the culture of the time has already fixed one of the opposites otherwise. Speculation, as philosophy, has here indeed suspended the opposition, but speculation, as system, has elevated something which in its ordinary familiar form is limited, to absolute status. The only aspect here relevant is the speculative, and this is simply not present for ordinary common sense. Viewed from this speculative aspect, the limited is something totally different from what it appears to ordinary common sense; [22] having been elevated into being the Absolute, it is no longer the limited thing that it was. The matter of the materialist is no longer inert matter which has life as its opposite and its formative agent; the Ego of the idealist is no longer an empirical consciousness which, as limited, must posit an infinite outside itself. The question that philosophy has to raise is whether the system has truly purified all finitude out of the finite appearance that it has advanced to absolute status; or whether speculation, even at its furthest distance from ordinary common sense with its typical fixation of opposites, has not still succumbed to the fate of its time, the fate of positing absolutely one form of the Absolute, that is, something that is essentially an opposite. But even where speculation has actually succeeded in freeing from all forms of appearance the finite which it has made infinite, ordinary common sense primarily takes offense over the name though it may take no other notice of the business of speculation. Speculation does indeed elevate finite things— matter, the Ego—to the infinite and thus nullifies them: matter and Ego so far as they are meant to embrace totality, are no longer matter and Ego. Yet the final act of philosophical reflection is still lacking: that is to say, the consciousness of the nullification of these finite things. And even though the Absolute within the system has still preserved a determinate form, in spite of the fact that this nullification has actually been accomplished, still the genuinely speculative tendency is unmistakable anyway. But ordinary common sense understands nothing about it, and does not even see the philosophic principle of suspending the dichotomy. It only sees the systematic principle by which one of the opposites is raised to the Absolute and the other nullified. So it has an advantage over the system with respect to the dichotomy. For there is an absolute opposition present in both of them. But in ordinary common sense there is *completeness* of opposition [whereas the system makes one of the opposites explicitly absolute]; and hence common sense is enraged on two counts.

Nevertheless, apart from its philosophical side, there accrues to a philosophical system of this kind, encumbered as it is with the defect of raising to the Absolute something that is still in some respect an opposite, another advantage and a further merit, which are not only incomprehensible but must be abhorrent to the ordinary intellect. The advantage is that by raising something finite to an infinite principle, the system has struck down with one stroke the whole mass of finitudes that adhere to the opposite principle. And the merit with regard to culture consists in having made the dichotomy that much more rigid and hence strengthened the urge toward unification in totality in the same measure.

Common sense is stubborn; it stubbornly believes itself secure in the force of its inertia, believes the non-conscious secure in its primordial gravity and opposition to [23] consciousness; believes matter secure against the difference that light brings into it just in order to reconstruct the difference into a new synthesis at a higher level. In northern climates this stubborness perhaps requires a longer period of time to be so far conquered that the atomic matter itself has become more diversified, and inertia has first been set in motion on its own ground by a greater variety of their combination and dissolution[23] and next by the multitude of fixed atoms thus generated. Thus the human intellect becomes more and more confused in its own proper doings and knowings, to the point where it makes itself capable of enduring the suspension of this confusion and the opposition itself.[24]

The only aspect of speculation visible to common sense is its nulli-

23. *Kombinieren und zersetzen derselben.* The reference of *derselben* is grammatically unclear: it may be either to "inertia" or to "atomic matter"; but the context is in favor of "atomic matter."

24. This paragraph relates the overcoming of "common sense" theories—and all forms of what Hegel and Schelling called *Unphilosophie*—by speculative idealism to the similar overcoming of Newtonian physics by Schelling (and his friends and followers) in the new "philosophy of Nature" for which the *Journal of Speculative Physics* was the official organ. It is not clear whether the analogy is meant simply as a metaphor, or whether a strict Spinozist parallel is intended. It is hard to believe that the paragraph is more than a metaphor, however, because a literal interpretation would seem to commit Hegel to an atomistic theory of mind. But the real thrust of the paragraph is precisely that we have to overcome our atomistic notions about matter.

fying activity; and even this nullification is not visible in its entire scope. If common sense could grasp this scope, it would not believe speculation to be its enemy. For in its highest synthesis of the conscious and the non-conscious, speculation also demands the nullification of consciousness itself. Reason thus drowns itself and its knowledge and its reflection of the absolute identity, in its own abyss: and in this night of mere reflection and of the calculating intellect, in this night which is the noonday of life, common sense and speculation can meet one another.

PRINCIPLE OF A PHILOSOPHY IN THE FORM OF AN ABSOLUTE BASIC PROPOSITION

Philosophy, as a totality of knowledge produced by reflection, becomes a system, that is, an organic whole of concepts, whose highest law is not the intellect, but Reason. The intellect has to exhibit correctly the opposites of what it has posited, as well as its bounds, ground and condition. Reason, on the other hand, unites these contradictories, posits both together and suspends them both. One might demand that the system as an organization of propositions should present the Absolute which lies at the basis of reflection in the fashion of reflection, that is, as the highest, or absolutely fundamental proposition. But such a demand at once entails its own nullity. For a proposition, as something posited by reflection, is something limited and conditioned on its own account. It requires another proposition as its foundation, and so on *ad infinitum*. Suppose that the Absolute is expressed in a fundamental proposition, validated by and for thinking, a proposition whose form and matter are the same. Then either mere sameness is posited, and the inequality of form and matter is excluded, so that the fundamental proposition is conditioned by this inequality.[25] In this

---

25. These and similar passages may perhaps be more easily understood by connecting them with Kant's distinction between analytic and synthetic judgments, a distinction which in Hegel's terms is typical of the reflective philosophy of the intellect and must be overcome in the speculative philosophy of Reason. The connection is by way of conceptual transformations which need not be actual historical steps.

The first set of transformations concerns the copula "is." The judgment "S is P" is taken to mean "S equals P." And "S equals P" is further taken to mean the same as "S is identical with P." Next, the identity relation is taken to be the

case the fundamental [24] proposition is not absolute but defective; it expresses only a concept of the intellect, an abstraction. Or else the fundamental proposition also contains both form and matter as inequality, so that it is analytic and synthetic simultaneously. In that case the fundamental proposition is an antinomy, and therefore not a proposition. As a proposition it is subject to the law of the intellect, the law that it must not contradict itself, that it cannot suspend itself,

---

form of the judgment while "S" and "P" are symbols for the matter (material, content, stuff) of the judgment.

The second set of transformations concerns the grammatical categories of subject and predicate. Paradigmatically, S is always taken to be a particular being and P a general concept or thought. So the first step is to replace the grammatical categories of subject and predicate by the ontological categories of being and thought. These, in turn, are tied to the epistemological categories of object and subject. Particular beings are objects; concepts or thoughts pertain to the subject. Finally, matter and form enter once more; for thought gives the form, and being gives the matter of the judgment.

If we take these two sets of transformations together, "S is P" becomes the expression of the identity of being and thought, of object and subject, of matter and form. But this is awkward. Within the idealistic current, the identity should be expressed as identity of thought and being and not of being and thought; of subject and object and not of object and subject; of form and matter and not of matter and form—just as, say, Queen Elizabeth would prefer to say that the Prime Minister is close to her rather than that she is close to the Prime Minister. Here, the equivocation of "subject" is a great help. The grammatical subject, whose correlate is the predicate, is allowed to swallow up the epistemological subject, whose correlate is the object; "S is P" becomes "subject is identical with object" ("S=O"). In the wake of that transformation, all other identities are reversed. Thought is identical with being; form with matter.

With these transformations as background, Hegel's treatment of the formulas "A=A" and "A=B" becomes somewhat more intelligible. A radical change in the meaning of "analytic" and "synthetic" is involved. In the language of the intellect any sentence is either analytic or synthetic. But in the language of speculation, in which Reason expresses itself, a proposition must be both analytic and synthetic; for a speculative proposition asserts the identity of the opposites, that is, of thought and being, of subject and object, of form and matter. That they are opposites is the synthetic element; that they are posited as identical is the analytic element. To the intellect, which takes "A=A" and "A=B" in isolation from one another, "A=A" would be the analytic judgment and "A=B" the synthetic judgment. The speculative élite, however, is aware of the intrinsic unity of what reflection separates into "A=A" and "A=B." Either "A=A" or "A=B" can function as the highest expression of Reason in the medium of intellect. Reason can see in either "A=A" or "A=B" the identity of what is antinomical to the intellect (although "A=B" is its more striking manifestation, to those at least who are only on their way from reflection to speculation, from intellect to

that it be something posited. As an antinomy, however, it does suspend itself.

It is a delusion that something merely posited for reflection must necessarily stand at the summit of a system as the highest or absolute and basic proposition; or that the essence of any system is expressible as a proposition that has absolute validity for thinking. This delusion makes the business of judging a system easy. For of any thought expressed by a proposition it can be shown very easily that it is conditioned by an opposite and therefore is not absolute: and one proves for this opposite that it must be posited, hence that the thought expressed by the fundamental proposition is a nullity. The delusion accounts itself all the more justified if the system itself expresses the Absolute which is its principle, in the form of a proposition or definition which is basically an antinomy, and for this reason suspends itself as something posited for mere reflection. For example, Spinoza's concept of substance, defined as both cause and effect, concept and being, ceases to be a concept because the opposites are united in a contradiction.

No philosophical beginning could look worse than to begin with a definition as Spinoza does. This offers the starkest contrast to 'founding and grounding,' or the 'deduction of the principles of knowledge,' or the laborious reduction of all philosophy to the 'highest facts of consciousness,' etc.[26] But when Reason has purified itself of the subjectivity of reflection, then Spinoza's artlessness which makes philoso-

---

Reason.) "A = A" obviously affirms identity; yet it acknowledges difference by placing "A" in the opposite roles of subject and predicate (which, according to the transformation rules, stand for thought and being). And "A = B" obviously affirms difference by placing different symbols in the opposite roles of subject and predicate, yet acknowledges their identity by " = ". Thus both "A = A" and "A = B" are analytic and synthetic at once. That is to say, they express in the language of reflection the identity of thought and being, subject and object, form and matter. Not only is Kant's distinction between analytic and synthetic "annulled," it is turned from a logical weapon against metaphysics into the heartbeat of metaphysics as speculation. Cf. pp. 109, 118 below.

26. "Founding and grounding" is Reinhold's special trademark: compare p. 88 above, and pp. 179–81 below. The other catchwords remind us first of Kant and of Fichte respectively. But probably Reinhold is the principal target of Hegel's irony throughout, since he first came to prominence as a disciple of Kant, and he had been an enthusiast for the new "science of knowledge" in its turn. He continued to use the vocabulary of both. In any case Hegel is certainly thinking of the contemporary epigones of the different "schools" of Critical Philosophy rather than of Kant and Fichte.

phy begin with philosophy itself, and Reason come forward at once with an antinomy, can be properly appreciated too.

If the principle of philosophy is to be stated in formal propositions for reflection, the only thing that is present, at the outset, as the object of this task is knowledge, i.e., in general terms the synthesis of the subjective and objective, or absolute thinking. But reflection cannot express the absolute synthesis in one proposition, if this proposition has to be valid as a proper proposition for the intellect. Reflection must separate what is one in the absolute Identity; it must express synthesis and antithesis separately, in two propositions, one containing the identity, the other dichotomy.

In $A = A$, as principle of identity, it is connectedness that is reflected on, and in this connecting, this being one, the equality, is contained in this pure identity; [25] reflection abstracts from all inequality. $A = A$, the expression of absolute thought or Reason, has only one meaning for the formal reflection that expresses itself in the propositions of the intellect. This is the meaning of pure unity as conceived by the intellect, or in other words a unity in abstraction from opposition.

Reason, however, does not find itself expressed in this onesidedness of abstract unity. It postulates also the positing of what in the pure equality had been abstracted from, the positing of the opposite, of inequality. One A is subject, the other object; and the expression of their difference is $A \neq A$, or $A = B$. This proposition directly contradicts the first. It abstracts from pure identity and posits the non-identity, the pure form of non-thinking,[27] just as the first proposition is the form of pure thinking, which is not the same thing as absolute thinking, or Reason. Only because non-thinking too, is thought, only because $A \neq A$ is posited through thinking, can it be posited at all.[28] In $A \neq A$, or $A = B$ there also is the identity, the connection, the "$=$" of the first proposition, but it is here only subjective, that is, only insofar as non-thinking is posited by thinking. But if non-thinking is posited for thinking this is entirely incidental to the non-thinking, it is a mere form for the second proposition. One must abstract from this form in order to have its matter pure.

27. See Reinhold, *Beyträge* I, 111.

28. *Kann er überhaupt gesetzt werden.* The most immediate and natural antecedent for *er* is "[*der Satz*] *A nicht = A.*" But the alert reader will soon notice that Hegel may very possibly mean "*der erste Satz*" (i.e., "$A = A$" or "the form of pure thinking").

This second proposition is as unconditioned as the first and *qua* unconditioned it is condition of the first, as the first is condition of the second. The first is conditioned by the second in that it is what it is through abstraction from the inequality that the second proposition contains; the second conditioned by the first, in that it is in need of a connection in order to be a proposition.

The second proposition has also been stated in the subordinate form of the principle of sufficient reason. Or rather, it was first brought down to this extremely subordinate meaning when it was turned into the principle of causality. A has a ground means: to A pertains an existence that is not an existence of A: A is a being posited that is not the being posited of A. Hence, $A \neq A$, $A = B$. If one abstracts from A's being something posited, as one must in order to have the second proposition in its purity, it expresses A's not being posited. To posit A as something posited and also as something not posited is already the synthesis of the first and second proposition.

Both propositions are principles of contradiction, but in an inverse sense. The first, the principle of identity, states that contradiction is $= 0$. The second proposition, insofar as one relates it to the first, states that contradiction is as necessary as non-contradiction. Taken separately (*für sich*) both propositions are posits on the same level. [But] if the [26] second one is so stated that the first proposition is connected with it at the same time, then it is the highest possible expression of Reason by the intellect. This connection of the two propositions expresses the antinomy; and as an antinomy, as an expression of the absolute identity, it makes no difference whether we posit $A = A$ or $A = B$ as long as each of them, $A = B$ and $A = A$, is taken as connection of both propositions. $A = A$ contains the difference of A as subject and A as object together with their identity, just as $A = B$ contains the identity of A and B together with their difference.

The intellect has not grown into Reason if it does not recognize the antinomy in the principle of sufficient reason which is a connection of both propositions. In that case the second proposition is not, *formaliter*, a new one for it: for the mere intellect $A = B$ does not say more than the first proposition and consequently it conceives A's being posited as B only as a repetition of A. That is to say, the intellect just holds fast to the identity and abstracts from the fact that when A is repeated as B or as posited in B, something else, a non-A, is posited and posited as A, hence, A is posited as non-A. If one reflects only on the formal aspect of speculation and holds fast to the synthesis of knowledge [only] in analytic form, then antinomy, that is, the contradiction that cancels itself, is the highest formal expression of knowledge and truth.

Once antinomy is acknowledged as the explicit formula of truth, Reason has brought the formal essence of reflection under its control. The formal essence still has the upper hand, however, if thought, [conceived merely] in its character of abstract unity, i.e., exclusively in the form of the first proposition as opposed to the second, is posited as the first truth of philosophy, and a system of the reality of cognition is supposed to be erected by analysis of the application of thinking.[29] In that case, the entire course of this purely analytic business will be as follows:

Thought, as infinite repeatability of A as A, is an abstraction, the first proposition expressed as activity. But now the second proposition is lacking, the non-thought. There must necessarily be a transition to it as the condition of the first; it, too, i.e., the matter, must be posited. Then the opposites will be complete; the transition from the first to the second is a certain kind of reciprocal connection between them, which is a very inadequate synthesis called an application of thought.[30] But even this weak synthesis goes counter to the presupposition that thought is a positing of A as A *ad infinitum*. For in the *application*, A is at the same time posited as non-A; and thought, in its absolute standing as infinite repetition of A as A, is suspended.

What is opposite to thought is, through its connection with thought, determined as something thought = A. But such a thought, such a positing = A is conditioned by an abstraction and is hence something opposite. Hence, that which is thought, besides the fact that it [27] has been thought = A, has still other determinations = B, entirely independent of being merely determined [as something thought] by pure thought. These other determinations are brute data for thought. Hence for thought as the principle of the analytic way of philosophizing, there must be an absolute stuff. We shall discuss this further below.[31] With this absolute opposition as foundation the formal programme, in which the famous discovery that philosophy must be reduced to logic[32] consists, is allowed no immanent synthesis save that

29. This paragraph is definitely aimed at Reinhold and Bardili. In the previous paragraph Hegel *may* have Jacobi in mind (as well).

30. See Reinhold; *Beyträge*, No. I, pp. 100 ff. (especially p. 106 ff). Compare pp. 188–92 below.

31. See pp. 188–9, 191–3, 194–7 below.

32. Reinhold, *Beyträge* I, 98.

provided by the identity of the intellect, i.e., the repetition of A *ad infinitum*. But even for this repetition the identity needs some B, C, etc. in which the repeated A can be posited. In order for A to be repeatable, B, C, D, etc. have to be [literally "are"] a manifold, in which each is opposed to the other. Each of them has particular determinations not posited by A. That is to say, there exists an absolutely manifold stuff. Its B, C, D, etc. must *fit in* with A, as best it can.[33] This fitting in without rhyme or reason takes the place of an original identity. The basic fault can be presented as follows. There is no reflection, in respect to form, on the antinomy of the A = A and A = B. This whole analytic approach lacks the basic consciousness that the purely formal appearance of the Absolute is contradiction. Such consciousness can only come into being where speculation takes its point of departure in Reason and in the A = A as absolute identity of subject and object.

TRANSCENDENTAL INTUITION

When speculation is viewed from the standpoint of mere reflection, the absolute identity appears in syntheses of opposites, i.e., in antinomies. The relative identities into which absolute identity differentiates itself are limited to be sure; they belong to the intellect and are not antinomic. At the same time, however, since they are identities, they are not pure concepts of the intellect. And they must be identities because nothing can stand as posited in a philosophy unless it is connected with the Absolute. But on the side of its connection with the Absolute, everything limited is a (relative) identity and hence something that is antinomic for reflection.—And this is the negative side of knowing, the formal aspect which, ruled[34] by Reason, destroys itself. Besides this negative side knowing has a positive side, namely intuition. Pure knowing, which would be knowing without intuition, is the nullification of the opposites in contradiction. Intuition without

33. The first edition printed "b, c, d, etc." here, but this seems to be just a typographical anomaly. Hegel emphasized *"sich fügen"* (fit in) because it is a technical term in Bardili's "reduction of philosophy to logic" (on which he is here commenting). Compare note 3 above and pp. 188, 190 below.

34. The editors of the New Critical Edition suggest that *regiert* may be a misprint for *negiert*—but it need not be; for Hegel has explained above, how when the intellect becomes Reason, it gives itself the law of self-destruction.

this synthesis of opposites, [on the other hand,] is empirical, given, non-conscious. Transcendental knowledge unites both reflection and intuition. It is at once concept and being. Because [28] intuition becomes transcendental, the identity of the subjective and objective, which are separated in empirical intuition, enters consciousness. Knowledge, insofar as it becomes transcendental, posits not merely the concept and its condition—or the antinomy of both, the subjective—but at the same time the objective, that is, being.

In philosophical knowledge, what is intuited is an activity of both intelligence and nature,[35] of consciousness and the unconscious together. It belongs to both worlds at once, the ideal and the real. It belongs to the ideal world because it is posited in the intelligence and, hence, in freedom. It belongs to the real world because it gets its place in the objective totality, it is deduced as a link in the chain of necessity. If we take up the standpoint of reflection or freedom, the ideal is the first, and essence and being are only schematized intelligence. If we take up the standpoint of necessity or being, thought is only a schema of absolute being. In transcendental knowledge both being and intelligence are united. Likewise, transcendental knowledge and transcendental intuition are one and the same. The variation of expression merely indicates the prevalence of the ideal or real factor.

It is of the profoundest significance that it has been affirmed with so much seriousness that one cannot philosophize without transcendental intuition.[36] For what would this be, philosophizing without intuition? One would disperse oneself endlessly in absolute finitudes. Whether these finitudes are subjective concepts or objective things and even though one may pass from one to the other, philosophizing without intuition moves along an endless chain of finitudes, and the transition from being to concept or from concept to being is an unjustified leap. Philosophizing of this sort is called formal. For thing as well as concept is, each taken by itself, just a form of the Absolute. Formal philosophizing presupposes destruction of the transcendental intuition, an absolute opposition of being and concept. If it talks of the unconditioned, it converts even that into something formal, say the form of an Idea that is opposed to Being for instance. The better

35. For the systems of Nature and Intelligence see pp. 160–71 below.

36. This is affirmed by Fichte (e.g. in the "Second Introduction to the Science of Knowledge," *Werke* I, 466–7, 472 [Heath and Lachs, pp. 41, 46]). The claim also recurs frequently (and even more explicitly) in Schelling. See, for instance, his *System of Transcendental Idealism,* Introduction § 4 or the lectures of 1802, *On University Education* ed. N. Guterman, p 49.

the method, the more glaring the results. To speculation, [on the contrary,] the finitudes are radii of the infinite focus which irradiates them at the same time that it is formed by them. In the radii the focus is posited and in the focus the radii. In the transcendental intuition all opposition is suspended, all distinction between the universe as constructed by and for the intelligence, and the universe as an organization intuited as objective and appearing independent, is nullified. Speculation produces the consciousness of this identity, and because ideality and reality are one in it, it is intuition.

POSTULATES OF REASON

As a work of reflection the synthesis of the two opposites posited by reflection required its completion; as antinomy that suspends itself, it needs its standing[37] in intuition. Speculative knowledge has to be conceived as identity of reflection and intuition. So if one posits only the share of reflection, which, as rational, is antinomic, but stands in a necessary connection with intuition, one can in that case say of intuition that it is postulated by reflection. Postulating Ideas is out of the question; for Ideas are the products of Reason or rather, they are the rational, posited as a product by the intellect.[38] The rational must be deduced in its determinate content, that is, it must be deduced starting from the contradiction of determinate opposites, the rational being their synthesis.[39] The only thing that can be postulated is the intuition that fills and sustains this antinomic aspect. This sort of 'Idea' that used to get postulated, is the 'infinite progress,' which is a mixture of empirical and rational elements: the intuition of time is empirical,

37. *Ihr Bestehen*: *ihr* may refer to "the synthesis," or (as Méry thinks) to "the two opposites," or again to "antinomy" (as we take it).

38. The "postulation of Ideas" is first discussed in Kant's "Dialectic of Pure Practical Reason" (*Akad.* V, 107–48). The crucial comment by Fichte about the right of the Ego to "postulate absolutely" is his footnote in *Werke* I, 260 (Heath and Lachs, p. 230). From Fichte's earlier use of the term (*Werke* I, 218; Heath and Lachs, p. 196) we can gather that he regarded the fundamental *theoretical* principle of his "science of knowledge": "The Ego posits itself as limited by the non-Ego" as a postulate. Hegel has both Kant's practical and Fichte's theoretical "postulates of Reason" in mind here.

39. See especially Kant's "Dialectic of Pure Practical Reason," *Akad.* V, 112–19; and Fichte, *Werke* I, 125–27 (Heath and Lachs, pp. 122–23). The whole procedure of the *Science of Knowledge* from this point onwards is here alluded to.

while the suspension of all time, its expansion to infinity (*Verunend-lichung*) is rational. But in the empirical progress, time is not purely infinitized, for in this progress time is supposed to have standing as something finite, as limited moments. It is an empirical infinitude. The true antinomy which posits both the limited and unlimited, not just side by side but together as identical, must *ipso facto* suspend the opposition. The antinomy postulates the determinate intuition of time, and this determinate intuition must be both the limited moment of the present and the unlimitedness of the moment's being self-externalized (*Aussersichgesetztsein*). That is to say, it must be eternity.—

It is equally impossible to postulate intuition as something that is opposed to the Idea or rather, to the necessary antinomy. The intuition that is opposed to the Idea is a limited existent, precisely because it excludes the Idea. Intuition is indeed postulated by Reason, but not as something limited; it is postulated in order to complement the one-sidedness of the work of reflection in such a way that the intuitive complement does not remain opposed to reflection but is one with it. In general one can see that this whole manner of postulating has its sole ground in the fact that the onesidedness of reflection is accepted as a starting point. This onesidedness requires, as the complement of its deficiency, the postulation of the opposite that is excluded from it. But this point of view places the essence of Reason in distorted perspective, for it here appears as something that is not self-sufficient but needy. When Reason recognizes itself as absolute, however, philosophy begins where reflection and its style of thinking ends, that is, it begins with the identity of Idea and [30] Being. Philosophy does not have to postulate one of the opposites for in positing absoluteness it immediately posits both Idea and Being, and the absoluteness of Reason is nothing else but the identity of both.

RELATION OF PHILOSOPHIZING TO A
PHILOSOPHICAL SYSTEM

The need of philosophy can satisfy itself by simply penetrating to the principle of nullifying all fixed opposition and connecting the limited to the Absolute. This satisfaction found in the principle of absolute identity is characteristic of philosophy as such. [For a philosophizing that did no more than this] the known, as to its content, would be something contingent; the dichotomies, from whose nullification the known emerged,[40] would have been given and would have vanished, but they would not themselves be reconstructed syntheses. The content of such philosophizing would have no internal coherence and would not constitute an objective totality of knowledge. But the philosophizing would not necessarily be abstract reasoning simply on account of the incoherence of its content. Abstract reasoning only disperses the posited into ever greater manifoldness; thrown into this stream the intellect drifts without an anchor, yet the whole extension of its manifold is supposed to stand fast unanchored. For true philosophizing on the other hand, even though it may be incoherent, the posited and its opposites disappear because it does not simply put them in context with other finite things, but connects them with the Absolute and so suspends them.

Since the finite things are a manifold, the connection of the finite to the Absolute is a manifold. Hence, philosophizing must aim to posit this manifold as internally connected, and there necessarily arises the need to produce a totality of knowing, a system of science. As a result, the manifold of these connections finally frees itself from contingency: they get their places in the context of the objective totality of knowledge and their objective completeness is accomplished. The philosophizing that does not construct itself into a system is a constant flight from limitations—it is Reason's struggle for freedom rather than the pure self-cognition of Reason that has become secure in itself and clear about itself. Free Reason and its action are one, and Reason's activity is a pure self-exposition.

In this self-production of Reason the Absolute shapes itself into an objective totality, which is a whole in itself held fast and complete, having no ground outside itself, but founded by itself in its beginning, middle and end. [31] A whole of this sort appears as an organization of propositions and intuitions. Every synthesis of Reason is united in speculation with the intuition corresponding to it; as identity of the conscious and non-conscious it is for itself in the Absolute and infinite. But at the same time, the synthesis is finite and limited, insofar as it is posited within the objective totality and has other syntheses outside itself. The identity that is least dichotomous—at the objective pole, matter, at the subjective pole, feeling (self-conscious-

40. We follow the text of the first edition. If, with the editors of Hegel's *Werke* (1832, 1845 and the "Jubilee" edition) one changed *aus deren Vernichtung es ging* to *auf deren Vernichtung es ging* one would get ". . . the dichotomies whose nullification was the aim. . . ."

ness)—is at the same time an infinitely opposed identity, a thoroughly relative identity. Reason, the faculty of totality (*qua* objective totality), complements this relative identity with its opposite, producing through their synthesis a new identity which is in turn a defective one in the face of Reason, and which completes itself anew in the same way. The method of the system should be called neither synthetic nor analytic. It shows itself at its purest, when it appears as a development of Reason itself. Reason does not recall its appearance, which emanates from it as a duplicate, back into itself—for then, it would only nullify it. Rather, Reason constructs itself in its emanation as an identity that is conditioned by this very duplicate; it opposes this relative identity to itself once more, and in this way the system advances until the objective totality is completed. Reason then unites this objective totality with the opposite subjective totality to form the infinite world-intuition, whose expansion has at the same time contracted into the richest and simplest identity.

It can happen that an authentic speculation does not express itself completely in its system, or that the philosophy of the system and the system itself do not coincide. A system may express the tendency to nullify all oppositions in the most definite way, and yet not pierce through to the most perfect identity on its own account. So in judging philosophical systems it is particularly important to distinguish the philosophy from the system. If the fundamental need has not achieved perfect embodiment in the system, if it has elevated to the Absolute something that is conditioned and that exists only as an opposite, then as a system it becomes dogmatism. Yet true speculation can be found in the most divergent philosophies, in philosophies that decry one another as sheer dogmatism or as mental aberration.[41] The history of philosophy only has value and interest if it holds fast to this viewpoint. For otherwise, it will not give us the history of the one, eternal Reason, presenting itself in infinitely manifold forms; instead it will give us nothing but a tale of the accidental vicissitudes of the human spirit and of senseless opinions, which the teller imputes to Reason, though they should be laid only to his own charge, because he does not recognize what is rational in them, and so turns them inside out.[42]

An authentic speculation, even when it does not succeed in con-

41. *Geistesverirrung*, the word that Reinhold used for d'Holbach's materialism. (See below p. 177.)

42. The model "teller" here is Reinhold. Hegel's own aim in all historical inquiries was always to "give the history of the one eternal Reason."

structing itself completely into a system, necessarily begins from the absolute identity. The dichotomy of the absolute identity into subjective and objective is a production by [or of] the Absolute. The basic principle then, is completely transcendental,[43] and from its standpoint there is no absolute opposition of the subjective and objective. But as a result the appearance of the Absolute is an opposition. The Absolute is not in its appearance, they are themselves opposites. The appearance is not identity. This opposition cannot be suspended transcendentally, that is to say, it cannot be suspended in such a fashion that there is no opposition in principle (*an sich*). For then appearance would just be nullified, whereas it is supposed to have being just like [the Absolute does]. It is as if one were to claim that the Absolute, in its appearance, had stepped out of itself. So, the Absolute must posit itself in the appearance itself, i.e., it must not nullify appearance but must construct it into identity.

The causal relation between the Absolute and its appearance is a false identity; for absolute opposition is at the basis of this relation. In the causal relation both opposites have standing, but they are distinct in rank. The union is forcible. The one subjugates the other. The one rules, the other is subservient. The unity is forced, and forced into a mere relative identity. The identity which *ought* to be absolute, *is* incomplete. Contrary to its philosophy, the system has turned into a dogmatism, it has either turned into realism positing objectivity absolutely, or into idealism positing subjectivity absolutely. Yet both realism and idealism emerged from authentic speculation, though this is more doubtful with respect to realism than to idealism.

Pure dogmatism, if it is a dogmatism of philosophy, remains within the opposition even as a tendency. The basic governing principle in it is the relation of causality in its more complete form as reciprocal interaction: the intelligible realm has effects upon the sensible realm

43. Kant generally uses the adjective "transcendental" to designate philosophical investigations into the possibility of synthetic *a priori* judgments. Schelling's use of the term in the *System of Transcendental Idealism* is cognate with this Kantian definition, for "transcendental philosophy" is there opposed to "philosophy of nature." But for Schelling, the ultimate principle of Identity is the goal both of "transcendental" and of "natural" inquiry; and with his "breakthrough" to a clear "intellectual intuition" of the "Absolute Identity," that principle itself could begin to be called a "transcendental" one. Until this "breakthrough" transcendentality is itself "something opposite" (as Hegel says of Fichte's "system" on p. 117 below).

or the sensible upon the intelligible.[44] In consistent realism and idealism the relation of causality plays only a subordinate role, even
though it appears to govern—for in realism the subject is posited as
produced by the object, and in idealism the object as produced by the
subject. But the causal relation is essentially suspended, for the producing is an absolute producing, the product an absolute product; that
is to say, the product has no standing apart from the producing; it is
not posited as something self-sustaining, as something that has standing prior to and independent of the producing, as is the case with the
pure causality relation, the formal principle of dogmatism. In dogmatism, the product is something posited by A and also, at the same
time, not posited by A, so A is absolutely only subject, and A = A
expresses merely an identity of the intellect. Even though philosophy
in its transcendental business makes use of the causal relation [33]
yet B, which appears to be opposed to the subject, is in its oppositeness a mere possibility and it remains absolutely a possibility, i.e., it
is only an accident.[45] Thus the true relation of speculation, the substantiality relation [i.e., the relation of substance and accident] is the
transcendental principle, though it appears under the guise of the
causal relation. Or again, we might express this formally[†] thus: genuine dogmatism acknowledges both principles A = A and A = B, but
they remain in their antinomy side by side, unsynthesized. Dogmatism does not recognize that there is an antinomy in this and hence
does not recognize the necessity of suspending the subsistence of the
opposites. The transition from one to the other by way of the causality relation is the only synthesis possible to dogmatism, and this is an
incomplete synthesis.

Notwithstanding this sharp difference between transcendental philosophy and dogmatism, the former is apt to pass over into the latter,
when it constructs itself into a system. This is the case if transcendental philosophy while [rightly] refusing to allow any real causal relation on the ground that nothing exists but the absolute identity in
which all difference and standing of opposites is suspended, yet introduces the causality relation, insofar as appearance is also supposed to

44. The reciprocal force of the "or" here makes it virtually equivalent to "and."
Hegel is using Kant's distinction between the intelligible (or "noumenal") and
the sensible (or "phenomenal") worlds to embrace at the same time various
other, more or less cognate, oppositions.
45. That is to say it inheres in the substance A (or it is an attribute of the One
Substance of the Identity Philosophy).

have a standing so that the Absolute must have a relation to appearance other than that of nullification. Thus appearance is turned into something subservient, and likewise[46] transcendental intuition is posited as something merely subjective and not objective, which is to say that the identity is not posited in the appearance. A = A and A = B remain both unconditioned whereas only A = A *ought* to be absolutely valid; that is, their identity is not set forth in their true synthesis which is no mere ought.

Thus in Fichte's system Ego = Ego in the Absolute.[47] The totality sought by Reason leads to the second proposition which posits a non-Ego. Not only is this antinomy of the positing of both complete, but also their synthesis is postulated. But in this synthesis the opposition remains. It is not the case that both, Ego as well as non-Ego, are to be nullified, but one proposition is to survive, is to be higher in rank than the other. The speculation at the basis of the system demands the suspension of the opposites, but the system itself does not suspend them. The absolute synthesis which the system achieves is not Ego = Ego, but Ego *ought* to be equal to Ego. The Absolute is constructed for the transcendental viewpoint but not for the viewpoint of appearance. Both still contradict each other. The identity was not also placed in the appearance, or [in other words] the identity did not also pass completely into objectivity.[48] Therefore transcendentality is itself something opposite, the subjective. One may also say that the appearance was not completely nullified.

In the following presentation of Fichte's system an attempt will be made to show that pure consciousness, the identity of subject and object, established as absolute in the system, is a *subjective* identity of subject and object. The [34] presentation will proceed by showing that the Ego, the principle of the system, is a subjective Subject-Object. This will be shown directly, as well as by inspecting [not only] the deduction of nature, [but also] and particularly, the relations of identity in the special sciences of morality and natural law and the relation of the whole system to the aesthetic sphere.

It will be clear from what has been said that we are concerned in this presentation with Fichte's philosophy as a system and not as au-

46. In Hegel's time, and with his pen, *also* still has, occasionally, the meaning "likewise" rather than "hence."

47. Hegel here goes on to discuss the opening sections of Fichte's *Science of Knowledge* (1794). See *Werke* I, 91–122 (Heath and Lachs, pp. 93–119).

48. This was the aim of Schelling's philosophy of nature.

thentic philosophizing.[49] As philosophy it is the most thorough and profound speculation, all the more remarkable because at the time when it appeared even the Kantian philosophy had proved unable to awaken Reason to the lost concept of genuine speculation.

49. We should remember that the title of the essay is "Difference Between Fichte's and Schelling's *System*"; *qua philosophy* there cannot be a difference between them.

Exposition of Fichte's System

The foundation of *Fichte's system* is intellectual intuition, pure thinking of itself, pure selfconsciousness, Ego = Ego, I am. The Absolute is Subject-Object, and the Ego is this identity of subject and object.[1]

In ordinary consciousness the Ego occurs in opposition. Philosophy must explain this opposition to an object. To explain it means to show that it is conditioned by something else and hence that it is appearance. Now, if empirical consciousness is shown to be completely grounded in, and not just conditioned by, pure consciousness, then their opposition is suspended as long as the explanation is otherwise completely shown—i.e., as long as it is not merely a partial identity of pure and empirical consciousness that has been shown. The identity is only a partial one if there remains an aspect of the empirical consciousness in which it is not determined by the pure consciousness, but is unconditioned. And as only pure consciousness and empirical consciousness are presented as the elements of the highest opposition, pure consciousness itself would then be determined and conditioned by the empirical consciousness so far as this was unconditioned. The relation would in this way be a sort of reciprocal relation, comprised of a mutual determining and being determined. It presupposes, however, an absolute opposition of the reciprocally effective

---

1. Hegel's exposition is based mainly on the *Grundlage der gesamten Wissenschaftslehre* of 1794. But Fichte's first explicit statement that "intellectual intuition" is the foundation of the system occurs in the "Second Introduction to the Science of Knowledge," § 5, *Werke* I, 463–8 (Heath and Lachs, pp. 38–42). "Intellectual intuition" is the identity of thought and being. Thus *Cogito ergo sum* becomes: "Whatever is aware of itself as thinking, knows itself as being"; or "In thinking, thinking thinks itself, and in thinking itself as thinking it knows itself as being." This is expressed as "the identity of thought and being"; and since thought (*das Denken*) is on the side of the subject, being is put on the side of the object. Thus the identity of thought and being is expressed also as "the identity of subject and object." To these identities of identities—(thought=intuition)= (thinking=being)=(subject=object)—the next paragraph adds the identity of pure consciousness with empirical consciousness, which by implication Kant did not reach, and which Fichte will be accused of having failed to reach also.

terms; and then it would be impossible to suspend their dichotomy in absolute identity.[2]

[35]   For the philosopher, this pure consciousness originates because he abstracts in his thinking from all the extraneous things that are not Ego and holds on only to the connection of subject and object. In empirical intuition, subject and object are opposites; the philosopher apprehends the activity of intuiting, he intuits intuiting and thus conceives it as an identity. This intuiting of intuiting is, on the one hand, philosophical reflection and as such opposed both to ordinary reflection and to the empirical consciousness in general which does not raise itself above itself and its oppositions. On the other hand, this transcendental intuition is at the same time the object of philosophical reflection; it is the Absolute, the original identity. The philosopher has risen into freedom and to the standpoint of the Absolute.

His task is now to suspend the apparent opposition of transcendental and empirical consciousness; and, in general terms, this is done by deducing the latter from the former. Of necessity, the deduction cannot be a transition to something alien. Transcendental philosophy aims just to construct the empirical consciousness not from a principle external to it, but from an immanent principle, as an active emanation or self-production of the principle. Something that is not constructed out of pure self-consciousness can no more occur in empirical consciousness than pure consciousness can be distinct in its essence from empirical conciousness. They are distinct in form, in just this way: what appears to empirical consciousness as object opposed to the subject, will be posited, in the intuition of this empirical intuiting, as identical. Thus empirical consciousness will be made whole by that which constitutes its essence even though it has no consciousness of this essence.

This task can also be expressed as follows: philosophy is to suspend pure consciousness as concept. When it is placed in opposition to empirical consciousness, intellectual intuition, the pure thinking of itself, appears as concept, that is to say, it appears as an abstraction from the whole manifold, from all inequality of subject and object. Of course, intellectual intuition is nothing but pure activity, doing, intuit-

---

2. *Die Entzweiung in absoluter Identität zu heben*: *in absoluter Identität* answers the question "Where?". "Whither" would require *in absolute Identität*. So *heben* must here be equivalent to *aufheben*.

ing; it is only present in the pure spontaneity which produces it and which it produces.[3] This act tears itself away from everything empirical, manifold, and opposite; it lifts itself to the unity of thinking, to Ego = Ego, to the identity of subject and object. But it has an aspect of opposition still; it is opposed to other acts. So it is capable of being determined as a concept, and it shares with its opposites a common higher sphere, the general sphere of thinking. Besides the thinking of itself, there is still other thinking, besides self-consciousness there is still a manifold of empirical [36] consciousness, besides the Ego as object there is a variety of other objects of consciousness. The act of self-consciousness differs decisively from all other consciousness in that its object is the same as the subject. Ego = Ego is in this regard opposed to an infinite objective world.

Transcendental intuition fails to produce philosophical knowledge in this way. On the contrary, philosophical knowledge becomes impossible when reflection gets control of transcendental intuition, opposes it to other intuitings, and holds fast to this opposition. This absolute act of free self-activity is the condition of philosophical knowledge, but it is not yet philosophy itself. Philosophy posits the objective totality of empirical knowledge as identical with pure self-consciousness, so that the latter becomes totally suspended as concept or opposite, and with it the former too. It is asserted that the only consciousness that exists is pure consciousness, Ego = Ego is the Absolute; all empirical consciousness is taken to be nothing but a pure product of Ego = Ego, and it is flatly denied that empirical consciousness is, or originates, an absolute duality, or that a positing could occur in it that would not be the positing of an Ego for and by the Ego. With the Ego's self-positing everything is posited and outside of it nothing. The identity of pure and empirical consciousness is not an abstraction from their original opposition. On the contrary, their opposition is an abstraction from their original identity.

Intellectual intuition is herewith posited as identical with everything, it is the totality. This identity of all empirical consciousness with pure consciousness is *knowledge*, and philosophy, knowing this identity, is the science of knowledge. Philosophy must show that empirical consciousness in all its manifoldness is identical with pure consciousness, and it must show this by its deed, through the real evolu-

---

3. Hegel here writes only *die sie hervorbringt*, which can be taken either way and is presumably meant both ways (as in the translation).

tion of the objective out of the Ego.[4] Philosophy must describe the totality of empirical consciousness as the objective totality of self-consciousness. The whole variety of knowledge is given to philosophy in Ego = Ego. To mere reflection this deduction appears as the contradictory enterprise of deducing the manifold from unity, duality from pure identity. But the identity of the Ego = Ego is no pure identity, that is, it does not arise through reflective abstraction. If reflection conceives of Ego = Ego as unity, it must at the same time conceive of it as duality. Ego = Ego is both identity and duplication at once: there is an opposition in Ego = Ego. Ego is subject on the one hand and object on the other. But what is set against the Ego is itself Ego; the opposites are identical. Hence, empirical consciousness cannot be viewed as stepping out of pure consciousness. If it were so viewed, then, of course, a science of knowledge starting from pure consciousness would be nonsensical. The basis of the view that empirical consciousness has stepped right out of pure consciousness is the above [37] abstraction in which reflection isolates its opposites. Reflection as intellect is in and of itself incapable of grasping transcendental intuition; and even if Reason has pushed through to self-cognition, reflection will, if it is given leeway, invert the rational into something opposite once more.

So far, we have described the purely transcendental side of the system, the side where reflection is powerless, but where Reason determines and describes the task of philosophy. Because of this genuinely transcendental aspect, it is all the more difficult either to apprehend the point of departure of that other side where reflection governs, or to hold on to it [as a whole]. For the retreat to the transcendental side remains always open for the propositions of the intellect into which reflection has inverted the rational. What we have to show, then, is that reflection does not have a subordinate place in the system, and that [on the contrary] the two standpoints, that of speculation and that of reflection, are absolutely necessary and without union at the center of the system.—In other words, Ego = Ego is the absolute principle of speculation, but the system does not display this identity. The objective Ego does not become identical with the subjective Ego;

4. This programme for philosophy appears to have originated with Schelling rather than with Fichte. On pp. 129–30 below Hegel speaks as if the language, at least, comes directly from Fichte. But we have not been able to trace his reference at that point either. The passage that Lasson refers to here (Fichte, *Werke* I, 43) can hardly be the source of anything that Hegel says either here or below.

they remain absolutely opposed to one another. The Ego does not find itself in its appearance, or in its positing; it must annul its appearance in order to find itself as Ego. The essence of the Ego and its positing do not coincide: *Ego does not become objective to itself.*

In the *Science of Knowledge* Fichte has chosen to present the principle of his system in the form of basic propositions. We have already enlarged upon the awkwardness of this approach.[5] The first basic proposition is absolute self-positing of the Ego, the Ego as infinite positing. The second is absolute oppositing, or positing of an infinite non-Ego. The third is the absolute unification of the first two by way of an absolute dividing (*Teilen*) of Ego and non-Ego and an apportioning (*Verteilen*) of the infinite sphere between a divisible Ego and divisible non-Ego. These three absolute basic principles set forth three absolute acts of the Ego. From this plurality of absolute acts it follows immediately that these acts and the principles are only relative. That is to say, the three acts, to the extent that they enter into the construction of the totality of consciousness, are merely ideal factors. Counterposed as it is to other absolute acts, Ego = Ego simply means pure consciousness as opposed to empirical consciousness. As such it is conditioned by abstraction from empirical consciousness, and the first basic proposition is as much a conditioned proposition as are the second and the third. The very plurality of absolute acts immediately indicates this even if their content were entirely unknown. But it is quite unnecessary to comprehend Ego = Ego, the [38] absolute self-positing, as something conditioned. On the contrary, we have viewed it above[6] in its transcendental significance as absolute identity (and not merely as an identity of the intellect). But in this form in which Ego = Ego is established as only *one* of several principles, it has no other meaning than that of pure consciousness as opposed to empirical consciousness, of philosophical reflection as opposed to common reflection.

[One might argue that] it is only for the sake of philosophical reflection that [Fichte] posits these ideal factors, that is, the pure positing and the pure oppositing. The point of departure for philosophical reflection is, to be sure, absolute identity; but precisely in order to describe the true essence of this identity, this reflection begins by

setting forth absolute opposites and binds them together to form the antinomy; and this is the only way in which reflection can expound

5. See above pp. 103–9.
6. See pp. 119–22 ff.

the Absolute, in order to take absolute identity out of the sphere of concepts at once, and to constitute it as an identity that does not abstract from subject and object but is the identity of subject and object. This identity cannot be so grasped that the pure self-positing and the pure oppositing are both activities of one and the same Ego. For then it would most assuredly not be a transcendental identity, but a transcendent one, in which the absolute contradiction of the opposites would be meant to subsist, and their union would be reduced to a union in the generic concept of activity. What is required is a transcendental union in which the contradiction of the two activities is itself suspended and a true synthesis, both real and ideal at once, is constructed out of the ideal factors. The third basic proposition gives this transcendental union: the Ego posits, within the Ego, a divisible non-Ego as opposed to a divisible Ego.[7] The infinite objective sphere, the opposite, is neither absolute Ego nor absolute non-Ego. Rather, it is that which envelops the opposites, that which is filled out by opposite factors whose relation is this: to the degree that the one is posited, the other is not; so far as the one rises, the other falls.

In this synthesis, however, the objective Ego is not identical with the subjective Ego. The subjective Ego is Ego, the objective is Ego + non-Ego. This synthesis is not an exposition of the original identity: pure consciousness, Ego = Ego, and empirical [consciousness], Ego = Ego + non-Ego, with all the forms in which the latter constructs itself, remain opposites. The incompleteness of this synthesis expressed by the third basic proposition is necessary if the acts of the first and second basic propositions are activities absolutely opposed one to the other; or in other words, no synthesis is basically possible at all. The synthesis is possible only if the activities of positing [39] and of oppositing are posited as ideal factors. But it certainly does seem to be self-contradictory to treat activities that are quite strictly not supposed to be concepts, simply as ideal factors. It makes no difference either in itself or with respect to a system whose principle is Identity, whether what is to be united, Ego and non-Ego, the subjective and the objective, are expressed as activities—positing and oppositing—or as products—objective Ego and non-Ego. Their being characterized as absolutely opposed to each other stamps them immediately as something merely ideal, and Fichte does recognize their pure ideality. He takes the opposites to be entirely different *before* the synthesis from what they are *after* the synthesis. *Before* the synthesis they are sup-

7. See Fichte, *Werke* I, 110 (Heath and Lachs, pp. 109–10).

posed to be "merely opposites and nothing else; the one is what the other is not, and the other is what the one is not [...] a mere thought without any reality and what is worse, a thought of mere reality.[8] As one comes in, the other goes out. But the one can only come in with the predicate of being the contrary of the other. Hence, where the one concept comes in, the other one comes in too, and nullifies it. So not even this one can come in, and nothing at all is present." Only "a beneficent deception of the imagination, which foisted a substratum upon the mere opposites, without being noticed" made it possible to think about them.[9]

It follows from the ideality of the opposite factors that they are nothing apart from the synthetic activity; only the latter posits them and their being opposite,[10] and their opposition is used only for the purpose of philosophical construction in order to make the synthetic faculty understandable. Productive imagination would be absolute identity itself, absolute identity represented as activity which, simply by positing the product, the boundary, posits at the same time the opposites as the bounding agents. It would only be valid to conceive the imagination as a synthetic faculty conditioned by opposites from the standpoint of reflection, which begins from the opposites and conceives intuition only as their union. But, in order to characterize this view as a subjective one pertaining to reflection, philosophical reflection would simultaneously have to establish the transcendental standpoint by recognizing that with respect to the absolute identity those absolutely opposed activities are nothing but ideal factors, thoroughly relative identities. In the absolute identity empirical consciousness is no less suspended than its antithesis, pure consciousness, which, as abstraction from the empirical, has an antithesis in it. It is only in this sense that the Ego is the transcendental center of both opposed activities and indifferent toward both. Their absolute opposition is significant only with respect to their ideality.

[40]   However, the synthesis expressed in the third proposition is imperfect. The objective Ego here is an Ego + non-Ego. This in itself already arouses the suspicion that the opposed activities [of the first two basic propositions] are not to be taken merely as relative identities, as ideal factors; though they can be so regarded if one considers only their relation to the synthesis, and abstracts from the title of ab-

8. Fichte: "a thought of a mere relation."

9. *Werke* I, 224–5 (Heath and Lachs, p. 200).

10. The German text allows also the following translation: "only the latter posits their being opposite and their ideality itself" (cf. Méry, p. 114).

soluteness that both activities carry with them just as the third one does.

This, however, is not the relation which the self-positing and the oppositing are meant to have mutually and towards the synthetic activities. Ego = Ego is absolute activity; in no respect should it be regarded as relative identity and as ideal factor. To the Ego = Ego a non-Ego is something absolutely opposed. Yet their union is necessary, and is the unique concern of speculation.[11] What union is possible, though, once absolute opposites are presupposed? Strictly speaking none at all, obviously. Or [to put the point another way] since the absoluteness of their opposition must be removed at least partially, and the third basic proposition must necessarily come in, even where opposition remains basic, only a partial identity is possible. Absolute identity is, of course, the principle of speculation; but like its expression, Ego = Ego, this principle remains only the rule whose infinite fulfillment is postulated but not constructed in the system.

The main point must be to prove that self-positing and oppositing are activities absolutely opposed to one another within the system. Fichte does say this directly, in so many words.[12] But this absolute opposition is just meant to be the very condition which alone makes productive imagination possible. Productive imagination, however, is the Ego only as theoretical faculty which cannot raise itself above the opposition. For the practical faculty, the opposition falls away; and it is only the practical faculty that suspends it.[13] So [to prove our claim] we have to show that the opposition is absolute for the practical faculty too, and that even in the practical faculty Ego does not posit itself as Ego: on the contrary, here again the objective Ego is an Ego + non-Ego and the practical faculty does not penetrate to Ego = Ego. Putting it the other way round: the absoluteness of opposition emerges from the incompleteness of the highest synthesis offered in the system. Opposition is still present in the highest synthesis.

Dogmatic idealism maintains its monism (*Einheit des Prinzips*) by denying the object altogether: it posits one of the opposites, the subject in its determinateness, as absolute. Likewise, the dogmatism which in its pure form is materialism, denies the subjective. If it is only the need for an identity of this sort that lies at the basis of

11. Compare pp. 90–1 above.
12. See Fichte, *Werke* I, 214–7 (Heath and Lachs, pp. 192–5).
13. Compare pp. 132–4 ff below.

philosophizing—the need for an identity that can be brought to pass by denying, and absolutely abstracting from, one of the opposites— [41] then it does not matter which of the two is denied, the subjective or the objective. Their opposition is in consciousness, and the reality of the objective, just as much as that of the subjective is founded in consciousness. Empirical consciousness offers no more and no less warrant for pure consciousness than for the thing in itself of the dogmatist. Neither the subjective nor the objective alone exhausts consciousness. The purely subjective is just as much an abstraction as the purely objective. Dogmatic idealism posits the subjective as the real ground of the objective, dogmatic realism the objective as the real ground of the subjective. Consistent realism denies consciousness as spontaneous self-positing activity altogether. But even when the object, which the realist takes to be the real ground of consciousness, is expressed as non-Ego = non-Ego, when he exhibits the reality of his object in consciousness, and is therefore validly challenged by the identity of consciousness as something absolute over and against his objective serialization of finites running on and on; then he must certainly abandon the form of his principle of pure objectivity. As soon as the realist admits that there is thinking, the analysis of thinking will lead to Ego = Ego. This is thinking expressed as a proposition; for thinking is a spontaneous activity of connecting opposites and the connection is the positing of the opposites as identical. Still, just as idealism validly asserts the unity of consciousness, so realism can validly assert its duality. The unity of consciousness presupposes a duality, connecting presupposes an oppositeness. Ego = Ego is opposed by an equally absolute proposition: the subject is not the same as the object. Both propositions are of the same rank.

Some of the forms in which Fichte has presented his system might mislead one into believing that it is a system of dogmatic idealism denying the opposite principle. Indeed, Reinhold overlooks the transcendental significance of the Fichtean principle which requires one to posit the difference of subject and object in Ego = Ego at the same time as their identity. He regards Fichte's system as a system of absolute subjectivity, that is, a dogmatic idealism.[14] But precisely what distinguishes Fichte's idealism is that the identity which it establishes is one that does not deny the objective but puts the subjective and the objective in the same rank of reality and certainty; and that pure and

14. Compare *Beyträge* I, 77, 82 ff., 124–5.

empirical consciousness are one. For the sake of the identity of subject and object I posit things outside myself just as surely as I posit
myself. The things exist as certainly as I do.—But if the Ego posits
things alone or itself alone—just one of the two terms or even both at
once but separately—then the Ego will not, in the system, come to be
Subject-Object to itself. True, the subjective is Subject-Object, but
the objective is not. Hence subject is not equal to object.

[42]   As *theoretical faculty*, the Ego is unable to posit itself with
perfect objectivity, and escape from the opposition. "Ego posits itself
as determined by non-Ego"[15] is that part of the third basic proposition, whereby the Ego constitutes itself as intelligence.[16] Now, the objective world has shown itself to be [not a substance but] an accident
of intelligence and the non-Ego, which intelligence posits itself as determined by, has shown itself to be something undetermined—every
determination of it is a product of intelligence. But still, there remains
one side of the theoretical faculty from which it is conditioned. To
wit, the objective world, in its endless determinacy through intelligence, still remains a something for intelligence which is at the same
time undetermined for it. The non-Ego has no positive character, to be
sure; but it does have the negative character of being something other,
i.e., something opposite in general. As Fichte expresses this: intelligence is conditioned by an impact, but the impact is in itself entirely
undetermined.[17] Because the non-Ego expresses only the negative,
something undetermined, even this character pertains to it only
through the Ego's positing. The Ego posits itself as not posited. The
positing of the opposite in general, the positing of something that is
absolutely undetermined by the Ego, is itself a positing of [and by]
the Ego. In this move the immanence of the Ego even as intelligence
is asserted in respect of its being conditioned by something other $= X$.
But this only gives the contradiction another form; it has now become
immanent itself. The Ego's positing of the opposite and its positing of
itself contradict each other, and the theoretical faculty is not able to
extricate itself from this opposition which therefore remains absolute
for it. Productive imagination is a hovering between absolute oppo-

15. Fichte, *Werke* I, 127 (Heath and Lachs, p. 123). In his initial statement of
the *third* or *grounding* principle (*Werke* I, 125–6, Heath and Lachs, p. 122) Fichte
speaks of Ego and non-Ego as limited (*beschränkt*) by one another. But he shifts
here to "determined" (*bestimmt*).

16. I.e., as *vorstellend*, as representing (or as having ideas of . . .). Cf. *Werke*
I, 227–46, 248 (Heath and Lachs, pp. 203–17, 219–20).

17. See Fichte, *Werke* I, 210-7, 248–51 (Heath and Lachs, pp. 189–95, 219–22).

sites; it can synthesize them at the boundary, but cannot unite their opposite ends.

Through the theoretical faculty, the Ego does not succeed in making itself objective to itself. It does not penetrate to Ego = Ego. Instead, the object originates for it as Ego plus non-Ego. Or in other words, pure consciousness is not shown to be equal to empirical consciousness.

The characteristics of a [Fichtean] transcendental deduction of an objective world can now be stated. Ego = Ego is the principle of speculation or of the subjective philosophical reflection which is opposed to empirical consciousness. It must prove itself objective as the principle of philosophy, and the proof will consist in the suspending of its opposition to empirical consciousness. This suspension must occur when pure consciousness produces out of itself a manifold of activities that is identical with the manifold of empirical consciousness. Thus Ego = Ego would show itself to be the immanent real ground of the totality of objects in their externality to one another (*des Aussereinander der Objektivität*). In empirical consciousness, however, there is an opposite, an X; and pure consciousness, since it is a positing of itself, can neither [43] produce this X from itself nor conquer it; instead, it must presuppose it. The question is this: is it the case that the absolute identity, insofar as it appears as theoretical faculty, cannot abstract entirely from subjectivity and from the opposition to empirical consciousness? Within the sphere of the theoretical faculty can it not become objective to itself, A = A? [Our own answer must be: No.] For this theoretical faculty, the Ego positing itself as Ego determined by the non-Ego is not a purely immanent sphere at all. Even within it every product of the Ego is also something not determined by the Ego. In so far as it produces the manifold of empirical consciousness out of itself, pure consciousness appears for this reason with the character of defectiveness. This primordial defectiveness of pure consciousness is accordingly what constitutes the possibility of a deduction of the objective world in general, and in the deduction the subjectivity of pure consciousness becomes most clearly apparent. The Ego posits an objective world because in positing itself it recognizes its own defectiveness, and consequently the absoluteness of pure consciousness falls away. The relation that is taken to hold between objective world and self-consciousness is that the former is the *condition* of the latter. Pure consciousness and empirical consciousness condition one another mutually, one is as necessary as the other. As Fichte puts it, the advance to empirical consciousness is made because pure consciousness is not a complete consciousness.[18] —In this reciprocal relation pure consciousness and empirical consciousness remain absolutely opposed. The identity which can come about is a highly incomplete and superficial one. Another identity is necessary, an identity which grasps both pure and empirical consciousness within itself and yet suspends them both as what they are.

We shall speak later of the form which the objective (or nature) gets in a deduction of this sort.[19] But the subjectivity of pure consciousness which results from the form of deduction that we have just discussed provides the key to another form of it, in which the production of the objective is taken as a pure act of free activity. If self-consciousness is conditioned by empirical consciousness, then empirical consciousness cannot be a product of absolute freedom. The free activity of the Ego would become only *one* factor in the construction of the intuition of an objective world. That the world is a product of the freedom of intelligence is the determinate and express principle of idealism. If Fichte's idealism has not succeeded in constructing a system upon this principle the reason for its failure will be found in the characteristic way in which freedom appears in this system.

Philosophical reflection is an act of absolute freedom. It lifts itself out of the sphere of givenness by an act of absolutely free choice (*mit absoluter Willkür*) and produces consciously what, in the empirical consciousness, intelligence produces non-consciously so that it appears to be given. In the sense in which the [44] manifold of necessary ideas arises for philosophical reflection as a system produced by freedom, the non-conscious production of an objective world is not asserted to be an act of freedom, for in this aspect empirical and philosophical consciousness are both the identity of self-positing. Self-positing, the identity of subject and object, is free activity.

In the above exposition of the production of the objective world out of pure consciousness or self-positing, an absolute positing of the

18. We have not been able to find this phrase in Fichte. The reference that Lasson gives (*Werke* I, 168 [Heath and Lachs, pp. 156–7]) does not contain it. The closest parallel that we have found is in the "Second Introduction" (1797): "This [intellectual] intuition, however, never occurs in isolation, as a complete act of consciousness; any more than sensory intuition occurs singly or renders consciousness complete" (*Werke* I, 463–4 [Heath and Lachs, p. 38]). Professor C. K. Hunter has kindly found for us the following passages dealing with the "completion" of consciousness or the "advance" to empirical consciousness: *Werke* I, 178 (Heath and Lachs, p. 164); *Werke* IV, 92 (Kroeger, *Ethics*, p. 95); *Werke* VI, 313 (Smith, I, 172–3).

19. See below, pp. 135–42.

opposite necessarily turned up.[20] If, now, the objective world is to be deduced as an act of freedom, this absolute positing of the opposite comes into view as a self-limiting of the Ego by itself; and productive imagination will be constructed from two factors, the indeterminate activity that moves toward the infinite, and the limiting activity that aims at finitization (*Verendlichung*). If the reflecting activity is likewise posited as an infinite one, then it, too, can be posited as an act of freedom, and the Ego limits itself freely. And it must be so posited because it is an ideal factor here, i.e., it is an absolute opposite. In this way, freedom and limit would not oppose each other, but would posit themselves as infinite—and as finite, which is just what appeared above as the opposition of the first and second basic proposition.[21] But now the limitation is something immanent, for it is the Ego that limits itself. The objects are only posited in order to explain this limitation; and the self-limiting of intelligence is the only real. Thus the absolute opposition which empirical consciousness sets up between subject and object is suspended; but it is transferred in another form into intelligence itself, and intelligence finds itself closed in by incomprehensible limits;[22] its law of self-limitation is absolutely incomprehensible to it. Yet it is precisely the incomprehensibility for ordinary consciousness of the opposition present in it, that is the spur to speculation. But the incomprehensible element still remains in the system in the form of the limits posited by intelligence itself. Yet to break out of this circle is the sole concern of the philosophical need.—

If freedom is set up against the limiting activity as self-positing against opposing, then freedom is conditioned, which must not happen; whereas if the limiting activity is posited as an activity of freedom [too]—as both self-positing and opposing were transferred into the Ego above[23]—then freedom is absolute identity but it contradicts its appearance, which is always something that is not identical, something finite and unfree. In the system freedom does not succeed in producing itself; the product does not correspond to the producing. The system, which starts out from self-positing, leads intelligence to its conditioned condition in an endless sequence of finitudes, without reestablishing it [as self-positing] in and through them.

20. See above, p. 129.

21. See pp. 123–5.

22. Here again *einmal* appears to be superfluous and we have omitted it (compare p. 95 above).

23. See p. 128.

Speculation cannot completely reveal its principle, Ego = Ego, in non-conscious productive activity; the object of the theoretical faculty necessarily [45] contains something not determined by the Ego. We are therefore directed to the practical faculty.[24] The Ego cannot succeed in positing itself as Ego = Ego or intuiting itself as Subject = Object through its non-conscious production; so the demand is still present that the Ego should produce itself practically as identity, as Subject = Object—that the Ego should metamorphose itself into the object. This supreme demand remains, in Fichte's system, a demand. Not only is it not dissolved into an authentic synthesis, it is fixed in the form of a demand; so that the ideal† is absolutely opposed to the real and the supreme self-intuition of the Ego and Subject-Object is made impossible.

Ego = Ego is postulated practically, and this is thought of as follows: Ego would become object for itself as Ego by entering into a relation of causality with the non-Ego, in which the non-Ego would disappear and the object would be something absolutely determined by the subject, so that the object would = Ego. Here the causality relation becomes the governing factor, which means that Reason, or the Subject = Object, becomes fixed as one of the opposites and that true synthesis is made impossible.

It is impossible for the Ego to reconstruct itself out of the opposition between subjectivity and the X that originates for it in a non-conscious producing, and so becomes one with its appearance. This impossibility is what is expressed in the fact that the highest synthesis revealed in the system is an *ought*. Ego *equals* Ego turns into Ego *ought* to equal Ego. The result of the system does not return to its beginning.

The Ego ought to nullify the objective world, it ought to have absolute causality with respect to the non-Ego. This is found [by Fichte] to be contradictory, for it would imply suspending the non-Ego; and the positing of the opposite, the positing of a non-Ego, is absolute.[25] So, the connection of pure activity with an object can only be posited as striving.[26] Because it represents Ego = Ego, the objective Ego that

24. For the discussion that follows (down to p. 135) see, in general, Fichte, *Werke* I, 246–85 (Heath and Lachs, pp. 218–51). We have given a few more precise indications (specifically those suggested by Buchner and Pöggeler). But these more specific indications are neither definitive nor exhaustive.

25. Compare Fichte, *Werke* I, 250–2, 254 (Heath and Lachs, pp. 221–2, 224–5).

26. Compare Fichte, *Werke* I, 261–2 (Heath and Lachs, pp. 230–1).

equals the subjective Ego, has at the same time an oppositing, and hence a non-Ego opposed to itself. The former is the ideal,† the latter is the real; and these two *ought* to be the same. This practical postulate of the absolute ought, expresses no more than the *thought* of a uniting of the opposition; it does not unite it in an intuition. It expresses only the antithesis between the first and second basic proposition.

At this point Ego = Ego has been abandoned by speculation and has fallen prey to reflection. Pure consciousness no longer functions as absolute identity; in its highest dignity it is [now] opposed to the empirical consciousness.

This makes the character of freedom in Fichte's system clear: it is not the suspension of the opposites, but the opposition to them, and in this opposition it gets fixed as negative freedom. Reason constitutes itself through reflection as a unity that is absolutely opposed by a manifold. The ought expresses this standing opposition; [46] it expresses the non-existence of the absolute identity. The pure positing, free activity, is posited as an abstraction, in the absolute form of something subjective. The transcendental intuition, from which the system starts, was, in the form of philosophical reflection which raises itself through absolute abstraction to the pure thinking of itself, something subjective. To get hold of transcendental intuition in its true formlessness it was necessary to abstract from this character of subjectivity; speculation had to detach this form from its subjective principle in order to raise this principle to the true identity of subject and object.[27] Instead, transcendental intuition as it pertains to philosophical reflection, and transcendental intuition as being neither subjective nor objective, still remain [in Fichte] one and the same. The Subject = Object does not get away anymore from difference and reflection. It remains a subjective Subject = Object to which appearance remains absolutely alien and which does not succeed in intuiting itself in its appearance.

The practical faculty of the Ego can no more achieve absolute self-intuition than its theoretical faculty could. Both alike are conditioned by an impact which, as a [brute] fact, cannot be derived from the Ego; the deduction of it amounts to a demonstration that it is the condition of the theoretical and practical faculty. The antinomy remains an antinomy and is expressed in striving, which is the ought as

27. This was what Schelling did.

activity. Now there is no way in which reflection can get hold of the Absolute except by antinomy; but the antinomy we have here is not the form in which the Absolute appears to reflection. On the contrary, this antinomical antithesis is what is fixed, it is the Absolute. As activity, namely as striving, it is supposed to be supreme synthesis, and the Idea of the infinite is to remain an Idea in the Kantian sense, i.e., it is something absolutely opposed to intuition.

This absolute opposition of Idea and intuition, and their synthesis which is nothing but a self-destructive demand, since it postulates a union which still must not happen—all this is expressed in the infinite progress. Absolute opposition is thus shoved into the form it had at a lower standpoint which had for a long time passed current as the true suspension of opposition and the highest solution of the antinomy by Reason. Existence prolonged into eternity involves both the infinity of the Idea and intuition within itself, but in forms which make their synthesis impossible. The infinity of the Idea excludes all manifoldness. Time, on the contrary, immediately involves opposition, extraneousness (*ein Aussereinander*). What exists in time is something that is opposed to itself, a manifold; and infinity is outside of time.— Space is similarly a [realm of] posited self: externality (*ein Aussersichgesetztsein*), but [47] because of its type of opposition it may be said to be an infinitely richer synthesis than time.[28] The preference that time acquires in that progress is supposed to take place in it, can only be grounded in the fact that striving is posited as something absolutely opposed to an outer world of sense and as something inward. Thus the Ego is hypostatized as absolute subject, as the unity of a point, and in popular parlance, as a soul.—[But] if time is to be totality, as infinite time, then time itself is suspended, and it was not necessary to take refuge in its name and in a progress of the lengthened existence. The true suspension of time is a timeless present, i.e., eternity, and in it striving falls away, and absolute opposition loses its standing. The lengthening of existence simply palliates the opposition in a synthesis of time, the poverty of which, instead of being fully supplied, just becomes more conspicuous as a result of this palliative union with an infinity that is absolutely opposed to it.

---

28. The parts of space are coexistent while the moments of time are not. Hence Spinoza speaks of "the face of the whole universe" as "the immediate infinite mode of extension"; whereas "duration" is always finite. This may be what Hegel has in mind here. We should note, in any case, that he certainly struggled to achieve a richer concept of time in his own later work.

All the further developments of what is contained in the striving, and all the syntheses of the oppositions that arise from the development carry within them the principle of non-identity. The further working out of the system belongs as a whole to consistent reflection; speculation has no part in it. Absolute identity is present only in the form of an opposite, namely as Idea. The incomplete causal relation is the ground of every synthesis of the Idea with its opposite. The Ego that posits itself in opposition, or in other words limits itself, is called the subjective Ego; and the Ego that tends toward the infinite is called the objective Ego. The joining of the two consists in this: the self-determining of the subjective Ego is made in accordance with the Idea of the objective Ego, of absolute spontaneity, of infinity; and the objective Ego, absolute spontaneity, is determined according to this Idea by the subjective Ego. Their determination is reciprocal. The subjective, ideal Ego receives, so to speak, the material of its Idea from the objective Ego; that is to say, it receives absolute spontaneity, indeterminateness. On the other hand, the objective, *real* Ego, the Ego tending toward the infinite, is bounded by the subjective Ego. But since the subjective Ego does its determining according to the idea of infinity, it suspends the bounding once more. While it makes the objective Ego finite in its infinity, it simultaneously makes it infinite in its finitude. In this reciprocal determination the opposition of finitude and infinity, of real determination and ideal indeterminateness endures. Ideality and reality remain disunited. In other words, the Ego is both *ideal* and *real* activity, the distinction being merely a matter of direction; it has united these different directions in particular incomplete syntheses such as drive and feeling, as will be shown below;[29] [48] but it does not achieve a complete exposition of itself in them. In the infinite progress of its lengthened existence it endlessly produces more parts of itself, but it never produces itself in the eternity of intuiting itself as Subject-Object.

The Ego remains a subjective Subject-Object because the subjectivity of transcendental intuition is held fast. This is most strikingly apparent in the *relation of the Ego to nature*.[30] We can see it both in the deduction of nature and in the sciences founded on that deduction.

29. See pp. 136–7.

30. For this part of Hegel's discussion (down to p. 142 below) see, in general, Fichte, *Werke* I, 285–322 (Heath and Lachs, pp. 251–81) and the *System der Sittenlehre* (1798), §§4–5 (*Werke* IV, 76–88; Kroeger, *Ethics*, pp. 79–91).

Because the Ego is subjective Subject-Object, there is a side from which it continues to have an object that is absolutely opposed to it and from which it continues to be conditioned by the object. As we have seen, the dogmatic positing of an absolute object is transformed in this idealism into a self-limiting that is absolutely opposed to free activity.[31] This being posited by the Ego is the deduction of nature, and it is the transcendental viewpoint. We shall see how far it goes and what its significance is.

As condition of intelligence[32] [Fichte] postulates a primordial determination [i.e., limitation]. Because pure consciousness is not complete consciousness, this appeared above[33] as necessity to proceed toward empirical consciousness. The Ego is to bound itself absolutely, to oppose itself absolutely; it is subject, and the limit is in and through the Ego. This self-bounding becomes a bounding both of the subjective activity, that is, of intelligence, and of the objective activity. The bounded objective activity is *drive*;[34] the bounded subjective activity is the *concept of purpose*. The synthesis of this twofold determination is *feeling*. Feeling unites cognition and drive; but at the same time it is something merely subjective.[35] It appears, to be sure, as something in general determinate in antithesis to the indeterminate, the Ego = Ego, and indeed as something subjective in antithesis to the objective Ego. It appears as something finite in general, as against both the infinite real activity and the ideal infinity, and in relation to the latter it appears as something objective. But [this Fichtean deduction does not work, for] in itself feeling is characterized as synthesis of the subjective and the objective, of cognition and drive, and because it is a synthesis, its antithesis to something indeterminate vanishes, whether the indeterminate opposite is an infinite objective or an infinite subjective one. Altogether, feeling is finite only from the point of view of reflection which produces this opposition of the infinite. In itself it is, like matter, something subjective and objective at the same time; it is identity insofar as identity has not reconstructed itself into totality.

Feeling as well as impulse appear as bounded, and "the manifestation of the bounded and the bounding in us is drive and feeling. The

31. See above pp. 130–1.
32. Compare n. 16 above.
33. See pp. 122–8.
34. See *System der Sittenlehre, Werke* IV, 105–7 (Kroeger, *Ethics*, pp. 109–11).
35. Compare Fichte, *Werke* I, 289 (Heath and Lachs, pp. 254–5).

original and determinate system of drives and feelings is *nature*. Consciousness of them[36] obtrudes on us and, at the same time, the substance in which this system of boundaries [49] is found is supposed to be the substance which freely thinks and wills, and which we posit as ourselves. So the nature that obtrudes is our nature,"[37] and Ego and my nature constitute the subjective Subject-Object: my nature is itself in the Ego.

What have to be distinguished here, however, are two kinds of *mediation* of the opposition of nature and freedom, of the originally limited and the originally unlimited; and it is essential to show that mediation occurs [in these] in different ways. This will show us the distinction between the transcendental standpoint and the standpoint of reflection in a new form; it is because the latter displaces the former that there is a difference between the starting point of this system and its result.

On the one hand, [the starting point is] Ego = Ego; freedom and drive are one and the same. This is the transcendental standpoint. "Part of what pertains to me is to be possible only through freedom, while another part is to be independent of freedom, just as freedom is independent of it; yet the substance to which both [the free and the non-free] pertain is all one and the same and is so posited. I who feel and I who think, I who am driven and I who make a decision with free will, am one and the same."[38] —"From the transcendental standpoint, my drive as natural being, and my tendency as pure spirit are the same basic drive (*Urtrieb*), the drive that constitutes my being; but it is viewed from two distinct aspects;"[39] the distinction exists only in appearance.

On the other hand, [in the result] freedom and drive are distinct, one is the condition of the other, one dominates over the other. Nature as impulse must, of course, be *thought* as determining itself through itself; "but it is characterized by its antithesis to freedom. [. . .] Nature determines itself must be translated into, nature *is* determined by its essence, *formaliter*, to determine itself; nature can never be indeterminate, as a free being can very well be; and *materialiter* too, nature is determined [to determine itself] just in one way and no other; unlike a free being, it does not have the choice between a cer-

---

36. *Derselben* may refer either to "drives and feelings" or to "nature."
37. Fichte, *Werke* IV, 109 (Kroeger, *Ethics*, pp. 113–4).
38. *System der Sittenlehre, Werke* IV, 108 (Kroeger, *Ethics*, p. 112).
39. *Ibid.*, p. 130 (Kroeger, *Ethics*, p. 135).

tain determination and its opposite."[40] The synthesis of nature and freedom provides now the following reconstruction of identity out of dichotomy into totality: I, as intelligence, as the undetermined—and I who am driven, Ego as nature, as the determined, shall become the same through the raising of impulse into consciousness. For then drive "comes within *my control*. [. . .] In the region of consciousness the drive does not act at all; I act or do not act according to it."[41] —That which reflects is *higher* than what is reflected: the drive of him who does the reflecting that is, of the subject of consciousness, is called the higher drive.[42] The lower drive, that is, nature, must be placed *in subservience to the higher*, that is, to reflection. This relation of subservience which one appearance of the self has to the other is to be the highest synthesis.

However, this latter identity and the identity of the transcendental viewpoint are totally opposed one to the other. Within the transcendental scope Ego = Ego, that is to say, the Ego is posited in a [50] relation of substantiality or at the least in a relation of reciprocity. By contrast in [Fichte's] reconstruction of identity one Ego dominates and the other is dominated; the subjective is not equal to the objective. They stand in a relation of causality instead; one of them goes into servitude, and the sphere of necessity is subordinated to that of freedom. Thus the end of the system is untrue to its beginning, the result is untrue to its principle. The principle was Ego = Ego; the result is Ego not = Ego. The former identity is an ideal-real one; form and matter are one. The latter is merely ideal, form and matter are divided; the identity is a merely formal synthesis.

This synthesis by way of domination comes about as follows. Pure drive aims at determining itself absolutely toward activity for the sake of activity. It is confronted by an objective drive, a system of limitations. In the union of freedom and nature, freedom surrenders some of its purity, and nature some of its impurity. In order for the synthetic activity to be pure and infinite still, it must be thought as an "objective activity whose final purpose is absolute freedom, absolute independence from all of nature. This final purpose can never be achieved; [it turns into] an infinite series through whose continuation the Ego would become absolutely equal to Ego.[43] Or in other words,

---

40. *Ibid.*, pp. 112–3 (Kroeger, *Ethics*, p. 117).
41. Fichte, *Werke* IV, 125–6 (Kroeger, *Ethics*, pp. 130–1).
42. Fichte, *Werke* IV, 131 (Kroeger, *Ethics*, p. 136).
43. Compare Fichte, *Werke* IV, 149 (Kroeger, *Ethics*, pp. 157–8).

the Ego suspends itself as object and therewith also as subject. But it should not suspend itself. There remains, then, for Ego only time, indefinitely extended, filled with limitations and quantities; our old friend the infinite progress must help out. Where one expects the supreme synthesis one finds always the same antithesis between a limited present and an infinity extraneous to it. Ego = Ego is the Absolute, is totality; there is nothing outside the Ego. In the system, however, the Ego does not get that far, and it never will, once time is to be mixed in; the Ego is absolutely infected with a non-Ego, and can only ever posit itself as a quantum of Ego.

It follows that both in the theoretical and in the practical respect *Nature* is something essentially determined and lifeless. In the theoretical respect, nature is self-limitation intuited, that is to say, it is the objective side of self-limitation. Inasmuch as it is deduced as condition of self-consciousness, and posited in order to explain self-consciousness, nature is simply something that reflection posits for the sake of the explanation, it is a [merely] ideal result. Since self-consciousness is shown to be conditioned by nature, nature is accorded the dignity of an independent standing equal to that of self-consciousness; but its independence is nullified again, because it is only posited by reflection and its fundamental character is oppositeness.

In the practical respect, it is the same story. Here the terms of the synthesis are self-determination without consciousness and self-determination by way of a concept, i.e., of natural drive and the drive toward freedom for freedom's sake.[44] In the synthesis nature becomes [51] something that the causality of freedom produces as a real result. The outcome is that the concept is supposed to be causal with respect to nature, and nature is supposed to be posited as absolutely determined.

Reflection may set up its analysis of the Absolute wholly in terms of an antinomy. One term of this antinomy is the Ego, i.e., indeterminateness, or self-determination, and the other is the object, determinateness. Since reflection recognizes both terms as original, it asserts of both that they are relatively unconditioned, and so also relatively conditioned. But now reflection cannot get beyond this reciprocity of mutual conditioning. It reveals itself as Reason by estab-

44. Each of these two basic drives tends towards a goal: the *Naturtrieb* tends towards enjoyment (*Genuss*), and the *Trieb der Freiheit* tends towards freedom itself. See especially Fichte, *Werke* IV, 128–31, 139–42 (Kroeger, *Ethics*, pp. 133–7, 145–9).

lishing this antinomy of the unconditioned that is conditioned. For through this antinomy reflection points towards an absolute synthesis of freedom and natural impulse; and in doing so, it has not maintained but nullified the opposition and the standing of the two terms or of either of them, and it has not maintained but nullified [the claim] that it is itself the Absolute and the eternal; it has thrown itself into the abyss of its perfection. On the other hand, if reflection asserts that it itself and one of its opposites is the Absolute and if it holds fast to the relation of causality, then the transcendental viewpoint and Reason have succumbed to mere reflection and to the intellect; the intellect has succeeded in fixing the rational as an absolute opposite in the form of an Idea. For Reason itself nothing is left but the impotence of self-suspending requirements and the semblance of a formal mediation of nature and freedom by the intellect through the mere *Idea* of the suspension of the antitheses, the *Idea* of the independence of the Ego and of the absolute determinacy of nature which is posited as something to be negated, something absolutely dependent. But the antithesis itself has not vanished. On the contrary, it has been made infinite; for as long as one of its terms has standing the other has too.

From this highest standpoint [of reflection] nature has the character of absolute objectivity, that is, of death; only from a lower standpoint does nature, as Subject-Object, have the semblance of life. Just as the Ego does not lose the form of its appearance as subject, when viewed from the highest standpoint [that Fichte reaches], so the character of nature as Subject-Object becomes a mere illusion, and absolute objectivity becomes its essence.

For nature is the non-conscious production by [or of] the Ego and [any] production by [or of] the Ego is a self-determining, so that nature itself is Ego, it is Subject-Object. "And just as my nature is posited, so there is also nature outside mine, for my nature is not the whole of nature [. . .] Nature outside myself [. . .] is posited in order to explain [. . .] my nature. Since my nature is determined as a drive, a determining of self by self, nature outside myself must also be determined in the same way, and this determination outside myself is the ground of the explanation of my nature."[45]

The products of reflection, such as cause and effect, whole and part, etc. must now be predicated in their antinomy of this [unconscious] determining of self by self. [52] In other words, nature must be posited as cause and effect of itself, as being whole and part at once, etc.

45. Fichte, *Werke* IV, p. 113 (Kroeger, *Ethics*, p. 118).

In this way nature takes on the semblance of being alive and organic.[46]

However, this standpoint of the faculty of reflecting judgment, from which the objective is characterized as something alive, turns out to be a lower standpoint.[47] For the Ego finds itself as nature only so far as it intuits just its original boundedness, and posits the absolute limitation of the basic drive objectively, or in other words when it posits itself objectively. From the transcendental standpoint, however, the Subject-Object is only acknowledged in pure consciousness, i.e., in unlimited self-positing; but this self-positing is confronted by an absolute positing of the opposite, which is thus determined as the absolute limit of the basic drive. Insofar as the Ego *qua* drive does not determine itself according to the Idea of infinity, and hence posits itself as finite, there is this finitude, there is nature;[48] [but the Ego] *qua* Ego is at the same time infinite and Subject-Object. Since the transcendental viewpoint posits only the infinite as Ego, it thereby separates the finite from the infinite. It extracts the subject-objectivity from what appears as nature, and there remains nothing to nature but the dead shell of objectivity. Nature, which was the finite-infinite before, is now deprived of its infinity and remains pure finitude opposed to Ego = Ego. What was Ego in it is pulled over to the subject. The transcendental viewpoint proceeds from the identity, Ego = Ego, in which there is neither subjective nor objective, to their differentiation, which continues to be [conceived] as oppositing contrasted with self positing, or with Ego = Ego; and as the transcendental viewpoint determines the opposites ever further, it, too, comes to a standpoint from which nature is posited for itself as Subject-Object. It should not be forgotten, however, that [for Fichte] this view of nature is only a product of reflection at a lower standpoint. In [his] transcendental deduction [of nature] the limit of the basic drive (posited as object, that is, nature) remains a pure objectivity absolutely opposed to the basic drive, the true being which is Ego = Ego, Subject = Object.

46. Compare Fichte, *Werke* IV, 113–5 (Kroeger, *Ethics*, pp. 118–9).

47. Compare pp. 151–4 below; also Hegel's criticism of Kant in *Faith and Knowledge*, pp. 85–92.

48. The German text reads *Insofern ich als Trieb . . . sich endlich setzt, ist dieses Endliche, die Natur*. This is what we have translated. However, if one were to delete the comma after *Endliche*, one would have "this finite is nature" (cf. Méry). And if one were to read *ist* [es] *dieses Endliche, die Natur*, one would have "it [the Ego] is this finite, [it is] nature." Either of these emendations makes good sense in this sentence, which confronts "Ego *qua* drive" with "Ego *qua* Ego."

This opposition is the condition in virtue of which the Ego becomes practical: [for as practical] the Ego must suspend its opposite. The suspension is thought of in such a way that one of the opposites is made dependent on the other. With respect to the practical sphere, nature is posited as absolutely determined by the concept. Insofar as nature is not determined by the Ego, the Ego has no causality, in other words, it is not practical. The standpoint which posited nature as living, disappears again; for the essence, the In-itself of nature, must now be nothing but a limit, a negation. From this practical standpoint, Reason is nothing but the dead and death-dealing rule of formal unity, given over into the hands of reflection which puts subject and object into the [53] relation of dependence of the one on the other, the relation of causality. So it comes about that the principle of speculation, identity, is wholly set aside.

In the exposition and deduction of nature, as it is given in [Fichte's] *System of Natural Law* the absolute opposition of nature and Reason and the domination of reflection reveal themselves in all their harshness.[49]

For any rational being (*Vernunftwesen*) must make unto itself a sphere for its freedom; it ascribes this sphere to itself. But it is only by antithesis that it is itself this sphere; the sphere is constituted only insofar as the rational being posits itself exclusively in it, so that no other person can have any choice within it. In ascribing the sphere to itself, the rational being essentially sets it over against itself also. The subject *qua* the Absolute, spontaneously active, and determining itself to the thinking of an object—sets up its own sphere of freedom outside itself, and posits itself divorced from it. Its connection with its sphere is merely a *having*. The basic character of nature is to be a world of the organic being, an absolute opposite; the essence of nature is atomistic lifelessness,[50] matter more or less fluid, or more or less tough and durable, matter which in a variety of ways is reciprocally cause and effect.[51] The concept of reciprocity does little to the

49. For this part of Hegel's discussion (down to p. 144 below) see in general Fichte, *Werke* III, 23–29, 56–85 (Kroeger, *Rights*, pp. 40–48, 87–125).

50. Hegel is here criticizing Fichte's deduction of the body as a necessary condition of a person's being the subject of rights. His complaint is that, because of its opposition to the Ego *qua* Ego, the body (and the organic in general) is for Fichte no more than a piece of atomistic matter, however complex the "articulation" (Fichte's word for organic structure) of the body may be.

51. Compare Fichte, *Werke* III, 68–70 (Kroeger, *Rights*, pp. 103–4).

total opposition of that which is merely cause or merely effect. Matter now becomes mutually modifiable in a variety of ways, but even the force for this impoverished union lies outside matter. Both the independence of the parts in virtue of which they are supposed to be organic wholes themselves, and the dependence of the parts on the whole, make up the teleological dependence on the concept; for the articulation [of matter] is posited in behalf of another being, the rational being who is essentially divorced from it. Air, light, etc. turn into atomistic, shapeable, moldable matter; and matter here is meant in a quite ordinary sense, i.e., it is something strictly opposed to that which posits itself.

By this route, Fichte comes closer than Kant to managing the antithesis of nature and freedom and exhibiting nature as an absolute effect and as dead. In Kant, too, nature is posited as absolutely determined. But it cannot be thought of as determined by what Kant calls understanding (*Verstand*),[52] for the variety of particular phenomena are left undetermined by *our human* discursive *understanding*; so they must be thought of as determined by *another* understanding. However, this determination by another understanding is to be taken merely as a maxim of our reflecting judgment.[53] Nothing is asserted about the actual existence of this other understanding. Fichte does not need this detour, this idea of a separate understanding that is other than human, in order to let nature become determined. Nature is determined immediately by and [54] for intelligence.[54] The latter sets absolute limits to itself and this self-limiting cannot be derived from Ego = Ego. It can only be deduced from it:[55] its necessity is to be

52. We follow the model of all or almost all English translators of Kant in rendering his *Verstand* as understanding. But the reader should remember that the word is the same as that which in its Hegelian use is here rendered throughout as *intellect*.

53. See above, note 6.

54. In the *Science of Knowledge* Fichte defines "intelligence" as "the Ego positing itself as *vorstellend*" (*Werke* I, 228; Heath and Lachs, p. 219). This is the theoretical Ego, the Ego that posits itself as limited or determined by the non-Ego. In Fichte's *Science of Rights* this theoretical Ego is the *Vernunftwesen*, or rational being. Once he has taken this first step in the self-limitation of the absolute Ego, Fichte makes a further descent to "persons" and finally to "individuals" (as persons having bodies).

55. Hegel does not explain this distinction between *Ableitung* and *Deduktion* (i.e., "transcendental deduction" à la Fichte) anywhere. But by *Ableitung* he probably means a simple and direct cognitive operation based on some elementary logical relation such as entailment or implication; whereas *Deduktion* is a

shown from the deficiency of pure consciousness. The intuition of this absolute limitedness of intelligence, of this negation, is objective nature.

Because of its consequences, nature's relation of dependence on the concept, the opposition of [nature to] Reason, becomes even more striking in the *two systems of the community of men.*[56]

This community is conceived as a community of rational beings, a community forced to take the detour through the dominion of the concept. Any rational being has a double aspect for any other: (a) it is a free, rational being; (b) it is modifiable matter, something that can be treated as a mere thing (*Sache*).[57] This separation is absolute and once it has, in all its unnaturalness, been made basic, there is no longer the possibility of a pure mutual connection in which the original identity could present and recognize itself. Rather, every connection is one of dominating and being dominated according to the laws of a consistent intellect. The whole edifice of the community of living beings is built by reflection.

The community of rational beings appears as one conditioned by the necessary limitation of freedom; freedom gives itself the law of self-limitation.[58] This concept of limitation constitutes a realm of freedom where every truly free reciprocal relation of life, every relation that is infinite and unlimited for itself, that is to say, beautiful, is nullified; for the living [being] is rent into concept and matter and nature goes into servitude.

Freedom is the characteristic mark of rationality; it is that which in itself suspends all limitation, and it is the summit of Fichte's system. In a community with others, however, freedom must be *surrendered* in order to make possible the freedom of all rational beings living in community. Conversely the community is a condition of freedom. So freedom must suspend itself in order to be freedom. This again makes

---

complex and indirect cognitive operation in which teleological and moral necessities are mixed with logical necessity through the use of the conveniently ambiguous German verb *sollen.* Thus for instance: if perfect moral autonomy is to be (*soll*), then such and such requirements must be (*soll*) fulfilled. And perfect moral autonomy ought to (*soll*) be. Therefore these requirements are necessarily (*soll*) fulfilled.

56. The "two systems" are the "Systematic Applications" of the *Science of Rights* (Fichte, *Werke* III, 92–303; Kroeger, *Rights*, pp. 137–387) and of the *System of Ethics* (Fichte, *Werke* IV, 157–365; Kroeger, *Ethics*, pp. 167–378).

57. Compare Fichte, *Werke* III, 86–87 (Kroeger, *Rights*, pp. 127–8).

58. Compare Fichte, *Werke* III, 86–93 (Kroeger, *Rights*, pp. 128–38).

it clear that freedom is here something merely negative, namely, absolute indeterminateness, i.e., it is a purely ideal factor as the self-positing was shown to be above:[59] freedom regarded from the standpoint of reflection. This freedom does not come upon itself as Reason, but as the rational being,[60] that is to say, in a synthesis with its opposite, a finite being. This synthesis of personality already includes the limitation of one of the ideal factors, which is what freedom here is. Reason and freedom in the rational being are no longer Reason and freedom but a singular entity. Hence the community of a person with others must not be regarded as a limitation of the true freedom of the individual but essentially as its enlargement. Highest community is highest freedom, both in terms of power and of its exercise. But it is precisely in this highest [55] community that freedom as an ideal factor and Reason as opposed to nature disappear completely.

If the community of rational beings were essentially a limitation of true freedom, the community would be in and for itself the supreme tyranny. But only freedom as indeterminacy, and as ideal factor is being limited at this point [in Fichte], so that tyranny does not yet arise in the community directly from this idea by itself. But it does arise in the highest degree from the way that freedom is to be limited, in order to make possible the freedom of the other rational beings. For freedom is not supposed to lose, through the community, its form of being something ideal and opposite; on the contrary it is going to be fixed in this form and made dominant. Through a genuinely free community of living connections the individual renounces his indeterminacy [which is what Fichte calls] his freedom. In a living connection there is only freedom in the sense that it includes the possibility of suspending itself and entering into other connections. That is to say, freedom as ideal factor, as indeterminacy, disappears. In a living relation, insofar as it is free, the indeterminate is nothing but the *possible*, it is neither something actual made dominant, nor a concept that commands. In the *System of Natural Law*, however, this suspension of indeterminacy is not what is understood as the free limitation of one's freedom. On the contrary, when limitation by the common will is raised to the status of law and fixed as a concept, true freedom, the possibility of suspending a determinate connection, is nullified. The living connection can no longer be indeterminate, so it is no longer rational but absolutely determined and made fast by the intellect. Life

59. See p. 133 and the subsequent discussion.
60. See note 54 above.

has given itself up to servitude. Reflection dominates it and has gained the victory over Reason.

This state of indigence and necessity[61] is asserted to be natural law. The assertion does not, of course, carry any implication that the highest goal would be the suspension of this state and the construction through Reason of an organization of life free from all bondage to the concept, an organization that takes the place of this non-rational community of the intellect. On the contrary, the state of indigence and its infinite extension over all the stirrings of life is accepted as an absolute necessity. This community under the dominion of the intellect is not presented [by Fichte] as one that is bound to make it its supreme law to suspend this indigence of life in which it is placed by the intellect, and to suspend this endless determination and domination in the true infinity of a beautiful community where laws are made superfluous by customs, the excesses of an unsatisfied life by hallowed joys, and the crimes of oppressed forces by the possibility of [56] activities directed toward great objects. But instead the lordship of the concept and the bondage of nature are made absolute and extended infinitely.

The intellect is bound to fall into the making of endless determinations. This exhibits in the most direct way the defectiveness of its principle, which is domination through the concept. Even [Fichte's] Need State[62] does entertain the aim of preventing its citizens from doing harm rather than avenging it when it is done. It follows that it must not only forbid the actual commission of offenses under [threat of] punishment, but it must obviate the possibility of offenses. And to this end it must prohibit "actions which, though they will hurt no one and seem entirely indifferent, will yet make the harming of others easier, and their protection or the discovery of the guilty more difficult."[63] Now, on the one hand, man submits to the State with no other desire but that of employing and enjoying his resources as freely as possible. But, on the other hand, there is simply no action at all from which the State could not with abstract consistency calculate some possible damage to others. And it is this endless possibility which the

61. *Stand der Not*: this condition is illustrated and discussed in Hegel's *Early Theological Writings* (e.g., Nohl, p. 262, Knox and Kroner, p. 208; and Nohl, pp. 373–4).

62. *Notstaat*: i.e., the State based on the conception of our natural condition as an "estate of need" (*Stand der Not*).

63. Fichte, *Werke* III, 294 (Kroeger, *Rights*, p. 377). Compare Hegel, *Philosophy of Right*, section 183.

preventive intellect and its coercive authority, the police, have to deal with.[64] So in this Ideal of a State there is no doing or stirring that is not bound to be subject to some law, subject to direct supervision and duly noticed by the police and the rest of the rulers; so that "in a State whose constitution is established on this principle, [. . .] the police know pretty well where every citizen is at any time of day and what he is doing"* (see page 155 of the second part [of Fichte's *Natural Law*]).[65]

---

64. Hegel actually says "its *Gewalt*, the duty of the police."

*Just how these determinations and their purpose get lost in their own endlessness will best be made clear by some examples. The whole variety of crimes possible in imperfect States is prevented by making the police more perfect. Thus with respect to counterfeit bills of exchange [cashable by bearer upon his own signature] and money, we see how, on pp. 148 ff. [*Werke* III, 297–8; Kroeger, *Rights*, p. 381]: "Anyone handing in a check must prove through his passport that he is this definite person, where he can be found, etc. The recipient [. . .] then simply adds on the back of the check to the name of the signer, 'With passport from such and such authority.'—Just two additional words to write and one or two additional minutes to inspect pass and person; otherwise the transaction is as simple as before." (Or rather simpler, for a cautious man will probably be on his guard and not accept a check, though it appears quite all right, from a man he does not know; and to inspect a pass and a person is infinitely more simple than to get to [57] know him a bit in some other way.)—"In case the check still turns out to be bad, the person will soon be found when the investigation has established who it is. Nobody is permitted to leave a place; he can be stopped at the gate." (The fact that our villages and many of our cities have no gates—not to speak of isolated dwellings—is no objection. On the contrary, the necessity of gates is herewith deduced.) "The traveller must state his destination, and this will be entered in the town's register and in his pass" (which entails the postulate that the gate attendant will be able to distinguish each traveller from all the other folk passing through the gate)—"The traveller will nowhere be received and accepted except at the destination entered in his pass. In the pass there is a factual description of the man (p. 146 [i.e., *Werke* III, 295; Kroeger, *Rights*, p. 379]) or, since descriptions must always remain ambiguous, a good portrait in its place in the case of persons who are important, and therefore able to pay for it" (in our case, persons capable of issuing bad checks). "The pass is made out of specially manufactured paper [. . .] exclusively owned and supervised by the highest authority and the subordinate authorities which have to *account* for the paper consumed. This paper will not be imitated, for there is need of only *one* pass for a false check, and that one pass would require too many preparations and the cooperation of too many arts." (Here it is postulated that in a well-ordered State the need for more than one single counterfeit passport could not arise. Factories for counterfeit passports, which are occasionally discovered in ordinary States, would find no customers.) Another State institution would also assist in preventing the counterfeiting of the privileged paper (p. 152 [i.e., *Werke* III, 299–300; Kroeger, *Rights*, pp. 382–3]). This is the institution

The determining and being determined are self-suspended in the infinity of the series to which they must proceed. The bounding of freedom must itself be infinite. This is the antinomy of a boundedness that is unbounded, in which the limitation of freedom and the State have disappeared. The theory has nullified its own principle, determination, by extending it to infinity.

[According to Fichte] ordinary States are inconsistent in that they extend their policing authority (*Ober-Polizei-Recht*) to just a few types of possible offenses. For the rest, they entrust the citizens to themselves. They do this in the hope that a citizen does not first [58] have to be barred (*beschränkt*) from modifying another citizen's modifiable matter through a concept and by means of a law. Yet every one of them could quite properly do so, for as a rational being he must in conformity with this freedom posit himself as determining the non-Ego and ascribe to himself the faculty of modifying matter in general. Imperfect States are imperfect because they must fix some antithesis or other; they are inconsistent because they do not follow their [chosen] antithesis through all [social] ties. But to make the antithesis which splits man absolutely into rational being and modifiable matter, infinite [as Fichte does] and then make determination endless, is a consistency that is self-suspending. So this inconsistency is what is most perfect in the imperfect States.

As a result of the absolute antithesis between pure drive and natural drive [Fichte's] *Natural Right* offers us a picture of the complete lordship of the intellect and the complete bondage of the living being. It is an edifice in which Reason has no part and which it therefore repudiates. For Reason is bound to find itself most explicitly in its self-shaping as a people (*Volk*), which is the most perfect organization that it can give itself. But that State as conceived by the intellect

---

aimed at "preventing the counterfeiting of coins; [. . .] since the State owns the monopoly of metals, etc., the State must not distribute the metals to the retailers without proof as to whom and for what use the received metals were issued." In the Prussian army a foreigner is supervised by only one trustee. In Fichte's state every citizen will keep at least half a dozen people busy with supervision, accounts, etc., each of these supervisors will keep at least another half dozen busy, and so on *ad infinitum*. Equally, the simplest transaction will cause an infinite number of transactions. [Hegel marked the quotations by using spread type, but they are sometimes rather free.]

65. Hegel refers to the first edition of 1798. See Fichte, *Werke* III, 302 (Kroeger, *Rights*, p. 386).

is not an organization at all, but a machine;[66] and the people is not the organic body of a communal and rich life, but an atomistic, life-impoverished multitude. The elements of this multitude are absolutely opposed substances, on the one hand the rational beings as a lot of [atomic] points, and on the other hand a lot of material beings modifiable in various ways by Reason, i.e., by intellect, the form in which Reason is here present. The unity of these elements is a concept; what binds them together is an endless domination. This absolute substantiality of the points makes the basis for an atomistic system of practical philosophy in which, as in the atomistic system of nature, an intellect alien to the atom becomes law in the practical sphere under the name of *Right*. This Right is a *concept* of totality which must confront every action as its opposite, for every action is a determined one; a concept that is to determine every action and thus kill the living element of true identity in it. *Fiat justitia, pereat mundus* is the law, and not even in the sense that Kant gave it: "let right be done though all the scoundrels in the world perish."[67] But rather in this sense: right must be done, even though for its sake, all trust, all joy and love, all the potencies of a genuinely ethical identity, must be eradicated root and branch, as we say.

We move on now to the system of the *ethical community of man*.

It is common ground for [Fichte's] *Ethics* and his *Natural Law* alike, that the Idea must absolutely dominate over drive, that freedom must dominate nature. What distinguishes them is this: in the *Natural Law*, the subservience of free beings to the concept is strictly the absolute end in itself[68] so that the fixed abstraction of the general will must here subsist apart and far from the individual, and have coercive authority over him. In the *Ethics*, on the other hand, concept and nature must be posited as united in one and the same person. In the State, Right alone is to govern, while in the realm of morality, duty will only [59] have power insofar as the individual's Reason acknowledges it as law.

Now, of course, it seems preferable to be one's own lord and bondsman than to be the bondsman of a stranger. But if in ethical life the relation of freedom and nature is supposed to become one of subjec-

66. Compare Hegel's "German Constitution" essay (Knox and Pelczynski, pp. 159–63) and his *Philosophy of Right*, section 183.

67. *Perpetual Peace*, Akad. VIII, 378; Beck, *On History*, p. 126.

68. Or: "subservience . . . to the concept in general is the absolute end in itself."

tive lordship and bondage, a suppression of nature by *oneself*, then this is much more unnatural than the relation in the Natural Law where the commanding power appears as something other, as something outside the living individual. In this relation, the living being has always a certain independence locked up within it; what is not at one with it (*einig*) is excluded from the self; the antagonist is an alien might. And even if faith in the oneness of the inner and the outer falls away still faith in one's inner harmony, an identity of character (*eine Identität als Charakter*) can endure; the inner nature is true to itself. In the *Ethics*, however, once the commander is transferred within man himself, and the absolute opposition of the command and the subservience is internalized, the inner harmony is destroyed; not to be at one, but to be an absolute dichotomy constitutes the essence of man. He must seek for unity; but with absolute non-identity at his very basis only a formal unity remains for him.

The formal unity of the concept, which is to govern, contradicts the manifold of nature (and vice versa); and the tug of war between them soon produces a significant drawback. The formal concept is to dominate. But the formal concept is empty, it must get its content through connection with [natural] drive; thus there arises an infinite number of possibilities to act. On the other hand, if science [i.e., here, practical philosophy] maintains the concept in its unity, then it has not achieved anything with an empty formal principle such as this.

The Ego is to determine itself to suspend the objective world, according to the Idea of absolute spontaneity. It is to have causality with respect to the objective Ego with which it therefore forms ties. The ethical drive becomes a mixed one[69] and hence it becomes as manifold as the objective drive itself, with the result that a great number and variety of duties arise. Their number can be greatly reduced if one sticks to the universality of concepts, as Fichte does; but in that event one has only formal basic propositions again. Opposition among the manifold duties occurs under the name of "collisions" and this leads to an important contradiction. If the duties deduced are absolute, they cannot collide. Yet they collide necessarily because they are opposite. Because the duties are equally absolute, choice is possible, and because of their collision, choice is necessary; and there is nothing present to do the deciding, except whim. If whim were to be excluded,

69. For the distinction between "pure" and "objective" (or natural) drive, and for the ethical drive as a mixture of both, see Fichte, *Werke* IV, 141–2, 151–2 (Kroeger, *Ethics*, pp. 148–9, 160–1).

the duties could not have the same degree of absoluteness. In that case we would have to say that one duty is more absolute than the other. This contradicts the concept, [60] for every duty is, as duty, absolute. Yet where there is such a collision, if one must act, absoluteness has to be given up and one duty preferred to another. So, if self-determination is to be possible, everything depends on finding the way to decide which concept of one's duty is to be preferred to the other, and on choosing among the conditional duties according to one's best insight. If whim and the contingency of inclinations are excluded from the self-determination of freedom through the highest concept, then self-determination now passes over into the contingency of insight and hence into sheer unawareness of what it is that decides a contingent insight. Kant, in his "Doctrine of Ethics," adds casuistic questions to every duty established[70] as absolute. Since we cannot suppose that, in doing this, he genuinely meant to scoff at the absoluteness of the duties he had established, we must obviously take it that he was rather seeking to indicate the necessity of casuistry in his "Doctrine of Ethics" and hence the necessity of not trusting one's own insight, because that is, of course, completely contingent. But it is precisely contingency that should be suspended by a "Doctrine of Ethics." Simply to exchange the contingency of inclinations for the contingency of insight cannot satisfy the ethical impulse which aims at necessity.

In *Systems of Ethics* and *Natural Law* like these [of Fichte] there can be no thought of a synthesis [of nature and freedom] or an indifference point;[71] for the polarity of nature and freedom is fixed and absolute. Transcendentality gets lost in appearance, and in the intellect which is the faculty of appearance. Absolute identity cannot find or establish itself here. Opposition remains absolutely fixed, even in its palliative, the infinite progress. It cannot be truly dissolved either for the individual in the indifference point which is the beauty of the soul and of the work [of art]; or for the complete and living commonweal of individuals in a [religious] community (*Gemeinde*).

70. Part II of the *Metaphysik der Sitten* (see, for example, *Akad.* VI, 422–3, 425, 427); *The Doctrine of Virtue*, translated by M. J. Gregor, pp. 86–7, 89–90, 91–2.

71. The metaphor of the "indifference point" derives from the phenomena of magnetism. The crucial fact to keep in mind is that if a simple bar magnet is broken at the "point of indifference" we obtain *two* magnets each with its own indifference point. The *old* indifference point is now the *North* pole of one magnet *and* the *South* pole of the other.

In his discussion of the duties of the various classes, Fichte does, to be sure, add a sort of last appendix to moral theory in which he speaks of the duties of the *aesthetic* artist.[72] He treats the aesthetic sense as a unifying bond between intellect and heart. Unlike the scholar who appeals only to the intellect and the [moral] folk teacher who appeals only to the heart, the artist addresses himself to "the whole mind in the unison of all its faculties."[73] Fichte therefore ascribes to the aesthetic artist and to aesthetic education "a supremely effective connection with the promotion of the rational purpose."[74]

Now, to begin with, it is incomprehensible, how in a science which is based, like this *System of Ethics*, on absolute opposition, there can be talk of a bond that unifies [61] intellect and heart, or of the wholeness of the mind. For, after all, absolute determination of nature according to a concept is the absolute domination of the intellect over the heart, a domination that is predicated on the suspension of their union. But then, too, the quite subordinate role that is allotted to aesthetic education shows how little it counts on the whole toward the completion of the system. Art is credited with a supremely effective connection with the promotion of the rational purpose, because "it prepares the soil for morality, so that when morality comes on the scene, it finds that half of its work is already done. Man has freed himself from the fetters of sensibility."[75]

It is remarkable how Fichte can express himself so well about beauty, when what he says is inconsistent with regard to his system; and he does not apply what he says to his system at all, but immediately proceeds to apply it wrongly to the idea of the ethical law.

"Art," Fichte says, "makes the transcendental point of view into the ordinary one. [. . .] From the former the world is made, from the latter it is given: from the aesthetic point of view the world is given as it is made."[76] —Through the aesthetic faculty we acknowledge a true union of the productive activity of the intelligence with the product that appears to it as given, of the Ego that posits itself as unlimited with the Ego that posits itself as being limited, or rather, a union

72. In the remainder of this section Hegel quotes liberally from section 31 of Fichte's *System of Ethics* (*Werke* IV, 353–6; Kroeger, *Ethics*, pp. 367–70).

73. Fichte, *Werke* IV, 353 (Kroeger, *Ethics*, p. 367).

74. Fichte, *Werke* IV, 354–5 (Kroeger, *Ethics*, p. 369).

75. Fichte, *Werke* IV, 354–5 (Kroeger, *Ethics*, p. 369).

76. Fichte, *Werke* IV, 353–4 (Kroeger, *Ethics*, pp. 367–8). Hegel marked this quotation himself by the use of spread type.

of intelligence with nature, where, precisely for the sake of this possible union, nature has another side than that of being a product of intelligence.[77] The acknowledgment of the aesthetic union of producing and product is something quite different from the positing of the absolute ought, the absolute striving, and the infinite progress. For these latter are concepts, which, as soon as this highest [aesthetic] union is acknowledged, announce themselves to be antitheses or only the syntheses of subordinate spheres, which are therefore in need of a higher synthesis.

The aesthetic view is further described as follows. "The given world, nature, has two sides: it is the product of our [self] limiting; and it is the product of our free, ideal[†] action. [. . .] Every shape in space should be viewed [. . .] as an utterance of the inner fullness and force of just the body that has that shape. But one who accepts the first viewpoint[78] sees nothing but forms that are distorted, oppressed, fear-ridden; he sees ugliness. He who accepts the second viewpoint sees vigorous fullness of nature, life and aspiration; he sees beauty."[79] —The action of intelligence in [Fichte's] *Natural Law* only produced nature as modifiable material; so it was not a free, ideal[†] action; it was the action of intellect, not of Reason.

The aesthetic view of nature is now applied to the ethical law; and certainly, the capacity for being regarded as beautiful cannot be an advantage that nature has over the ethical law. "The ethical law commands absolutely and crushes all natural inclinations. He who looks at it in this fashion, relates himself to it like a slave. But the ethical law [62] is still, at the same time, the Ego itself, it comes out of the inner depth of our own being (*Wesen*); and if we obey it, we obey in the end only ourselves. He who looks upon it thus, sees it aesthetically."[80] 'We obey ourselves' means 'our natural inclination obeys our ethical law.' But in the aesthetic intuition of nature as the "expression of the inner fullness and force of bodies" the sort of sundered condition that belongs to obedience does not occur at all; while we do find it in ethi-

---

77. The text could also be translated: "nature has another side, as being a product of intelligence." (Compare Méry, p. 137). But compare the following quotation from Fichte.

78. Fichte: "to view every shape in space as limitation by the adjacent bodies" (*Werke* IV, 354; Kroeger, *Ethics*, p. 368).

79. Fichte, *Werke* IV, 354 (Kroeger, *Ethics*, p. 368).

80. Fichte, *Werke* IV, 354 (Kroeger, *Ethics*, p. 368). Hegel marked this quotation himself by the use of spread type.

cal life, according to this system, because in self-obedience we intuit natural inclination as bounded by its neighbour Reason, and drive as subservient to concept. This necessary viewpoint of [Fichte's] *Ethics,* far from being aesthetic, is precisely the one that reveals distorted, fear-ridden, oppressed forms, or ugliness.

If the ethical law demands autonomy only in the sense of a determination by and through concepts; if nature can receive its due simply through a limiting of freedom according to the *concept* of the freedom of many rational beings; if these two types of oppression are the highest modes in which man constitutes himself as man, then there is no place for the aesthetic sense either in its pure form, as unlimited self-enjoyment, or in its limited appearances, that is to say, in civil justice (*bürgerliche Rechtlichkeit*) and in morality. For the aesthetic sense must be taken in its largest scope, as the perfected self-shaping of the totality within the union of freedom and necessity, of consciousness and the non-conscious; and in the aesthetic sense all determination according to concepts is so thoroughly suspended that all this business of the intellect (*verständige Wesen*) with domination and determination is ugly and hateful to it (*hässlich und zu hassen*) wherever it comes across it.

Comparison of Schelling's Principle
of Philosophy with Fichte's

The basic character of Fichte's principle, as we have shown, is that the Subject-Object steps out of its identity and is unable to reestablish itself in it because the different [i.e., pure and empirical consciousness] gets transposed into the causal relation. The principle of identity does not become principle of the system; as soon as the formation of the system begins, identity is abandoned. The system itself is a consistent product of the intellect, a mass of finitudes, which the original identity [63] cannot draw together into the focus of totality or to its absolute self-intuition. The Subject-Object, therefore, turns itself into a subjective Subject-Object and it does not succeed in suspending this subjectivity and positing itself objectively.

The principle of identity is the absolute principle of Schelling's system as a *whole*. Philosophy and system coincide. Identity does not lose itself in the parts, still less in the result.

For absolute identity to be the principle of an entire system it is necessary that *both* subject and object be posited as Subject-Object. In Fichte's system identity constitutes itself only as subjective Subject-Object. [But] this subjective Subject-Object needs an objective Subject-Object to complete it, so that the Absolute presents itself in each of the two Subject-Objects, and finds itself perfected only in both together as the highest synthesis that nullifies both insofar as they are opposed. As their point of absolute indifference, the Absolute encloses both, gives birth to both and is born of both.

If the formal task of philosophy is taken to be the suspension of dichotomy,[1] Reason may try to solve it by nullifying one of the opposites and exalting the other into something infinite. This in effect [*der Sache nach*] is what happened in Fichte's system. But, in this solution, the opposition remains. For the opposite that is posited as Absolute is conditioned by the other, and just as it stands firm, so does the other. Both of the opposites, subject as well as object, must be suspended if the dichotomy is to be suspended; and they will be suspended as subject and object, if they are posited as identical. In the absolute identity subject and object are related to each other, and thus nullified; so

---

1. Compare pp. 90–91 above.

far there is nothing present for reflection and knowledge. Any philosophizing that cannot achieve systematic form gets to this point. It is satisfied with the negative side, where everything finite is drowned in the infinite. It might, of course, emerge again as knowledge, and it is a matter of subjective contingency whether this kind of philosophizing is bound up with the need for a system or not. But if this negative side is itself the principle, there must not be any way out to knowledge, since all knowledge has one foot in the sphere of finitude. Mystic rapture [Schwärmerei] holds fast to this intuition of colorless light; there is manifoldness in it only because it fights against the manifold. It lacks consciousness of itself, it is not aware that its contraction is conditioned by an expansion.[2] So it is onesided, because it holds fast to an opposite and turns the absolute identity into an opposite. In the absolute identity subject and object are suspended, but because they are within the absolute identity they both have standing too. This standing is what makes a knowledge possible; for in knowledge their separation is posited up to a point. The separating activity is reflection; considered in isolation, reflection suspends identity and the [64] Absolute, and every cognition should strictly be considered an error because there is a separating in it. This aspect of cognition— that it is a separating and its product is something finite—turns all knowledge into something limited and hence into a falsehood. But inasmuch as every knowledge is at the same time an identity, there is no absolute error.—

The claims of separation must be admitted just as much as those of identity. When identity and separation are placed in opposition to each other, both are absolute, and if one aims to maintain identity through the nullification of the dichotomy, they [identity and dichotomy] remain opposed to each other. Philosophy must give the separation into subject and object its due. By making both separation and the identity, which is opposed to it, equally absolute, however, philosophy has only posited separation conditionally, in the same way that such an identity—conditioned as it is by the nullification of its opposite—is also only relative. Hence, the Absolute itself is the identity of identity and non-identity; being opposed and being one are both together in it.

In its separating, philosophy cannot posit the separated [opposites]

---

2. For the first mention of this antinomy see p. 114 above. Hegel returns to the problem of reconciling the principles of "contraction" and "expansion" at the end of the essay—see below pp. 192–5.

without positing them in the Absolute. Otherwise they would be pure opposites, having no character save that the one is not if the other is. This connection with the Absolute is not [the same as] their being suspended again, for then there would be no separation. Rather, they are to remain separate and must not lose this character when they are posited in the Absolute or the Absolute in them. Indeed, both must be posited in the Absolute, for what right could one of them have to priority over the other? And it is not only a matter of equal right, but of equal necessity; for if only one of them were connected with the Absolute and not the other, they would be posited as essentially unequal, their union would be impossible, and so would philosophy's task of suspending the dichotomy. Fichte posited only one of the opposites in the Absolute, or in other words, as the Absolute. For him, the right and the necessity reside in self-consciousness; for only self-consciousness is a self-positing, a Subject-Object, and it does not first have to be connected with the Absolute as something higher; rather self-consciousness is itself the Absolute, that is, it is absolute identity. It has a stronger right to be posited as the Absolute, precisely because it posits itself; whereas the object does not: it is only posited by consciousness. But this is only a contingent status for the object, a fact which becomes clear from the contingency of the Subject-Object posited as self-consciousness; for this Subject-Object is itself conditioned. Its standpoint is therefore not the highest. It is Reason posited in a limited form, and it is only from the standpoint of this limited form that the object appears as something that is not self- [65] determining, but absolutely determined. Both of them, therefore, must be posited in the Absolute, or the Absolute must be posited in both forms while yet both of them retain separate standing. The subject, then, is subjective Subject-Object, and the object is objective Subject-Object, and since a duality is now posited, each one of the opposites is opposed to itself and the partition goes on *ad infinitum*. Hence, every part of the subject and every part of the object is itself in the Absolute, an identity of subject and object; every cognition is a truth just as every speck of dust is an organization.

It is only because the object itself is a Subject-Object that Ego = Ego is the Absolute. For it is only when the objective is itself Ego, only when it is itself Subject-Object, that Ego = Ego does not change into Ego ought to be equal to Ego.

Because both subject and object are Subject-Object, the opposition of subject and object is real; for both are posited in the Absolute and through it they have reality. The reality of opposites and real opposition only happen because of the identity of the opposites.* If the object is an absolute object, it is something merely ideal and the opposition is likewise merely ideal. Since the object is merely ideal[†] and not in the Absolute, the subject, too, becomes something merely ideal. The Ego as the self-positing, and the non-Ego as the self-oppositing are such ideal[†] factors. It is no help [to claim] that the Ego is sheer life and quickness, is doing and acting themselves, the most real[†] [*Allerrealste*], the most immediate in the consciousness of everyone. As soon as the Ego is placed in absolute opposition to the object, it is nothing real,[†] but is only something thought, a pure product of reflection, a mere form of cognition.[3] And out of products of mere reflection identity cannot construct itself as totality; for they arise through abstraction from the absolute identity which can only relate itself to them immediately through nullification, not through construction. Infinity and finitude, indeterminateness and determinateness, etc. are reflective products of the same sort. There is no transition from the infinite to the finite, from the indeterminate to the determinate. The transition as synthesis becomes an antinomy; for reflection, which

---

* Plato expresses real opposition through absolute identity thus: "The truly beautiful bond is that which makes itself and what it binds one [. . .]. For whenever, of any three numbers, or masses, or forces, the middle is such that what the first is for it, it is for the last, and conversely, what the last is for the middle, the middle is just that for the first, then since the middle has become the first and last, and the last and first conversely, have both become the middle, in this way they will all necessarily be the same; but things which are the same as against each other are all one."

[The passage comes from *Timaeus* (31c-32a). Hegel used the "Bipontine" edition of Plato, which included the Latin translation of Marsilio Ficino, 11 vols. (Zweibrugge, 1781–86). His rendering of Plato is a fairly literal one, and we have tried to translate it accordingly. For comparison, and to facilitate understanding, here is the version of Cornford: "And of all the bonds the best is that which makes itself and the terms it connects a unity in the fullest sense; and it is of the nature of a continued geometrical proportion to effect this most perfectly. For whenever, of three numbers, the middle one between any two that are either solids (cubes?) or squares is such that, as the first is to it, so it is to the last, and conversely as the last is to the middle, so is the middle to the first, then since the middle becomes first and last, and again the last and first become middle, in that way all will necessarily come to play the same part toward one another, and by so doing they will all make unity." (*Plato's Cosmology*, p. 21).]

3. In this paragraph, at least, Hegel seems to use the forms *reell, real*, and *ideell, ideal* quite indifferently. (The reader should note that *except where marked with a dagger* [†] "ideal" *always* represents *ideell* and "real" represents *reell*).

separates absolutely, cannot allow a synthesis of the finite and the infinite, of the determinate and the indeterminate [66] to be brought about, and it is reflection that legislates here. It has the right to allow a unity that is only formal, once the dichotomy into the infinite and the finite, which is its work, has been permitted and accepted. But Reason synthesizes them in the antinomy, and so nullifies them. An ideal opposition is the work of reflection, which totally abstracts from absolute identity; while a real opposition, on the other hand, is the work of Reason, which posits the opposites, identity and non-identity, as identical, not just in the form of cognition, but in the form of being as well. And the only real opposition of this kind is the one in which subject and object are both posited as Subject-Object, both subsisting in the Absolute, and the Absolute in both, and hence reality in both. For this reason it is only in real opposition that the principle of identity is a real principle. If the opposition is ideal and absolute, identity remains a merely formal principle, for it is posited in only one of the opposite forms, and cannot claim recognition as Subject-Object. A philosophy based on a formal principle becomes itself a formal[†] philosophy. After all, as Fichte says somewhere,[4] his own system would be only formally correct for God's self-consciousness—a consciousness in which everything would be posited through the Ego's being posited. But, on the other hand, if the matter, the object, is itself a Subject-Object, then the separation of form and matter can drop out, and the system, like its principle, is no longer merely formal, but formal and material at the same time: everything is posited through absolute Reason. Only in real[†] opposition can the Absolute posit itself in the form of the subject or of the object; and only then can there be a transition of subject into object or of object into subject in their essence: the subject can become objective to itself because it is originally objective, that is, because the object itself is Subject-Object, or the object can become subjective because originally it is just Subject-Object. Both subject and object are Subject-Object. This is just what their true identity consists in, and so does the true opposition they are capable of. When they are not both Subject-Object, the opposition is merely ideal and the principle of identity is formal. Where the identity is formal and the opposition is ideal, nothing more than an incomplete synthesis is possible. Or in other words, the identity, insofar as it synthesizes the opposites, is itself just a quantum, and the differ-

4. See Fichte, *Werke* I, 253 (Heath and Lachs, p. 224).

ence is qualitative;[5] in the fashion of the categories where the first, for example, reality, is posited in the third, and so is the second, but only quantitatively.[6] On the other hand, if the opposition is real, it is merely quantitative. The principle is simultaneously ideal and real, it is the only quality; and the absolute, which reconstructs itself out of the quantitative difference, is not a quantum, but totality.

[67]   To posit true identity of subject and object, both must be posited as Subject-Object; each of them is now capable of being, on its own, the object of a special science. Each of these sciences requires abstraction from the principle of the other. In the System of Intelligence the objects are nothing in themselves; nature only has standing in consciousness. That the object is a nature, and that intelligence, as consciousness, is conditioned by it—this is what we abstract from [in the System of Intelligence]. In the System of Nature, on the other hand, we forget that nature is something known; the ideal[†] determinations nature receives in science, are also immanent in it. Still this mutual abstraction is not a onesidedness of the sciences; it is not a subjective abstraction from the real principle of the other science, supposedly made for the sake of knowledge, and destined to disappear at a higher standpoint. It is not here the case that, considered in themselves, the objects of consciousness which idealism takes to be nothing but products of consciousness, are properly something absolutely different and have an absolute standing outside consciousness (*ausser dem Wesen des Bewusstseins*); or that nature, on the other hand, which is posited in its science as self-determining and having its own ideal[†] side (*in sich selbst ideell*) is, considered in itself, only object, and any identity Reason recognizes in nature is only a form lent to it by knowledge. We abstract not from the inner principle, but only from the peculiar form of the other science, and our purpose is to obtain purity for each, that is to say, the inner identity of both. Abstraction from what is peculiar to the other is abstraction from onesidedness. Nature and self-consciousness are *in themselves* as they are posited by speculation in their respective science. They are so in themselves because it is Reason that posits them. Reason posits them as Subject-Object, hence as the Absolute; the Absolute is the only In-itself. Reason posits them as Subject-Object, because it is Reason

5. Lasson simply deletes this semicolon in the text of the first edition. Glockner preserves it. Méry, who follows Lasson, discusses this difficult passage at length (pp. 183–5, note *m*).

6. See Kant, *Critique of Pure Reason*, A 80, B 106; B 111.

itself that produces itself as nature and as intelligence, and cognizes itself in them.

The standpoints of the two sciences differ but do not contradict each other; and this is so because of the true identity in which subject and object are posited, both being Subject-Object, and because the opposition of subject and object is therefore a real one, so that each is capable of passing over into the other. If subject and object were absolutely opposed and only one of them were Subject-Object, the two sciences could not stand side by side in equal dignity. Only the one standpoint would be that of Reason. It is only because one and the same [Absolute] is being constructed in the necessary forms of its existence in both of the two sciences that either of them is possible at all. They appear to contradict each other because in each of them the Absolute is posited in a form opposite to that of the other, and this contradiction is not suspended by asserting that just one of the two is the unique science, [68] and nullifying the other one from the standpoint of that one. The higher standpoint from which the onesidedness of both sciences is truly suspended is the standpoint which recognizes the same Absolute in both of them. The science of the subjective Subject-Object has hitherto been called transcendental philosophy; that of the objective Subject-Object, philosophy of nature. Insofar as each is opposed to the other, the subjective has priority in transcendental philosophy, the objective in the philosophy of nature. In both of them the subjective and objective are placed in the relation of substantiality.[7] In transcendental philosophy, the subject, as intelligence, is the absolute substance and nature is an object, an accident. In the philosophy of nature, the absolute substance is nature, of which the subject, intelligence, is only an accident. Now, the higher standpoint is not one that suspends one or the other of the two sciences, and asserts that the subject alone, or the object alone is the Absolute. Nor is it a standpoint which mixes the two sciences together.

What happens when they are mixed together is this. If what belongs to the science of nature is mixed up in the system of intelligence, transcendent hypotheses arise.[8] Because of the false semblance

7. Compare Kant, *Critique of Judgment*, section 73.

8. If "transcendent" in Kant meant "beyond those limits of any possible experience which *The Critique of Pure Reason* established," "transcendent" here means "below that authentic union of the dichotomies which the speculative philosophy establishes."

of a union of consciousness and the non-conscious, these can be blinding. They pretend to be natural and, in fact, they do not fly beyond the palpable. The fiber theory of consciousness is an example.[9] On the other hand, if intelligence as such is mixed up in the doctrine of nature, hyperphysical, and especially teleological explanations result. Both of these mixture blunders arise from the urge to explain. For the sake of explanation intelligence and nature are put into a relation of causality, the one being the ground, and the other that which is grounded. Nothing is achieved in this way, however, except that the opposition gets fixed as absolute, and through the semblance of a merely formal identity—such as causal identity is—the way to absolute unification is completely cut off.

The other standpoint from which the contradictory aspect of the two sciences is supposed to be suspended depends on denying that one or the other of the two sciences is a science of the Absolute. Dualism may very well fall in with the science of intelligence; and yet still allow that things [in the objective realm] are proper beings (*Wesen*); with this in mind it can take the science of nature to be such a system of the proper being of things: let each of the two sciences be as valid as it likes; there is room for both to stay peacefully side by side. The trouble with this view is that the essence of the two sciences as sciences of the Absolute has been overlooked; for the Absolute is no [mere] juxtaposition.

Or there is yet another standpoint which denies that one or other of the two sciences is a science of the Absolute. This is the one [69] which would suspend the positing of the principle of one science in the Absolute, or the positing of the Absolute in the appearance of this principle. The most remarkable example in this regard is the standpoint of what is ordinarily called transcendental idealism. We have maintained that this science of the subjective Subject-Object is one, and only one of the [two] integrating sciences of philosophy. We have shown that this science is onesided when it claims to be science par excellence and we have exhibited the shape that nature has from

9. Méry suggests that the *Traité des membranes* (Paris, 1800) of M. F. X. Bichat (1771–1802) may be meant. But (i) it is unlikely that Hegel was so completely *au fait* with medical research in 1801; and (ii) when he did read Bichat he always regarded him with a respect that was well merited (see the *Philosophy of Nature*, additions to sections 354–5). Méry's other candidate, J. C. Lossius (1748–1813), is a much more probable target. His book *Physical Causes of Truth* (1775) "attempts to explain contradictions as 'conflicts between nerves' " (L. W. Beck, *Early German Philosophy*, p. 322 n.).

its standpoint. But we still want to consider here the form which the science of nature assumes when it is constructed from this standpoint.

Kant acknowledges nature: he posits the object to be something undetermined (by understanding)[10] and he views nature as Subject-Object in that he treats the product of nature as an end of nature, as purposeful without a concept of purpose, as necessary without being mechanistic, as identity of concept and being. But at the same time this view of nature is supposed to be merely teleological,[11] that is to say, it only serves validly as a maxim for our limited human understanding whose thinking is discursive and whose universal concepts do not contain the particular phenomena of nature. This *human* perspective is not supposed to affirm anything concerning the reality of nature. The perspective remains wholly subjective, therefore, and nature purely objective, something merely thought. The synthesis of nature as determined and yet also not determined by understanding, is supposed to remain a mere Idea in a sensuous understanding; and *for us men* it is quite impossible that explanation in the mechanical mode should ever converge with purposiveness. These positions adopted in the critical philosophy are on a most subordinate, non-rational plane because they posit human reason in strict opposition to absolute Reason. All the same, they do rise to the *Idea* of a sensuous intellect, and sensuous intellect is Reason. Yet *in itself*, that is to say, in Reason, the convergence of mechanism of nature and purposiveness of nature is not supposed to be impossible. But Kant has not given up the distinction between what is *in itself possible* and what is *real*. Nor has he raised the necessary supreme Idea of a sensuous intellect to reality.[12] So in his science of nature[13] he cannot, in the first place,

10. *Verstand*: see note 52 on p. 143 above.

11. Compare the *Critique of Judgment*, sections 62–68 (*Akad.* V, 362–84).

12. This curious remark about a *sinnliche Verstand* refers to Kant's discussion of the "intuitive intellect" in the *Critique of Judgment*, sec. 77 (*Akad.* V, 405–10; Meredith, *Teleological Judgment*, pp. 60–7). In fact the whole "Dialectic of the Teleological Judgment" (sections 69–78) should be studied here, especially sections 75–78. The *Critique of Judgment* is more helpful than any of Kant's scattered remarks about "intellectual intuition" and "intuitive intellect (or understanding)" in the *Critique of Pure Reason* (for which see Norman Kemp Smith's index). Fichte's attempts to revise the Kantian conception of intellectual intuition and intuitive intellect (see for instance *Werke* I, 471–4; Heath and Lachs, pp. 45–7) also throw some light on the way Schelling and Hegel went about their more radical transformation.

13. Hegel now turns his attention to Kant's *Metaphysical Foundations of Natural Science* (1786).

allow any insight into the possibility of basic forces; and in the second place, a science of nature of this kind, a science for which nature is matter—i.e., something absolutely opposite, something that does not determine itself—can only construct a mechanics. And even with all the poverty of its forces of attraction and repulsion, it has yet made matter too rich; for force is something internal that produces something external, it is a self-positing = Ego, and from the purely idealistic viewpoint no such thing can pertain to matter. [Kant][14] conceives matter simply as the [70] objective, as that which is opposed to the Ego. For him, attractive and repulsive forces are not merely superfluous; they are either purely ideal, in which case they are not forces, or else they are transcendent. The only construction of phenomena that he can allow is mathematical, not dynamical.[15] The phenomena must be given, and they are filtered by the categories. Now this filtering may produce all sorts of correct concepts, to be sure, but it does not confer any necessity on the phenomena; and the chain of necessity is the formal aspect of what is scientific in the construction. The concepts remain contingent with respect to nature just as nature does with respect to the concepts. For this reason correctly constructed syntheses by way of the categories would not necessarily have to be corroborated by nature itself. Nature can only offer variegated displays that could count as contingent schemata for laws of the understanding, exemplary by-plays whose living peculiarity would fade away precisely because only the determinations of reflection [i.e., the categorized aspects] are recognized in them. And conversely the categories are only impoverished schemata of nature.

If nature is only matter, if it is not Subject-Object, then no scientific construction of nature is possible for which knower and known (*Erkennendes und Erkanntes*) are necessarily one. A Reason which has made itself into reflection by opposing itself to the object absolutely, can only proceed by deduction when it lays down more about nature a priori than its universal character as matter. This universal

14. The intended subject of this and the next two sentences is not quite certain. Hegel's *er* could refer to "the purely idealistic viewpoint." For "Kant" we have to go back to the beginning of a long and complex sentence.

15. For this basic distinction see *Critique of Pure Reason*, B 110. (Kant's various discussions of it in the first Critique are easily located with the aid of N. K. Smith's index.) But the essential context of Hegel's discussion here is in the *Metaphysical Foundations of Natural Science*. See *Akad*. IV, 467–79 and 496–553 (especially p. 470). See also Kant's "Comment" regarding "Explication 4" of the "Phoronomy" (*Akad*. IV, 486–7; Ellington, p. 27).

character remains basic; the manifold further determinations are posited for and by reflection. A deduction of this kind gives the illusion of a-priority because it posits the concept, the product of reflection, as something objective. Because it posits nothing else, it remains, of course, immanent. Essentially this kind of deduction is identical with the view [Wolff's] that acknowledges only external purposiveness in nature. The sole distinction is that this deduction develops more systematically from a determinate point, for example, from the body of the rational being;[16] but in both views nature is something absolutely determined by the concept, i.e., by something alien to it. The teleological view which only acknowledges nature as determined according to external purposes, has an advantage in respect of completeness, for it is able to absorb the manifold of nature as it is given in experience. [Fichte's] deduction of nature, on the other hand, has a determinate point of departure and because of the latter's incompleteness, it postulates more and more—that is what the deduction consists of. It is immediately satisfied with what it postulates, and the postulation is supposed to supply directly whatever the concept requires. Whether an actual natural object can really supply what is required by itself is of no concern to the deduction, which can only find this out by experience. If the directly postulated object cannot be found in an adequate form in nature, then another object is deduced, and so on, until the purpose is found to be fulfilled. The order of these deduced objects depends upon the definite ends that serve as points of departure, and it is only to the extent that the objects [71] have a connection with respect to this end, that they are coherent among themselves. Properly speaking, however, they are not capable of an inner coherence. For if the object that was directly deduced is found by experience to be inadequate to the concept that has to be satisfied, then this single object, since it is infinitely determinable externally, gives rise to an infinite dispersion. The only way in which this dispersion could be avoided at all, would be for the deduction to draw its various points into a circle; but it cannot establish itself at the inner center of the circle because from the outset it is outside it.[17] Concept and object are mutually external to each other.

So then [we have seen that] neither of the two sciences can establish itself as the only one, neither can suspend the other. For then the Absolute would be posited in only *one* form of its existence; and as

16. It is clear that Hegel's example is now Fichte once more, rather than Kant.
17. Literally "it is at the outer center."

soon as it posits itself in the form of existence, it must posit itself in a duality of form; for appearing and dichotomy [of subject and object] are the same thing.

Both sciences present the Absolute as it emerges from the lower levels of one form of its appearance and gives birth to itself as the totality in this form. Because of this inner identity, the two sciences are equal as to their coherence and their sequence of stages. They corroborate each other. One of the older philosophers put it somewhat like this: the order and coherence of ideas (the subjective) is the same as the coherence and order of things (the objective).[18] Everything is in *one* totality only: the objective totality and the subjective totality, the system of nature and the system of intelligence are one and the same; to any subjective determination there corresponds the very same objective determination.

As sciences they are objective totalities and proceed from one limited item to another. But each limited item is itself in the Absolute and is thus internally unlimited. It loses its external limitedness by being placed in the systematic context of the objective totality. In this totality it has truth even as a limited item, and to determine its place is to know it.—Jacobi said that systems are organized structures of not-knowing.[19] We have only to add that the non-knowing—the cognition of single items—becomes knowledge by becoming organized.

Apart from this external equality which holds between these sciences insofar as they are mutually isolated, their principles also necessarily permeate each other directly. The principle of the one is the subjective Subject-Object, and of the other the objective Subject-Object; hence the system of subjectivity also contains the objective, and the system of objectivity contains the subjective. Nature is an immanent ideality just as intelligence is an immanent reality. The two poles of cognition and being [72] are present in each, so that each has also the point of indifference in itself; but in one system the ideal pole prevails, in the other the real pole. In nature, the ideal pole does not reach the point of absolute abstraction, that posits itself over and against the infinite expansion as a point within itself. This is how the ideal pole constructs itself in Reason. In the intelligence, the real pole

---

18. Spinoza, *Ethics*, Part II, prop. VII.

19. Jacobi, *Werke* III, 29. *Jacobi an Fichte*: "Our sciences, *taken merely as such*, are games which the human spirit invents to pass its time. In these games the human spirit *organizes only its ignorance* without coming a hair's breadth closer to *what is true.*"

does not achieve the envelopment of the infinite, which in this contraction posits itself as infinitely outside itself. This is the way the real constructs itself in matter.

Each of the two systems is both a system of *freedom* and a system of *necessity* at the same time. Freedom and necessity are ideal factors, so they are not in real opposition. Hence the Absolute cannot posit itself as Absolute in either of these two forms; and the philosophical sciences cannot be, the one a system of freedom, the other a system of necessity. A freedom set apart like that would be a formal freedom, just as a necessity set apart would be a formal necessity. Freedom is the character of the Absolute when it is posited as something inner, something that remains unlimited even when it posits itself in a limited form, i.e., in definite points of the objective totality. That is to say, it remains what it is, even when it is viewed as opposed to its being; and when so viewed, it is viewed as something inner, hence as capable of relinquishing its being and passing into another appearance. Necessity is the character of the Absolute viewed as something outer, as an objective totality, hence as a [system of] externality whose parts, however, have no being apart from the whole [system] of objectivity. Intelligence and nature are in real opposition because they are posited in the Absolute. For this reason, the ideal factors, freedom and necessity, pertain to both of them. But whim and contingency have their place only from subordinate standpoints and are banished from the concept of the science of the Absolute. For whim is only the semblance of freedom, it is a freedom wholly abstracted from necessity, or from freedom as a totality—and this abstraction can only take place where freedom is already posited within a single sphere[20] —just as contingency, which is what corresponds to whim in the realm of necessity, is the positing of single parts as if they were for themselves, and did not exist solely in and through the objective totality. The truth, however, is that necessity belongs to intelligence just as it does to nature. For since intelligence is posited in the Absolute, the form of being pertains to it, too: it must split itself and appear; it is a fully developed organization of cognition and intuition. Every shape that it assumes is conditioned by opposed shapes, and if their abstract identity is isolated from the shapes themselves as free-

---

20. *Innerhalb einer einzelnen Sphäre*: probably this means "within the sphere of a singular [rational] agent." (Compare the following remark about contingency. If this view is right, then "freedom as a totality" refers to the politically articulated autonomy of the *Volk*.)

dom, this freedom is only an ideal pole of the indifference point of intelligence—the other immanent pole here being an objective totality. [73] And on the other side, nature has freedom. For nature is not a stillness of being, it is a being that becomes; or in other words, it is not split and synthesized from the outside, it sunders itself and unites itself by itself; and in all of its shapes it posits itself freely, not just as something limited, but as the whole. Its non-conscious development is a reflection of the living force which, endlessly splitting itself, yet posits itself in every limited shape and is identical [in all of them]. To this extent no configuration of nature is limited, each is free.—

Hence, the science of nature is the *theoretical part* of philosophy, and the science of intelligence its *practical part*; but at the same time each science has for itself a theoretical and a practical part of its own in its turn. In the system of nature, identity at the level of light, is alien to heavy matter, not in itself but as a potency; it is an alien [force] which splits and integrates matter into cohesion and produces a system of inorganic nature. In the same way for the intelligence that produces itself in objective intuitions, identity is not present at the level of self-positing. The identity does not cognize itself in the [objective] intuition. The identity produces both [the system of inorganic nature and the world of objective intuitions] without reflecting upon its action; and both are therefore the concern of a theoretical part. The intelligence, however, does cognize itself in the will, and places itself as itself [i.e., consciously] within objectivity nullifying the intuitions that it produced non-consciously. And equally nature becomes practical in organic nature in that light joins its product and becomes internal. In inorganic nature, light posits the point of contraction outside in crystallization as an external ideality. In organic nature, light forms itself as something internal, into the contraction that is the brain; already at the level of plant life, there is the blossom in which the inner light-principle disperses itself in colors and rapidly fades away in them. Yet through the polarity of the sexes the inner light posits itself as both subjective and objective in the plant; and it does so still more firmly in the animal: the individual seeks and finds itself in another. In the animal the light remains more intensely inward; it posits itself as more or less changeable voice, or in other words, it posits animal individuality as something subjective in universal communication: it posits itself as cognizing and to be recognized. The identity [of the inner light] is set forth by the science of nature through the *reconstruction* of the moments [i.e., moving powers] of inorganic nature from the inside outwards. Because of this the science has a practical part. [For instance] reconstructed [i.e., repeated at the organic level] practical magnetism is the suspension of the gravity that expands itself outwardly into poles; it is the recontraction of gravity into the point of indifference which is the brain, and the transposition of the two poles into the inner life, as a pair of indifference-points, such as nature has already set up [outwardly] in the elliptical orbits of the planets.[21] Electricity, reconstructed from the inside, posits the sexual difference of organisms. Each organism produces [74] the [sexual] difference through itself, posits itself ideally on account of the lack [it feels], finds itself objectively in another organism.—Nature, so far as it becomes practical through the chemical process has put the third which mediates between the two different organisms back into them as something inward. The third appears as a tone, an inward sounding that produces itself. Like the third body of the inorganic process,[22] this sounding [an animal voice] is without potency and passes away; it extinguishes the absolute substantiality of the different beings and brings them to the indifference of mutual self-recognition, an ideal[†] positing which does not die out again in a real identity, as the sexual relation does.

We have thus far set the two sciences with their inner identity against each other. In one of them, the Absolute is subjective in the form of cognition, in the other it is objective in the form of being. Because they are placed in opposition to each other, being and cognition become ideal factors or forms; each of them is present in both sciences, but in one science cognition is matter and being is form, while in the other being is matter and cognition is form. The Absolute is the same in both, and is set forth by the sciences not merely as opposite in form, but insofar as the Subject-Object posits itself in them. Hence the sciences themselves are not just ideally, but really opposed, and for this reason they must also be treated as a single coherent science forming one continuous whole. Insofar as they are opposed to each other, they are, to be sure, internally closed in themselves and form totalities; but the totalities are at the same time only relative, and as such they tend toward the point of indifference. As

21. The construction of the planetary orbits by way of a line with two indifference points was a principal task of Hegel's Latin dissertation *On the Orbits of the Planets* (1801; already drafted in German before the present essay was written).

22. The reference is probably to the acid medium between the two poles of a Voltaic pile.

identity and relative totality, the indifference point always lies within the sciences themselves; but as absolute totality it lies outside them. But inasmuch as both sciences are sciences of the Absolute and their opposition is real, they are the poles of the indifference [point] and cohere with one another at this point itself; they are themselves the lines which link the pole with the center. The center is itself doubled, however, identity being one, and totality the other, and in this perspective the two sciences appear as the progressive evolution, or self-construction, of identity into totality.

The indifference point towards which the two sciences strive (inasmuch as they are opposed when looked at in terms of their ideal factors) is the whole regarded as a self-construction of the Absolute; this is their ultimate peak. The point of transition, the middle term through which identity constructing itself as nature passes over to identity constructing itself as intelligence, is the internalization of the light of nature, the lightning stroke of the ideal upon the real, as Schelling calls it,[23] its self-constitution as point. This [75] point is Reason, the turning point of both sciences; and it is the ultimate apex of nature's pyramid, its final product, the point of arrival at which it becomes complete. But as a point it must likewise expand into a nature. Science establishes itself at this point as its center and divides from here into two parts, assigning the non-conscious production to one side and the conscious production to the other. But at the same time science knows that intelligence as a real factor takes the whole self-construction of nature on the other side over into its own realm —it has all that precedes it or stands beside it within itself; and it knows, too, that nature as a real factor has equally immanent in it what is set against it in science. In this knowledge all the ideality of the factors together with their onesided form is suspended; this is the unique higher standpoint where both sciences are lost in each other: for the division between them is acknowledged to be just a scientific one, and the ideality of the factors is only posited for the purposes of science.

This view is immediately only negative. It simply suspends the separation of the two sciences and of the forms in which the Absolute has posited itself. It is not a *real* synthesis, it is not the absolute indifference point where these forms are nullified in that they both subsist united. The original identity expanded its non-conscious contrac-

---

23. The reference is to "Darstellung meines Systems der Philosophie" (1801) § 145, Zusatz 3. See Schelling, *Werke* IV, 205.

tion—subjectively feeling, objectively matter—into the objective to-tality, the endlessly organized arrays and sequences of space and time. Against this expansion the original identity set the subjective totality, the contraction which is self-constitutive by nullifying the expansion, in the self-cognitive point of (subjective) Reason. The original iden-tity must now unite both in the self-intuition of the Absolute, which is becoming objective to itself in completed totality. It must unite them in the intuition of God's eternal human Incarnation, the beget-ting of the Word from the beginning.[24]

This intuition of the self-shaping or objectively self-finding Abso-lute can be viewed once more as a polarity, by positing one of the factors of the equilibrium as predominant, consciousness, on the one hand, or the non-conscious on the other.[25] In *art* this intuition appears more concentrated in a point, and consciousness is stricken down. This happens either in art properly speaking or in religion. In art properly speaking, the intuition appears as a work which, being ob-jective, is enduring, but can also be regarded by the intellect as an external dead thing; it is a product of the individual, of the genius, yet it belongs to mankind. In religion the intuition appears as a living

---

24. This is the first explicit reference to Hegel's life-long concern with the in-terpretation of the Christian dogma of the Trinity. The Son, or Second Person of the Trinity, has always been identified by orthodox theologians with the *Logos* or Word referred to in the first chapter of the Gospel of John. According to the Creeds, God the *Father* created the world, but the Son was *"begotten, not made"* and *"begotten of the Father, before all worlds."* John, however, says of the *Logos* "by him (it) all things were made, and without him (it) was not anything made, that was made." Hegel seems to have been more influenced by John than by Genesis or the Creeds. We know that sometime between 1800 and 1804 he at-tempted to lay out his philosophy of Nature schematically as a "Divine Triangle" based on the Trinitarian dogma (see Rosenkranz, *Hegels Leben*, pp. 101–2). If we take the present passage together with the similar remark in *Faith and Knowl-edge* (Cerf and Harris, p. 81) we can see clearly that Hegel did not interpret the distinction between the "begetting of the Son" and the "creation of the world" in an orthodox way. By treating the "creation" as the "moment of difference" in the "begetting" he could legitimately assert "all things came to be through the *Logos* and apart from it not even one thing came to be that did come to be," (which is what John asserts in the most literal translation possible). Also he could avoid the philosophical inconvenience of a creation of the world *in time* (which does appear to be implied by the *priority* which the Nicene Creed gives to the beget-ting of the *Logos*). For the way Hegel himself distinguished "the Son" from "the world" in the summer of 1802 see Rosenkranz' reports of his lecture-manuscripts (*Hegel's Leben*, pp. 133–41).

25. The relation of art, religion and speculation set out in the following pas-sage is discussed above in our introduction, pp. 51–2.

(e)motion (*Bewegen*) which, being subjective, and only momentary, can be taken by the intellect as something merely internal; it is the single individual. In *speculation*, the intuition appears more as consciousness, and as extended in consciousness, as an activity of subjective Reason which suspends objectivity and the non-conscious. Whereas the Absolute appears in art, taken in its true scope, more in the form of [76] absolute being, it appears in speculation more as begetting itself in its infinite intuition. But though speculation certainly conceives the Absolute as becoming, it also posits the identity of becoming and being; and what appears to speculation as self-begetting is at the same time posited as the original absolute being which can only come to be so far as it is. In this way, speculation can rid itself of the preponderance that consciousness has in it; the preponderance is in any case something inessential. Both art and speculation are in their essence divine service—both are a living intuition of the absolute life and hence a being at one with it.

Speculation, then, and its knowledge are at the point of indifference, but not essentially and demonstrably [*an und für sich*] at the true point of indifference. This will depend on whether speculation recognizes itself to be only one side of it or not. Transcendental philosophy is *one* science of the Absolute, for the subject is itself Subject-Object and to that extent Reason. But if this subjective Reason posits itself as the Absolute, then it is a pure Reason, i.e., a formal Reason, whose products, the Ideas, are the absolute opposite of a sensibility or nature, and can serve the phenomena only as the rule of a unity that is alien to them. In setting the Absolute into the form of a subject, this science has an immanent boundary. Only by recognizing this boundary and being able to suspend itself and the boundary—and that, too, scientifically—does it raise itself to the science of the Absolute and to the absolute indifference point. For there used to be much talk about the boundary stakes of human Reason, and even transcendental idealism acknowledges "incomprehensible limits" of self-consciousness, "in which we happen to be enclosed."[26] But since the limits have traditionally been given out as boundary stakes of Reason, and nowadays as incomprehensible, science recognizes its incapacity to suspend itself by itself, i.e., not by a *salto mortale*; or in other words, its incapacity to abstract again from the subjective in which it has posited Reason.

---

26. See Fichte, "Ueber den Grund unseres Glaubens an eine göttliche Weltregierung" (*Werke* V, 184).

Transcendental philosophy posits its subject as a Subject-Object and is thus one side of the absolute point of indifference. So the totality is in it, certainly. The entire philosophy of nature falls, as knowledge, within its sphere. And one can no more prevent the Science of Knowledge—though it would be only part of [a complete] transcendental philosophy—from laying claim to the form it gives to knowledge [i.e., the title of absolute science] and from laying claim to the identity which is in knowledge than one can prevent logic from doing the same thing. That is to say, one cannot prevent them from isolating the form as consciousness and constructing the appearance for themselves. However, this identity, separated from all the manifold that is known, as pure self-consciousness, shows itself to be a relative identity in that it cannot get away from being conditioned by an opposite in any of its forms.[27]

Intellectual intuition is the absolute principle of philosophy, the one real ground and firm standpoint in Fichte as well as in Schelling. [77] Expressed for reflection, this is the identity of subject and object. In science, intellectual intuition becomes the object of reflection, and for this reason philosophical reflection is itself transcendental intuition. Philosophical reflection makes itself into the object and is one with it: this is what makes it speculation. Hence Fichte's philosophy is an authentic product of speculation. Philosophical reflection is conditioned, or [to put it another way] the transcendental intuition enters consciousness through free abstraction from the whole manifold of empirical consciousness, and in this respect it is something subjective. When philosophical reflection becomes its own object, it is taking something conditioned as the principle of its philosophy. In order to grasp transcendental intuition in its purity, philosophical reflection must further abstract from this subjective aspect so that transcendental intuition, as the foundation of philosophy, may be neither subjective nor objective for it, neither self-consciousness as opposed to matter, nor matter as opposed to self-consciousness, but pure transcendental intuition, absolute identity, that is neither subjective nor

27. Hegel wants to exhibit the latest "philosophical revolution" as a degenerate form of what he calls in *Faith and Knowledge* "the reflective philosophy of Subjectivity." The "boundary stakes of Reason" were established in Locke's *Essay Concerning Human Understanding* (see *Faith and Knowledge*, pp. 68–9). Fichte set up the "Science of Knowledge" as the whole of philosophy (within its "incomprehensible limits"). Finally Bardili (seconded by Reinhold) proclaimed the "reduction of philosophy to Logic" (see p. 79 above and pp. 179, 186–8, 192–5 below).

objective. As the object of reflection transcendental intuition becomes subject and object. Philosophical reflection posits these products of pure reflection in the Absolute in their abiding opposition. Opposition as it pertains to speculative reflection is no longer an object and a subject, but a subjective transcendental intuition and an objective transcendental intuition. The former is the Ego, the latter is nature, and both are the highest appearances of absolute, self-intuiting Reason. These two opposites, whether they are called Ego and nature, or pure and empirical self-consciouness, or cognition and being, or self-positing and oppositing, or finitude and infinity, are together posited in the Absolute. Ordinary reflection can see nothing in this antinomy but contradiction; Reason alone sees the truth in this absolute contradiction through which both are posited and both nullified, and through which neither exists and at the same time both exist.

[ON REINHOLD'S VIEW AND PHILOSOPHY] [1]

It still remains for us to say something about *Reinhold's view of Fichte's and Schelling's philosophy* and something about his own philosophy.

As for his *view of Fichte and Schelling,* to begin with, he has overlooked the difference between these philosophies as systems, and, in the second place, he has not taken them as philosophies.

Reinhold seems to have not the slightest inkling that for years there has been a philosophy other than pure transcendental idealism before the public. It is marvellous how he manages to see nothing but an [abstract] principle in philosophy as Schelling has established it, nothing but Egoity, the principle that makes subjectivity comprehensible. [2] Reinhold can say all in one breath that Schelling "discovered that the Absolute so far as it is not mere subjectivity, is nothing more, and cannot be anything more [78] than mere objectivity or mere nature as such:" and that the *way to* this discovery was the positing of the Absolute in the absolute identity of intelligence and nature. [3] So, at one stroke he presents Schelling's principle thus: (a) the Absolute, so far as it is not mere subjectivity, is mere objectivity and, hence, not

---

1. This heading is not in the first edition (a new page begins with some blank space left).

2. Compare *Beyträge* I, 86–7.

3. See *Beyträge* I, 85–6.

the identity of both, and (b) the Absolute is the identity of both. Quite the reverse: the principle of the identity of subject and object had to become the road to the insight that the Absolute as identity is neither mere subjectivity, nor mere objectivity. Later on he presents the relation of the two sciences correctly. They are "two different views," not, certainly [as he says], "of one and the same thing (*Sache*)" but [as he goes on to say], "of the absolute self-sameness, of the all-one."[4] And precisely for this reason neither the principle of the one nor that of the other science is mere subjectivity or mere objectivity. Still less is that in which alone they permeate each other, pure Egoity. Pure Egoity, like nature, gets swallowed up in the point of absolute indifference.

One who is committed to love of and faith in truth, and is not taken in by system, will easily convince himself, so Reinhold opines, that the fault of this solution lies in the way the problem was formulated.[5] But it is not quite so easy to detect where the fault in Reinhold's description of what Schelling conceived to be philosophy lies, nor how it was possible for him to get hold of it in the way that he has done.

It will not help to point to the Introduction of [Schelling's *System of*] *Transcendental Idealism* itself where the relation of transcendental idealism to the whole of philosophy is established, along with the concept of this whole, for in his discussions of the *System of Transcendental Idealism* Reinhold confines himself to this Introduction, and he sees in it the opposite of what is there. Nor is it any use to draw attention to certain passages in it, where the true viewpoint is most definitely expressed; for Reinhold himself adduces the most definite passages in his first discussion of this system.[6] These passages assert that *in one* and only one [of the two] necessary basic sciences of philosophy namely in Transcendental Idealism, the subjective is the *first*;[7] not that it is the first principle of all philosophy—which is how it is at once turned upside down in Reinhold—; and as purely subjective it is not even the principle of transcendental idealism—it is the subjective *Subject-Object* that is the principle.

For those who are capable of not taking definite statements to mean the opposite of what they say, it may perhaps not be superflu-

---

4. *Ibid.*, p. 86.

5. *Ibid.*, p. 87.

6. Reinhold does not actually quote any passages or give specific references in his first *Beurteilung* of Schelling's system (*Beyträge* I, 85–9).

7. Schelling, *Werke* III, 342–3.

ous to draw attention to the second issue of the first volume of the
Journal for Speculative Physics—leaving aside the introduction to the
System of Transcendental Idealism itself, and of course the more recent issues of the *Journal*.[8] In Volume I, no. 2, [79] Schelling expresses himself as follows: "The philosophy of nature is a physical
explanation of idealism;—in the far distance nature has already sown
the seed for the height it achieves in Reason.—The philosopher is
only apt to overlook this, because already in his first act he takes up
his object, at its highest level, that is, as the Ego, as consciousness.
Only the physicist sees through this illusion. The idealist is right in
making Reason the self-creator of everything. He has on his side the
very intention of nature with respect to man; but precisely because it
is the intention of nature, the idealism [of creative Reason] becomes
itself something explicable; and the theoretical reality of idealism coincides with this intent.—When men finally learn to think in a purely
theoretical way, *in an exclusively objective way without any admix-
ture of the subjective*, they will learn to understand this."[9]

Reinhold claims that the main weakness of [modern] philosophy
hitherto is this: that thinking has so far been regarded as having the
character of a merely subjective activity. He demands that we should
attempt to abstract from the subjectivity of thinking.[10] Now, abstraction from what is subjective in the transcendental intuition is the basic
characteristic formula (*der formelle Grundcharakter*) of Schelling's
philosophy. This is inherent, not only in the passages quoted, but in
the very principle of his whole system. It is expressed even more
definitely in the *Journal for Speculative Physics*, vol. II, no. 1, in the
discussion of Eschenmayer's *Objections to the Philosophy of Nature*,
objections which are *derived from the grounds of transcendental
idealism* where the totality is posited only as an Idea, a thought, or
in other words as something subjective.[11]

As far as *Reinhold's view of what is common to both systems* is
concerned, i.e., their being both speculative philosophies, from Reinhold's own peculiar standpoint they must appear to be personal pe-

8. Hegel is referring especially to the first issue of the second volume of *Zeit-
schrift für spekulative Physik*. This issue contained both the controversy with
Eschenmayer (see note to p. 79 above) and the new "Exposition of My System of
Philosophy."

9. The emphasis is Hegel's rather than Schelling's. The quotation is very much
abbreviated and rather free (see Schelling, *Werke* IV, 75–7).

10. Compare the passages Hegel quotes on pp. 97 above and 187 below.

11. See Schelling, *Werke* IV, 86–104 (compare note 1 on p. 79 above).

culiarities, so they do not appear to him as philosophies at all. The most essential business, theme and principle of philosophy according to Reinhold is to ground the reality of cognition by way of analysis, that is, by separation.[12] So speculation whose supreme task is to suspend the separation of subject and object in their identity, can, of course, have no significance at all; and thus the most essential aspect of a philosophical system, that of being speculation, cannot come into consideration; it will be nothing but a personal peculiarity and a more or less serious case of mental aberration.[13] Materialism, for example, appears to Reinhold only as a sort of mental aberration that is not indigenous to Germany, and he fails to recognize in it the authentic [80] philosophical need to suspend the dichotomy that takes the form of spirit and matter.[14] If the western locality of the culture from which this system emerged keeps it at a distance from another country the question then is: whether this distance does not originate in an opposite onesidedness of [that country's] culture. And even if the scientific value of materialism may be quite small, still we should not fail to appreciate that [in D'Holbach's] *Système de la Nature*, for example, a spirit that is profoundly bewildered by its time is speaking out, and reproducing itself in science. We should not fail to see how the grief over the universal deceit of its time, over the bottomless corruption of nature, over the infinite lie that was called truth and justice,—how this grief, that spreads through the whole, has still kept enough strength to construct for itself the Absolute which had taken flight from the phenomena of life, and to construct it as truth, out of genuinely philosophical need, and with authentic speculation, in a science which appears in a form concordant with the local principle of objectivity—while German culture, on the contrary, nestles down in the form of subjectivity—to which love and faith belong—and often without speculation.

Since the analytical way of philosophizing rests on absolute opposition, it is bound to overlook the philosophical [i.e., speculative] aspect of philosophy precisely because the latter aims at absolute synthesis. It must therefore strike the analyst as a most extraordinary thing that Schelling, as Reinhold puts it, introduced the joining of the

---

12. Compare pp. 86–7 above and *Beyträge* I, passim (especially pp. 1 ff., 90 ff.).

13. *Geistesverirrung*. In *Beyträge* I, 86, Reinhold calls Schelling's principle "the *non plus ultra* of all aberration (*Verirrung*) in speculation thus far, and even of all possible aberration."

14. *Beyträge* I, 77.

finite and the infinite into philosophy[15]—as if philosophy were any-thing else but the positing of the finite in the infinite. In other words, it strikes him as the most extraordinary thing that philosophizing should be introduced into philosophy.

Reinhold not only overlooks the speculative, philosophical aspect of Fichte's and Schelling's systems altogether. He even regards it as an important discovery and revelation when the principles of this philosophy transform themselves for him into what is most idiosyn-cratic of all things; and what is most universal, the identity of subject and object, is transformed into what is most particular, namely the very personal, individuated individuality of Messrs. Fichte and Schel-ling.[16] Still it is understandable and necessary enough that Reinhold should thus tumble from the mountain peak of his limited principle and his own peculiar view into the abyss of his limited view of these systems. But it is an unnecessary and spiteful twist for him to explain the private oddity of these systems in terms of ethical corruption (*Unsittlichkeit*). Reinhold uses this explanatory twist in a preliminary way in the *Deutsche Mercur*, and he will use it more extensively in the next issue of the *Contributions*,* and the explanation consists in saying that in these systems ethical corruption has been given the form of a principle and of philosophy. We can call this a wretched evasion, a convenient outlet for embittered malice, etc.; indeed we can scold and miscall it as we like, for this sort of thing is fair game. It is true that a philosophy issues from its time, and if one wants to call the [81] fragmentation of the time its ethical corruption, then philoso-phy issues from that corruption; but it does so in order to reestablish man from within himself, against the confusion of the time and in order to restore the totality which the time has rent.

As for *Reinhold's own philosophy*, he gives a public history of it to the effect that in the transmigrations of his philosophical soul

15. What Reinhold said was: "It was reserved for *Schelling* to introduce the *absolute finitude of the infinite* into philosophy" (*Beyträge* I, 85).

16. Reinhold boasts of this "secret" that he has "revealed" in *Beyträge* I, 153–4 (cf. *ibid.*, p. 146). Bardili gives the same individualistic interpretation of ideal-ism (*Grundriss*, section 15, p. 112).

* Since this was written he has done so.

[Reinhold's article in Wieland's *Neuer Deutscher Merkur* (1801, n. 3, pp. 167–93) had a preliminary note which announced: "This essay consists of fragments from a treatise in the *second volume* of my *Contributions* etc." So Hegel knew what to expect. The "treatise" (*Beyträge* II, 104–40) was entitled: "On Autonomy as the Principle of the *Practical* Philosophy of the Kantian School—and of the *Whole* Philosophy of the School of Fichte and Schelling."]

he first wandered into Kant's philosophy, and after laying that aside, into Fichte's; from there into Jacobi's, and, after he had left that too, he moved in on Bardili's *Logic*.[17] According to the *Contributions* (p. 163) "he limited his occupation with Bardili's *Logic* to sheer learning, pure receiving and *following* its thought in the most exact meaning of the term in order to subdue his pampered imagination and let the new rationalistic models expel the old transcendental ones from his brain."[18] After this discipline he has now begun to work up Bardili's *Logic* in his *Contributions* (to a more convenient Survey of the State of Philosophy at the Beginning of the 19th Century). These *Contributions* take the occasion of an event so important for the cultural progress of the human spirit as the dawning of a new century to "congratulate the new century upon the fact that the cause of all philosophical revolutions was actually discovered and so overcome at its very heart—no earlier and no later than in the next to last year of the 18th century."[19] *La révolution est finie* has been very frequently decreed in France. Similarly, Reinhold has already announced several endings of the philosophical revolution. He now recognizes the final end of the ends, even though "the bad consequences of the transcendental revolution will persist for some time." But he adds the question "whether he might not be mistaken once again and whether even this true and genuine end might not again be only the beginning of still another wrong turning."[20] The question should rather be whether this end, incapable as it is of being an end, could possibly be the beginning of anything.

The founding and grounding tendency, the tendency to philosophize before getting to philosophy has here finally succeeded in expressing itself completely. It has found out just what should be done: philosophy is to be transmuted into the formal element of cognition, that is, into logic.[21]

Philosophy as a whole grounds itself and the reality of its cognition, both as to form and as to content, within itself. The founding and grounding tendency on the other hand, with all the crowded press of its corroborations and analyses, its becauses and insofars, its there-

17. This "public history" is in *Beyträge* I, "Vorrede" and pp. 118–34.

18. This acknowledged quotation is actually a conflation of two passages on the page Hegel refers to. But it is fairly exact. The context is a letter to Bardili.

19. Hegel here conflates a passage on p. III of Reinhold's "Vorrede" with a remark on pp. V–VI.

20. The quotations and echoes come from Reinhold's "Vorrede," p. IV–VI.

21. Compare note 3 to p. 79 above and pp. 186–8, 192–5 below.

fores and ifs neither gets out of itself nor into [82] philosophy. To the rootless worry that grows ever greater the busier it is, every investigation is premature, every beginning is rashness, and every philosophy is a mere preparatory exercise.[22] Science claims to found itself upon itself by positing each one of its parts absolutely, and thereby constituting identity and knowledge at the beginning and at every single point. As objective totality knowledge founds itself more effectively the more it grows, and its parts are only founded simultaneously with this whole of cognitions. Center and circle are so connected with each other that the first beginning of the circle is already a connection with the center, and the center is not completely a center unless the whole circle, with all of its connections, is completed: a whole that is as little in need of a particular handle to attach the founding to as the earth is in need of a particular handle to attach the force to that guides it around the sun and at the same time sustains it in the whole living manifold of its shapes.

But the founding-hunt is always busy searching for the handle, and making the run-up for living philosophy. Making the run-up becomes its true work; its very principle makes it impossible for it to arrive at knowledge and philosophy. Logical cognition, if it actually does advance toward Reason, must be led to the result that it nullifies itself in reaching Reason; it must recognize antinomy as its supreme law. Reinhold's theme is the application of thinking, and thinking is defined as the infinite repeatability of A as A in A through A.[23] Of course, this is antinomical too; for in application A is in actual fact posited as B. But [Reinhold has] no awareness and no recognition of the presence of this antinomy; thinking, its application and its stuff rest peacefully side by side. For this reason thinking, as the faculty of abstract unity, is, like cognition, merely formal [in Reinhold] and all the foundations are supposed to be only problematic and hypothetical until such time as, in the progress through the problematic and hypothetical, we stumble upon "the arch-true in our truth and upon truth through the arch-true."[24] But, to begin with, this is impossible, for from what is formal in an absolute sense one cannot reach anything

---

22. Compare pp. 86–9 above.

23. Compare p. 97 above; and Reinhold, *Beyträge* I, 108.

24. Hegel (or his printer) made a slip in transcribing Reinhold here which we have corrected. The first edition read "Unwahre" in place of the second "Ur-wahre": ". . . and upon truth through what is untrue."

material; the formal and the material are absolutely opposed.[25] Still less can one arrive at an absolute synthesis—which must be more than a mere fitting together. And in the second place, nothing at all is ever founded by way of the hypothetical and the problematic. The alternative to all this is to connect cognition with the Absolute, so that it becomes an identity of subject and object, of thinking and its stuff, but then cognition is no longer formal; that awkward thing, knowledge, has arisen; and the founding that was meant to come first [83] has got lost again. The fear of slipping into knowledge has no recourse left but to comfort itself with its love, and its faith, and its fixed tendency to keep on to the end with its analyzing, methodizing and storytelling.

If making the run-up does not get one over the ditch, the blame is shoved, not onto its perennial repetition, but onto its method. The true method is supposed to be the method whereby knowledge has already been pulled over to this side of the ditch, to the playground where the running is done. This is the method whereby philosophy is reduced to logic.

We cannot pass at once to the consideration of this method which is to transfer philosophy into the region of the run-up. We must first talk about the *presuppositions* Reinhold believes are necessary for philosophy—in other words, we must talk about the run-up for the run-up.

The [first] *antecedent condition* for philosophizing is what Reinholds calls the *love of truth* and certainty; this is the condition with which the effort to ground cognition must start.[26] And since this will

---

25. "Stuff" is the most indefinite category here. The implicit contrast is with an activity that molds or shapes "stuff." For this activity the "stuff" is "(raw) material" as opposed to "shaped result." But in the "shaped result" the "matter" can be distinguished from the "form" (and hence the "material" side can be opposed to the "formal" side). Thus there is an unavoidable ambiguity of contrast when "material" is used as a substantive. We use "material" only in contrast to "formal." There are other ambiguities which only the context can clarify (and sometimes it does not do it very adequately). Thus "form" as *essential* is opposed to "matter," while "form" as *accidental* is opposed to "content." "Matter" is often contrasted with "mind" or "spirit"; and "materialism" always contrasts with "idealism" but "ideal" generally contrasts with "real." "Materiality" might be contrasted with "spirituality"—but we use it only to translate *Materiatur*, which seems to be Bardili's "raw material" synonym for "stuff," or his "prime matter" as contrasted with the "form" supplied by the "application of thought."

26. Compare p. 88 above. The reference is to *Beyträge* I, 67.

be quickly and easily assented to, he does not dilly-dally over it. And indeed, [we agree that] the object of philosophical reflection cannot possibly be anything else but the true and the certain. However, if consciousness is filled with this object, then a reflection on the subjective, in the form of some love, can find no room in it. It is reflection which first makes the love by fixing the subjective; and of course it makes the love that has so sublime a concern as truth into something utterly sublime—and the individual [Reinhold] who postulates truth because he is animated by this love is utterly sublime too.

The second essential condition of philosophizing is the *faith in truth* as truth, and this, Reinhold thinks, will not be so easily assented to as the love of it. The word faith alone would have sufficiently expressed what he meant to express. With regard to philosophy one might speak of the faith in Reason as being genuine health. The superfluity of the phrase, "faith in truth as truth," instead of making it more edifying, introduces something odd. The main thing is that Reinhold seriously declares that *he should not be asked "what faith in truth is. For he to whom this [. . .] is not clear in himself does not have, and does not know, the need* to find it confirmed in knowledge which can solely proceed from this faith. He does not understand himself in this question," and so Reinhold *"has nothing further to say to him."*[27]

If Reinhold has faith that he is justified in postulating [truth]— then we can with equal justification find in the postulate of transcendental intuition the presupposition that there is something that is superior to, and elevated above, all proof and, following from this, the right and necessity of postulating. Reinhold himself admits that Fichte and Schelling have described [84] transcendental intuition, the activity peculiar to pure Reason, as an acting that returns upon itself.[28] But Reinhold, for his part, has nothing to say to anyone who might want to ask for a description of this faith of his. Still he does do more than he feels himself bound to do; he defines faith at least by setting it in an antithesis with knowledge: faith is "holding something to be true, with no firm foundation in knowledge."[29] The definition of what it is to know will be developed by pursuing the problematic and hypothetical founding; there too the sphere that is common to knowl-

---

27. Hegel used spread type to indicate his quotation—more exactly delimited by our quotation marks (see *Beyträge* I, 69).

28. See *Beyträge* I, 141.

29. *Ibid.*, p. 68.

edge and faith will be marked out and thus the description will be completed.

Although Reinhold believes that a postulate has spared him the trouble of further argument, it still appears strange to him that Messrs. Fichte and Schelling go in for postulating. He takes their postulate to be an idiosyncrasy "in the consciousness of certain extraordinary individuals endowed with a special sense for postulating, in whose writings pure Reason itself has published its knowledge that is action and its action that is knowledge."[30] Reinhold thinks (p. 143) that he, too, was once a member of this magic circle, and that, having escaped from it, he is now well situated to reveal the secret. His tale told out of school amounts to this: that for him what is most universal, the activity of Reason, is transformed into what is most particular, into Messrs. Fichte and Schelling's idiosyncracy.[31] —Anyone to whom Reinhold's love and faith are not clear on their own account, and to whom he has nothing further to say, must similarly view him as a member of the magic circle of an arcanum whose possessor, as representative of love and faith, pretends to be furnished with a peculiar sense, an arcanum that establishes and presents itself in the consciousness of this extraordinary individual, an arcanum that seeks to publish itself in the world of sense through [Bardili's] *Outline of Logic* and the *Contributions* in which this *Outline* is being worked up, etc.

The postulate of love and faith sounds a bit nicer and gentler than that queer requirement of a transcendental intuition; the public will be more edified by a gentle postulate, and it will be put off by the rough postulate of the transcendental intuition;—but this is not a relevant contribution to the main issue.

We come now to the *main presupposition* which, finally, is of more direct concern to philosophizing. What must be presupposed antecedently, in order even for the attempt at philosophy to be thinkable, is the arch-true,* as Reinhold calls it, [85] that which is true and cer-

---

30. *Ibid.*, p. 140.
31. Compare note 16 above.
*[84] Reinhold here retains Jacobi's language, but not his thought. As he says [*Beyträge* I, 126] he had to quit him. When Jacobi speaks of Reason as the faculty for *presupposing the true* [in his "Letter to Fichte," *Werke* III, 32; compare *Beyträge* I, 124], he sets up the true, as the true *being* (*Wesen*) in contrast with formal† [85] truth; but as a sceptic he denies that the true being could be humanly *known*. Reinhold, on the contrary, says that he has learned to think the true—through a formal† proof (*Begründen*). In Jacobi's view, the true cannot be found in any such thing.

tain for itself, the [inconceivable] ground of explanation for everything that is conceivably true. But what philosophy begins with must
be the truth that is the first conceivable one—and indeed it must be
the conceivable, i.e., the true first one, which in the meantime is only
problematically and hypothetically presupposed in philosophy as a
striving. In philosophizing as knowledge, however, the first will only
prove itself to be the one possible first solely if and when and so far
as one can first show with absolute certainty how and why the first
conceivable truth, and the possibility and actuality of the cognizable,
as well as of cognition, are possible through the arch-true as the arch-
ground of everything manifested in the possible and the actual, and
how and why it is true because of the arch-true, which, "outside of
its relation to the possible and the actual in which it manifests itself,
is the absolutely inconceivable, the absolutely inexplicable and the absolutely unnameable."[32]

We can see that where the Absolute has the form of the arch-true,
as it does here, philosophy is not concerned with producing knowledge and truth through Reason. We can see that [Reinhold's] Absolute in the form of truth is not the work of Reason, because it is
already in and for itself something true and certain, that is, something
cognized and known. Reason cannot assume an active relation to the
Absolute. On the contrary, if Reason were active in any way, if the
Absolute were to receive any form through it, the activity would have
to be viewed as an alteration of the Absolute, and an alteration of the
arch-true would be the production of error. So [for Reinhold] philosophizing means absorbing into oneself with absolute passive receptivity something that is already [in and by itself] fully completed knowledge. One cannot deny that this sort of approach has its conveniences.
But there is no need for a reminder that outside of cognition, whether
it be belief or knowledge, truth and certainty are absurdities, and that
the Absolute becomes something true and certain solely through the
spontaneous activity of Reason. But once the convenient device of
presupposing a ready made arch-true is adopted, it is easy to comprehend how odd the claim must appear that thinking should be up-

---

32. Only the last part of this sentence is (as shown) a direct quotation from
Reinhold (*Beyträge* I, 73). But Hegel did not mark off the direct quotation from
the exaggerated caricature of Reinhold's style which he himself furnished as its
context. We have to remember that, for the learned public of the time, Reinhold
and Jacobi were luminaries (almost) as bright as Fichte and more prominent than
Schelling. But perhaps only Reinhold himself would immediately know how
much was quotation here, and how much was burlesque.

graded to knowledge by the spontaneous activity of Reason, or again the claim that nature should be created for consciousness by science, or the claim that the Subject-Object is nothing save what it makes itself by its own activity. According to that convenient habit of thought, the union of reflection and the Absolute in knowledge takes place in perfect accord with the Ideal of a philosophical utopia in which the Absolute itself readies itself for being something true and known, and [86] surrenders itself for total enjoyment to the passivity of a thinking which only needs a mouth agape. Strenuous creative construction, in assertoric and categorical statements, is banished from this utopia. A problematic and hypothetical shaking of the tree of knowledge, which grows in a sandy grounding, brings the fruit tumbling down, already chewed and self-digested. When the entire business of a philosophy is reduced to wishing to be nothing but a problematic and hypothetical trial and prelude, the Absolute must necessarily be posited as arch-true and known;—for how else could truth and knowledge issue from the problematic and hypothetical?

But if and insofar as the presupposition of philosophy consists in that which is inconceivable in itself and arch-true, then because and insofar as this is so, the presupposition can only announce itself in a truth that is conceivable. Philosophizing cannot begin from something arch-true but inconceivable; it must begin from a truth that is conceivable. —But not only is this conclusion [of Reinhold's] quite unproven; the fact is rather that one has to draw the opposite conclusion. If the presupposition of philosophy were the arch-true that is inconceivable, then the arch-true would be announcing itself in its opposite, that is, falsely, if it were to announce itself in something conceivable. One would rather have to say that, though philosophy must begin with, advance through and terminate in concepts, the concepts must be inconceivable. For within the limitation of a concept, the inconceivable is suspended instead of being announced. The union of opposite concepts in the antinomy—which is a contradiction for the faculty of concepts—is the assertoric and categorical appearance of the inconceivable. It is not its problematic and hypothetical appearance; but in virtue of its immediate relation with the inconceivable the antinomy is the true revelation of the inconceivable in concepts, the revelation that is possible through reflection. According to Reinhold, the Absolute is only inconceivable *outside* of its relation to the actual and the possible in which it manifests itself, which is to say that it can be cognized in the possible and the actual. But this would only be cognition through the intellect and not cognition of the Absolute. For when Reason intuits the relation of the actual and possible to the Absolute, it thereby suspends the possible and actual as possible and actual.[33] These determinations vanish from the sight of Reason along with their opposition. Thus Reason knows, not external appearance as revelation, but the essential being that reveals itself; and it is obliged to recognize that a concept for itself, the abstract unity of thinking, is not an announcing of that being, but its disappearance from consciousness. Of course, in itself the essential being has not disappeared, but it has disappeared from a speculation of this kind. [87]

We now pass to the consideration of what the *true business* of a *philosophy reduced to logic* is. Its business is this: "Through the analysis of the application of thinking as thinking, the arch-true is to be discovered and established along with the true, and the true is to be discovered and established through the arch-true."[34] We can see the various absolutes required for this.

(a) "*Thinking* does not first become thinking in and through its application, and as something applied."[35] Instead, it is its *inner* character that must here be understood, and this is "the infinite repeatability of one and the same in one and the same and through one and the same. This is the pure identity [. . .] the absolute infinity that excludes all externality from itself, all temporal and spatial order."[36]

(b) Totally different from the thinking itself is the *application of thinking*. "It is certain that thinking and application of thinking are not at all the same. It is equally certain that in and through the application

(c) some third thing $= C$ must be added to thinking. This is the matter for the application of thinking."[37] This materiality[38] which is partly nullified by thinking, and partly fits into it, is postulated. The warrant and the necessity for accepting and presupposing matter is to be found in the fact that thinking could not possibly be applied if there were none. Matter cannot be what thinking is; for,

33. Compare Kant, *Critique of Judgment*, section 76.
34. *Beyträge* I, 91.
35. *Ibid.*, p. 100.
36. *Ibid.*, pp. 106–7. Compare pp. 97 and 175.
37. *Ibid.*, p. 110 (the citation is abbreviated but direct). What follows is summarized from *ibid.*, pp. 111–12.
38. *Materiatur.* See above, note 25.

if it were the same, it would not be another, and no application could take place because the inner character of thinking is unity. Hence, the inner character of matter is just the opposite, in other words it is manifoldness. What used formerly to be simply accepted as given in experience, has since Kant's time been postulated, and this sort of thing they call "remaining immanent." It is only within the subjective realm, under such names as "facts of consciousness," that empirically given laws, forms or what you will, are still permitted. The objective realm must be postulated.

To begin, then, with Reinhold's concept of thinking. As we have already noted above, he locates the basic mistake of all recent philosophy in the basic prejudice and bad habit of taking thinking to be a merely subjective activity. He asks that for the present and provisionally we should make the attempt to abstract from all subjectivity and objectivity of thinking.[39] But it is not difficult to see that this basic mistake or basic prejudice emerges at full strength when thinking is taken to be pure unity, the unity that abstracts from all materiality and is therefore its opposite—especially when this abstraction is followed, as it must be, by the postulate of a matter essentially distinct from and independent of thinking. Thinking, here, is essentially not the identity of subject and object, which is how it [88] must be characterized as the activity of Reason; and it is only in this way, through thinking being both subject and object at once, that abstraction is made from subjectivity and objectivity. In Reinhold's view, on the other hand, the object is a matter postulated for thinking, so that thinking is nothing but a subjective affair. So even if one wanted to accede to Reinhold's request, and abstract from the subjectivity of thinking, and posit thinking as being both subjective and objective, and hence as having neither of these predicates, one would still not be permitted to do it. For through the opposition of something objective, thinking is determined as something subjective; absolute opposition becomes the theme and principle of a philosophy that has fallen into reduction through logic.

As the principle is, so the synthesis turns out of course. In his popular jargon Reinhold calls it an "application"; but even in this anemic shape, from which the two absolute opposites would not profit much towards their synthesis, the synthesis does not agree with Reinhold's

39. Compare p. 97 above where the passage is more directly quoted. See also p. 176.

claim that the first theme of philosophy should be something conceivable. For even the slight synthesis called application involves a transition of the unity into a manifold, a union of thinking and matter, and hence includes what is called the inconceivable. To be capable of synthesis, thinking and matter must not be absolutely opposed to each other; they must be posited as originally one, and so we would be back with that tiresome identity of subject and object in transcendental intuition, the thinking that is insight (*intellectuelles Denken*).

In this preliminary and introductory exposition, however, Reinhold does not adduce everything in [Bardili's] *Outline of Logic* which might serve to tone down the sort of difficulty that is involved in the absolute opposition. In addition to the postulated matter and its deduced manifoldness, the *Outline* also postulates an inner capacity and suitability of matter to be thought. Besides the materiality that is to be annulled in thinking, there must be something that cannot be annulled by thinking; and even the perceptions of a horse do not lack it. It is a form that is independent of thinking, and since *by the law of nature* form cannot be destroyed by form, the form of thinking *has to fit itself* into it. In other words, besides the materiality that cannot be thought, besides the thing in itself, there must be an absolute stuff which can be represented and is independent of the representing subject, though in representation it is connected with the form.[40] Reinhold always calls this connecting of the form with the stuff 'application of thinking' and he avoids the expression 'representation' used for it by Bardili. It has, indeed, been asserted that [Bardili's] *Outline of Logic* is nothing but [Reinhold's] *Elementary Philosophy* warmed over.[41] It does not seem, however, that the reviewer was ascribing to Reinhold the intention of wanting to re-introduce the *Elementary* [89] *Philosophy* in the [supposedly] almost unchanged form [of Bardili's *Outline*] to a philosophical public which no longer appreciates it. He meant rather that, in his sheer receiving and pure learning of logic, Reinhold had all unknowingly gone to school with himself.

40. These ideas recur continually in Bardili's *Grundriss der Logik*.

41. This was asserted (anonymously) by Fichte in a review of Bardili's *Grundriss* published in the Erlangen *Literatur Zeitung* (30/31 October, 1800—see now *Werke* II, 491). It is virtually certain that Hegel knew who wrote this review. Reinhold's *Elementar-Philosophy* consisted of three volumes: (1) *Versuch einer neuen Theorie des menschlichen Vorstellungsvermögens* (1789); (2) *Beiträge zur Berichtigung bisheriger Missverständnisse der Philosophie* (1790); (3) *Fundament des philosophischen Wissens* (1791).

In the *Contributions* Reinhold himself proposes the following arguments against this view of the matter:

[1] *First*, he [Reinhold] had not looked for his *Elementary Philosophy* in Bardili's *Outline of Logic*. Instead, he had seen in it a certain kinship with idealism. Indeed, because of the bitter scorn with which Bardili referred to Reinhold's theory every time he had occasion to mention it, he would have expected to find any philosophy rather than his own in Bardili's.

[2] The words "representation," "represented," and "mere representation" etc. consistently occur in Bardili's *Outline* in a sense radically opposed to the sense in which they were used by the author of the *Elementary Philosophy*, a fact he [Reinhold], must know better than anyone else.

[3] Anyone who claims that the *Outline* is in any imaginable sense a recasting of Reinhold's *Elementary Philosophy* makes manifest the fact that he has not understood the book he is reviewing.[42]

We don't have to go into the first argument, about the "bitter scorn." The others are assertions whose cogency can be gleaned from a brief comparison of the main features of [Reinhold's] *Theory*[43] with [Bardili's] *Outline*.

According to Reinhold's *Theory*, "the essential constituents of representations, which form their inner conditions," are:

(a) a stuff of representation, which is given to the receptivity and whose form is manifoldness,

(b) a form of representation, which is produced by spontaneity. This form is unity.[44]

According to Bardili's *Logic*,

(a) thinking, an activity whose basic character is unity.

(b) a matter whose character is manifoldness.

(c) both in Reinhold's *Theory* and in Bardili's *Logic* the connecting of the two elements (a) and (b) to each other is called "representing," except that [nowadays] Reinhold always says "application of think-

---

42. Although Hegel puts this passage in quotation marks it is in the main only a paraphrase (from *Beyträge* I, 128–9; the context is an "Open Letter" to Fichte).

43. The *Versuch einer neuen Theorie des menschlichen Vorstellungsvermögens* (more usually abbreviated as *Versuch*) appeared in 1789. It was the first volume of the *Elementar-Philosophie* (see n. 41 above).

44. See *Versuch*, pp. 227–91, especially pp. 230, 235, 255, 264, 267, 283. (By "*Vorstellung* in its narrowest sense" Reinhold means "what sensation, thought, intuition, concept, and Idea have in common": *Versuch*, p. 214.)

ing."[45] Furthermore, form and stuff, or thinking and matter are equally self-subsistent in both books.[46]

With further reference to matter:

(a) one part of it, both in the *Theory* and in the *Logic*, is the *thing in itself*. In the *Theory* this is the object itself insofar as it cannot be represented, and yet can no more be denied than the representable objects themselves;[47] in the *Logic* it is the materiality that is to be annulled in thinking, the aspect of matter that is unthinkable.[48]

[90] (b) In the *Theory* the other part of the object is the familiar stuff of the representation,[49] and in the *Logic*, the indestructible form of the object, a form that is independent of thinking and into which the form of thinking must *fit itself* since form cannot annul form.[50]

This, then, is the bipartite character of the object. On the one hand an absolute materiality. Thinking cannot *fit itself into* it; indeed, it does not know what to do with it except to annul it, that is, to abstract from it. On the other hand, a property that again pertains to the object independent of all thinking, and yet a form that makes it suitable to be thought and which thinking must fit into as well as it can. And across this bipartite character of the object, thinking must plunge headlong into life.[51] Thinking comes to philosophy with a broken neck from the tumble into such absolute duality. Although the forms of the duality may change unceasingly, it always gives birth to the same non-philosophy. Not unlike the man who was unknowingly hosted to his own perfect satisfaction from his own cellar, Reinhold finds all hopes and wishes fulfilled in this freshly garnished version of his own doctrine, and finds the philosophical revolutions

---

45. As Reinhold does not seem to use this expression at all in his *Versuch*—which aims to be quite Kantian—we must choose between assuming that Hegel really meant to write "Bardili always says 'application of thinking,' or else assuming that he is referring to the Reinhold of the moment who had gone to school under Bardili.

46. Hegel's report here seems to be contrary to what Reinhold himself says in the *Versuch*, pp. 244 ff. Hegel seems to be replacing Reinhold's "form" and "matter" in the *Vorstellung* either by its subject and object, or by the thing-in-itself and the subject-in-itself.

47. See *Versuch*, section XVII, pp. 244–55.

48. Compare *Grundriss*, pp. 31, 35, 39–40, 67, etc.

49. See *Versuch*, pp. 230 ff. and 304 ff.

50. See *Grundriss*, pp. 81, 115.

51. Bardili speaks of thinking "plunging headlong" into life (*Grundriss der Logik*, p. 69); and he uses the expression *sich fügen* (fit in) frequently (e.g., *ibid.*, pp. 114–5).

are at an end in the new century. In the universal reduction of philosophy through logic perpetual peace[52] can now come at once upon the philosophical scene.

Reinhold begins his new labor in this philosophical vineyard—as the *Political Journal* also begins every issue[53]—with the story that, over and over again, things have turned out differently from what he had predicted. They turned out "different from what he had proclaimed at the outset of the revolution, different from the way he was trying to advance it in mid course, different from the goal which he believed it had attained towards its end; he asks if he might not be mistaken a fourth time."[54] Besides, if the number of previous mistakes can facilitate the calculation of probability, and be relevant with respect to what is called an authority, then we may add several other mistakes to these three that Reinhold acknowledges from the *Contributions* of this authority[55] who cannot [by this criterion] actually be one.

For instance, on p. 126 Reinhold felt compelled to abandon forever the intermediate standpoint that he believed he had found between Fichte's and Jacobi's philosophy.[56]

On p. 129 he believed, wished, etc. "that the essential core of Bardili's philosophy could be shown to follow from that of Fichte's and vice versa," and "he tried quite seriously to convince Bardili that he was an idealist." But Bardili was not to be convinced; on the contrary, it was Reinhold who was forced by Bardili's letters (p. 130) to give up idealism altogether.

52. The echo of Kant's title can be heard here.

53. The *Politische Journal* was edited by a committee of scholars in Hamburg. We have not been able to discover whether it was still being published at this date. If it had ceased publication before July 1801 then "used to" is the proper rendering of *sonst*.

54. *Beyträge* I, iii–iv. In spite of Hegel's quotation marks, this is not quite a direct quotation. Hegel has turned Reinhold's first personal locutions into the third person and omitted his specification of references. The 'proclamation at the beginning' was in the *Letters on the Kantian Philosophy*; the labors in the middle were in the *Versuch*; and Reinhold thought the revolution had reached its end in Fichte's *Wissenschaftslehre*.

55. We read *von dieser* instead of *vor dieser*.

56. The transcendental idealists accused Jacobi of "dogmatism" (by which they meant what in pre-Wittgensteinian epistemological controversies would have been classified as realism—more particularly as an empirical realism with a religious basis). Hegel's assault on Jacobi's empirico-religious realism can be found in the "Jacobi" section of *Faith and Knowledge*.

[91]   As the attempt with Bardili was a failure, Reinhold appealed urgently to Fichte to take the *Outline* to heart (p. 163), exclaiming: "What a triumph it would be for the good cause if Fichte could manage to penetrate through the bastion of his own terminology and yours (Bardili's) to achieve unity with you!"[57] We all know how this turned out.[58]

Finally, with respect to Reinhold's historical views, it should not be forgotten that things are not the way he thought when he believed he could see the whole system in one part of Schelling's philosophy, and when he took this philosophy to be what is usually called idealism.

How things will turn out in the end for the logical reduction of philosophy is not easy to predict. As a device for keeping oneself out of philosophy, while continuing to philosophize, it is too serviceable not to be in demand. But it carries its own verdict along with it. For since it must choose one of the many possible forms of the standpoint of reflection, everyone else may create another form for himself at his own pleasure. This sort of thing is what is called "an old system being pushed out by a new system," and so it must be called, since one is forced to take the reflective form for the essence of the system. Reinhold himself, for instance, managed to see in Bardili's *Logic* a system different from the one in his own *Theory*.

The *founding program* aims to reduce philosophy to logic. In it *one side of the universal need of philosophy appears* and fixes itself; and as an appearance it must take its necessary, definite and objective place in the manifold of cultural tendencies which are connected with philosophy, but which assume a rigid shape before they arrive at philosophy itself. At every point on the line of its development, which it produces until it reaches its own completion and perfection, the Absolute must curb itself and organize itself into a pattern; and it appears as self-forming in this manifold.

Where the need of philosophy does not reach to the centre of philosophy, it shows up the two sides of the Absolute, which is at the same time inner and outer, essence and appearance, in a sundered

57. This quotation is from one of the published letters of Reinhold to Bardili. Reinhold subsequently published their correspondence as a book (Munich, 1804) with the subtitle "On the Essential Being of Philosophy and the Non-Being of Speculation."

58. This is probably a reference to Fichte's review of Bardili's *Grundriss der Logik* (Fichte, *Werke* II, 490–504); Reinhold commented on this review (in *Beyträge* I, 113–34) and Fichte retorted again in a pamphlet (Tübingen, 1801; see *Werke* II, 504–34).

form, inward essence and outward appearance separately. Outward appearance becomes for itself the absolute objective totality. It becomes the manifold dispersed *ad infinitum*, which manifests its nonconscious coherence with the Absolute in its striving towards infinite multitude. One must be just to this unscientific effort: in its striving to expand the empirical infinitely it does feel the need for totality; even though precisely because of this striving [towards infinity] the stuff [of experience] necessarily wears very thin in the end. This laboring over the infinite objective [92] stuff constitutes the opposite pole to that of density, which strives to remain within the inward essence and cannot emerge from the contraction of its sterling stuff into scientific expansion. Through its infinite bustling the empirical labor causes a stir in the deadness of the essential being that it deals with, though it does not introduce life. And whereas the Danaides could never fill up [their jars] because the water forever ran out[59] these empirical labors do not come to fruition because by constantly pouring water into their ocean they give it an infinite breadth. The Danaides could not achieve satisfaction because there always remained something that still needed to be watered; the empirical bustling, on the contrary, finds eternal nourishment in the immeasurable surface. Taking its stand upon the proverb that no created spirit penetrates into Nature's inwardness,[60] empiricism gives up hope of creating spirit

59. Forty-nine of the fifty daughters of Danaus murdered the husbands they were forced to marry. For this they were condemned in Hades to pour water into a sieve (or alternately a pot with a hole in it). Hegel does not mention the utensil so we cannot be sure which version he had in mind, but he had probably read Lucretius, who speaks of a pot (III, 1009). It is quite likely that he also has in mind Plato's comparison of the sensual man's life to a leaky pot (*Gorgias*, 493–4). If this is right then he means to contrast the endless flowing *away* of experience in practical life, with its endless flowing *in* upon the theoretical investigator.

60. Hegel referred to Albrecht von Haller's pious poem "Human Virtues" several times in his books and lectures. This is the first occasion—but see also *Faith and Knowledge*, (p. 174). Lines 289–90 of the poem, which achieved the status of a proverb, ran: "Ins Innre der Natur dringt kein erschaffner Geist / Zu glücklich, wenn sie noch die äussre Schale weist" ["To Nature's heart there penetrates no mere created mind / Too happy if she but display the outside of her rind"—Wallace]. In 1820 Goethe published a response, "Heiteres Reimstück": "Ins Innre der Natur / O du Philister! / dringt kein erschaffner Geist / . . . / Glückselig! wenn sie nur / Die äussre Schale weis't / Das hör' ich sechzig Jahre wiederholen / Ich fluche drauf, aber verstohlen: / Sage mir tausend tausend Male / Alles giebt sie reichlich und gern; / Natur hat weder Kern noch Schale, / Alles ist sie mit einem Male." (Adapting Wallace slightly we may render the comment

and an inwardness itself, and bringing its dead [stuff] to life as Na-ture.—The inward gravity of the enthusiast, on the other hand, scorns the water through whose addition the stuff might have been able to crystallize itself into a living shape. The seething urge, that originates in the natural necessity to take shape, repels the possibility of shape, and dissolves nature into spirits, forming it into shapeless shapes. Or, where reflection prevails over fancy, genuine scepticism comes into being.[61]

---

thus: "I swear—of course but to myself—as rings within my ears / That same old warning o'er and o'er again for sixty years, / And thus a thousand thousand times I answer in my mind:— / With gladsome and ungrudging hand metes Na-ture from her store; / Nature has neither core nor rind / But all in each both rind and core has evermore combined." This response delighted Hegel as soon as he saw it. He cited it in the *Encyclopaedia* of 1830 [§ 140 Anm.].)

61. Here the cultural situation of Germany is characterized through an analogy drawn from Schelling's "construction" of the *Potenz* of *light* in his philosophy of nature (compare what Hegel says about this on pp. 168–9 above, and the discus-sion in the Introduction, pp. 55–6). At this "level," the active power of light is alien to the dark and dead matter which is the *dependent* focus of gravitational force. But in the phenomena of crystallization this opposition is overcome. The crystal *forms itself* by precipitation from a watery medium; and instead of sim-ply repelling light, it focuses it, reflects it in an intensified form, or breaks it up and transforms it, etc. In Schelling's construction, water, which is the medium of crystallization, is said to be *potenzlos* (i.e., unable to give itself shape, unable to crystallize *itself*). (*Darstellung* [1801], section III, *Werke* IV, 182).

The formal principle of identity in the logic of Reinhold and Bardili is similar-ly *potenzlos* (i.e., unable to generate and shape its own content). Anyone who accepts the *Ding an sich* will find that his *absolute* or philosophical knowledge is thus watery. From the point of view of a speculative comprehension of nature as a whole, all the labors of the empirical scientists, when poured into the formal patterns of such a logic as this, are an ocean of water poured into a leaky pot or through a sieve. It runs away uselessly and no philosophical insight into nature is gained. This is the point of Hegel's Danaid metaphor.

On the other side stands the mystic who has an "intuition" of the absolute Whole. He has the (dark, impervious) raw material for crystallization, but he needs the water of finite experience as a medium. Then his mystic fervor can crystallize into genuine speculative knowledge. (The remark about "shapeless shapes" may be a glancing hit at Schleiermacher, whose religious ideal is said to be "art without the work of art" in *Faith and Knowledge*.)

The birth of "genuine scepticism" through the prevailing of "reflection over fancy" should most probably be taken as comment on the outcome of Kant's third Critique. Hegel would be more willing to grant the status of a *genuine* sceptic to Kant himself than to a declared sceptic among the epigones, like G. E. Schulze. This is evident from his long review of Schulze, published in 1802, for which see *N.K.A.* IV, 197–238.

A false mid-point between these two poles [of dispersal into empirical acquaintance and contraction into religious enthusiasm] is constituted by a popular philosophy, a philosophy of formulae, which has grasped neither of the poles. This popular philosophy thinks it can not only please both sides by leaving the essence of each unchanged, but also let them cling together by a modification of the principles. It does not embrace both poles within itself, but rather causes the essence of both of them to disappear in its superficial modification and neighborly union. Thus popular philosophy is a stranger to both of the principles as it is to [speculative] philosophy. From the pole of dispersal, popular philosophy takes the principle of opposition. The opposites, however, are not supposed to be mere appearances and concepts *ad infinitum*, but one of them is itself something infinite and inconceivable. In this way the enthusiast's desire for something supersensuous should be satisfied. But the principle of dispersal despises the supersensuous, just as the principle of enthusiasm despises opposition to the supersensuous or [the granting of] standing for a limited entity alongside it. [Speculative] philosophy in its turn, rejects every semblance of being a mediating position that popular philosophy seeks to confer on its principle of the absolute non-identity of the finite and the infinite. That which has died the death of dichotomy philosophy raises to life again through the absolute identity. And through Reason, which devours both [finite and infinite] and maternally posits them both equally, philosophy strives towards the consciousness of this identity of the finite and the infinite, or in other words, it strives towards knowledge and truth.[62]

62. This paragraph compares two ways of mediating the extremes of finite cognition and infinite enthusiasm. "Popular" philosophy offers a false mean in which each extreme is allotted to a world of its own (and each world is an object of belief or faith rather than of genuine knowledge). Thus the "principle of opposition" between subject and object is preserved in both realms. In this world experience continually accumulates, but the ultimate reality eludes us and makes its home in the other. This side-by-side conciliation is unacceptable to serious adherents of either principle. (If we want to put a name to this extreme it is worth remembering that Fichte remarked on the "formula-method" that Bardili used to achieve a standpoint between Fichte's and Jacobi's: *Werke* II, 491.)

The true mean of speculative philosophy suspends the principle of opposition and replaces faith with knowledge. It unites the rational identity of the empiricist with the density of religious experience in a philosophical "crystallization." Thus the opposed *principles* of the two poles are reunited in the absolute indifference point. The one world of nature and intelligence is seen from the standpoint of the divine creative act: the "begetting of the Word from the beginning."

Bibliographic Index

All works referred to in Hegel's text or in the translator's introduction and notes are listed here (and identified as fully as possible) *except* classical and medieval authors (e.g., Aristotle, Lucretius), where the reference can be found in any good modern edition (where a specific edition has been cited—e.g., Cornford's translation of the *Timaeus*—details are included).

Baillie, Sir James Black. See Hegel, *Phenomenology of Mind*.

Bardili, Christoph Gottfried (1761–1808). *Grundriss der Ersten Logik*. Stuttgart: Löflund, 1800.

Beck, L. W. *Early German Philosophy: Kant and His Predecessors*. Cambridge, Mass.: Belknap Press of Harvard University Press, 1969.

Bichat, Marie François Xavier (1771–1802). *Traité des Membranes en général et des diverses membranes en particulier*. Paris: Richard, Caille et Ravier, An VIII (1799/1800).

Brown, John (1735–88). *The Elements of Medicine*. 2 vols. London, 1788. (First published in Latin, Edinburgh 1780; German translation, Copenhagen, 1796.)

Chisholm, Roderick M. See Fichte. *Die Bestimmung des Menschen* (*The Vocation of Man*).

Croce, Benedetto (1866–1952). *What is Living and What is Dead in the Philosophy of Hegel*. Translated from the third Italian ed. (1912) by Douglas Ainslie. London: Macmillan, 1915.

Düsing, Klaus. "Spekulation und Reflexion." *Hegel-Studien* 5 (1969): 95–128.

Ellington, James. See Kant, *Metaphysical Foundations of Natural Science*.

Eschenmayer, Adam Karl August (1770–1852). "Spontaneität = Weltseele oder das höchste Prinzip der Naturphilosophie." *Zeitschrift für spekulative Physik*, II, 1800–1801, 1–68.

————. *Sätze aus der Naturmetaphysik*. Tübingen: Cotta, 1797.

Fichte, Johann Gottlieb (1762–1814). *Antwortschreiben an Prof. Reinhold*. Hamburg: Perthes, 1801. Reprinted in *Werke* II, 504–31.

————. *Die Anweisung zu einem seligen Leben oder die Religionslehre*. Leipzig, 1806. (English translation by William Smith, *The Way to the Blessed Life*, in *Popular Works*, Vol. II.)

————. *Appellation an das Publikum*. Jena/Leipzig: Gabler; Tübingen: Cotta, 1799. Reprinted in *Werke* V.

————. *Die Bestimmung des Menschen*. Berlin: Vossische Buchhandlung, 1800. Reprinted in *Werke* II. (*The Vocation of Man*, translated by William Smith and edited by R. M. Chisholm, Indianapolis and New York: Bobbs-Merrill, Library of Liberal Arts, 1956.)

————. *Briefwechsel*. Edited by Hans Schulz. 1930. Hildesheim: Georg Olms Verlag, 1967.

——. "Erste Einleitung in die Wissenschaftslehre." *Philosophisches Journal*, V. Jena/Leipzig: Gabler, 1797. Reprinted in *Werke* I. (For translation see *Science of Knowledge*.)

——. "Zweite Einleitung in die Wissenschaftslehre." *Philosophisches Journal*, VI. Reprinted in *Werke* I. (For translation see *Science of Knowledge*.)

——. *Grundlage des Naturrechts*. 2 vols. Jena and Leipzig: Gabler, 1796, 1797.

——. *Grundlage der gesammten Wissenschaftslehre*. Leipzig: Gabler, 1794. (Reprinted in *Werke*. [For translation see *Science of Knowledge*].)

——. *Popular Works*. Translated by William Smith. 2 vols. London: Trübner, 1889.

——. *Sämmtliche Werke*. Edited by I. H. Fichte. 8 vols. Berlin: Veit, 1845–46.

——. *Science of Knowledge* (*Wissenschaftslehre*, 1794, with the First and Second Introductions). Edited and translated by Peter Heath and John Lachs. New York: Appleton-Century-Crofts, 1970.

——. *The Science of Rights*. Translated by A. E. Kroeger. London, 1889. Reprinted by Routledge and Kegan Paul, 1970.

——. *System der Sittenlehre*. Jena and Leipzig: Gabler, 1798.

——. *System of Ethics*. Translated by A. E. Kroeger. London, Trübner, 1897.

——. *Über der Begriff der Wissenschaftslehre*. Weimar: Industrie-Comtoir, 1794. Revised and augmented, Jena and Leipzig: Gabler, 1798. Reprinted in *Werke* I.

——. "Über den Grund unseres Glaubens an eine göttliche Weltregierung." *Philosophisches Journal*, VIII, 1799. Reprinted in *Werke* V.

——. Review of Aenesidemus [G. E. Schulze], *Über Reinholds Elementarphilosophie, Jenaer Allgemeine Literaturzeitung*, 1794. Reprinted in *Werke* I.

——. Unsigned review of Bardili's *Grundriss, Literatur-Zeitung, Erlangen*, II, 1800, 214–15. Reprinted in *Werke* II.

Fuhrmans, Horst. See Schelling, *Briefe*.

Goethe, Johann Wolfgang von (1749–1831). "Faust. Ein Fragment" in *Goethes Schriften*, vol. 7. Weimar: Goschen, 1790. Reprinted in *Werke*, Berlin edition, Aufbau Verlag, VIII, 69–143.

——. "Faust: Der Tragödie Erster Teil" in *Goethes Werke*, vol. 8. Tübingen: Cotta, 1808. Reprinted in *Werke*, Berlin edition, Aufbau Verlag, VIII, 145–300. (Translated by W. Kaufmann, Garden City, N.Y.: Doubleday, Anchor Books, 1961.)

——. "Allerdings. Dem Physiker" in *Zur Morphologie*, vol. I, 1821. Reprinted in *Werke*, Berlin edition, Aufbau Verlag, I, 555–56.

Haller, Albrecht von. "Die Falschheit der menschlichen Tugenden." In *Versuch Schweizerischer Gedichte*. Bern, 1732.

Haldane, Edward S. and Simson, Frances H. See Hegel, *Lectures on the History of Philosophy*.

Harris, Henry Silton. *Hegel's Development I: Toward the Sunlight (1770–1801)*. Oxford: Clarendon Press, 1972.

Heath, Peter and Lachs, John. See Fichte, *Science of Knowledge*.

Hegel, Georg Wilhelm Friedrich (1770–1831). *On Art, Religion, Philosophy*. Edited by J. G. Gray. New York: Harper Torchbooks, 1970.

——. *Briefe von und an Hegel*. Edited by Johannes Hoffmeister and Rolf Flechsig. 4 vols. Hamburg: F. Meiner, 1961 (*Briefe*).

————. *De Orbitis Planetarum*. Jena: Seidler, 1801. Reprinted in *Erste Druckschriften*.

————. *Differenz des Fichte'schen und Schelling'schen Systems der Philosophie*. Jena: Seidler, 1801. (For current editions see Hegel, *Erste Druckschriften*, *Gesammelte Werke*, and *Sämtliche Werke*.)

————. *Early Theological Writings*. Translated by T. M. Knox with an introduction, and fragments translated by Richard Kroner. Chicago: University of Chicago Press, 1948.

————. *Hegels Erste Druckschrift*. (Jean Jacques Cart, *Vertrauliche Briefe*.) Göttingen: Vandenhoek and Ruprecht, 1970.

————. *Erste Druckschriften*. Edited by Georg Lasson. Leipzig: F. Meiner, 1928. (The texts of this edition of *Differenz des Fichte'schen und Schelling'schen Systems der Philosophie* and of *Glauben und Wissen* were each reprinted separately at Hamburg by Meiner in 1962.)

————. *Faith and Knowledge*. Translated by Walter Cerf and H. S. Harris. Albany: State University of New York Press, 1976.

————. *Gesammelte Werke*, Band 4, *Jenaer Kritische Schriften*. Edited by Hartmut Buchner and Otto Pöggeler. Hamburg: F. Meiner, 1968. (The present translation is based on the text of this edition, and the pagination of this edition is indicated herein [*N.K.A.*].)

————. *Glauben und Wissen* in *Kritisches Journal der Philosophie*, Band 2, n. 1. Tübingen: Cotta, 1802. (For current editions see Hegel, *Erste Druckschriften and Gesammelte Werke*.)

————. *Lectures on the History of Philosophy*. Translated by E. S. Haldane and F. H. Simson. 3 vols. London: Routledge and Kegan Paul, 1892. Reprinted 1955.

————. *Logic*. Translated from the *Encyclopaedia of the Philosophical Sciences* by William Wallace. Second edition, Oxford: Clarendon Press, 1892. Reprinted 1975.

————. *Natural Law*. Translated by T. M. Knox, with an introduction by H. B. Acton. Philadelphia: University of Pennsylvania Press, 1975.

————. *Phänomenologie des Geistes*. Edited by Johannes Hoffmeister. Hamburg: F. Meiner, 1952.

————. *Philosophy of Nature*. Translated by A. V. Miller. Oxford: Clarendon Press, 1970. (Also translated by M. J. Petry, 3 vols. London: Allen and Unwin, 1970).

————. *Philosophy of Right*. Translated with notes by T. M. Knox. Oxford: Clarendon Press, 1945.

————. *Political Writings*. Translated by T. M. Knox with an introductory essay by Z. A. Pelczynski. Oxford: Clarendon Press, 1964.

————. *Premières Publications*. Translated by Marcel Méry. 3d edition. Paris: Ophrys, 1970. (French translation of *Difference* and *Faith and Knowledge* with analytical introductions and explanatory notes.)

————. "Das System der spekulativen Philosophie" (1803–04). First published in *Jenenser Real Philosophie* I, edited by J. Hoffmeister. Leipzig: Meiner, 1931. Critical edition in *Gesammelte Werke*, Band 6, *Jenaer Systementwürfe* I, edited by K. Düsing and H. Kimmerle. Hamburg: Meiner, 1975.

————. *Sämtliche Werke*. "Jubilee edition" edited by H. Glockner. Stuttgart: Frommann, 1927–30 (see vol. I for *Differenz*).

————. *Theologische Jugendschriften*. Edited by Hermann Nohl. Tübingen: Mohr, 1907. Reprinted 1968.

————. *System der Sittlichkeit*. Edited by Georg Lasson. Hamburg: Meiner, 1967. (Reprinted from *Schriften zur Politik und Rechtsphilosophie*, second edition, 1923.)

————. "Über das Wesen der philosophischen Kritik." (Introduction for) *Kritisches Journal der Philosophie*, I, Heft 1. Tübingen, 1802. Reprinted in *Gesammelte Werke* IV, 117–28.

————. "Die Verfassung Deutschlands." (Written 1799–1802, first complete publication in) Hegel, *Schriften zur Politik und Rechtsphilosophie*, edited by G. Lasson. Leipzig: F. Meiner, 1913 (second edition, 1923). Translated in *Political Writings*.

————. "Verhältniss des Scepticismus zur Philosophie." *Kritisches Journal der Philosophie*, I, Heft 2. Tübingen, 1802. Reprinted in *Gesammelte Werke* IV, 197–238. (French translation by B. Fauquet. Paris: Vrin, 1972.)

————. "Wie der gemeine Menschenverstand die Philosophie nehme" (review of Krug). *Kritisches Journal der Philosophie*, I, Heft 1, 1802. Reprinted in *Gesammelte Werke* IV, 174–87.

————. *Werke* (Complete edition edited by a committee of his friends), Duncker and Humblot, 1832 ff. Vol. I: *Philosophische Abhandlungen*. Edited by K. L. Michelet. 1832 (second edition, 1845).

Hegel-Studien. Bonn: Bouvier, 1961 ff.

Hegel, Hannelore: *Isaak von Sinclair zwischen Fichte, Hölderlin und Hegel*. Frankfurt a. M.: Klostermann, 1971.

Herder, Johann Gottfried (1744–1803). *Gott: Einige Gespräche*. First edition, 1787. Second edition, revised, Gotha, 1800. Both editions collated in *Werke* XVI (and in the translation below).

————. *God: Some Conversations*. Translated by F. H. Burkhardt. Indianapolis: Bobbs-Merrill, 1940.

————. *Sämmtliche Werke*. Edited by B. Suphan et al. 33 vols. Hildesheim: Georg Olms Verlag, 1967.

Hoffmeister, Johannes. See Hegel, *Phänomenologie des Geistes*.

Holbach, Paul H. D. Baron d', *Système de la Nature*. Paris, 1770. German translation, 1783.

Jacobi, Friedrich Heinrich (1743–1819). *An Fichte*, Hamburg: Perthes, 1799. Reprinted in *Werke* III.

————. *Über die Lehre des Spinoza in Briefen an den Herrn Moses Mendelssohn*. Neue verm. Ausg. Breslau: Loewe, 1789. Reprinted in *Werke* IV, i.

————. *Werke*. 6 vols. Leipzig: Fleischer, 1812–25. Reprinted Darmstadt: Wissenschaftliche Buchgesellschaft, 1968.

Kant, Immanuel (1724–1804). *Critik der reinen Vernunft*. Riga: Hartknoch, 1781 [=A]. Second edition improved throughout, 1787 [=B] (the two editions collated by R. Schmidt. Hamburg: Meiner, 1930).

————. *Critique of Pure Reason*. Translated from R. Schmidt's collation of editions A and B by Norman Kemp Smith. London: Macmillan, 1933. (The pagination of both A and B is indicated in the margin.)

————. *Critik der praktischen Vernunft*. Riga: Hartknoch, 1788. Reprinted in *Akad.* V.

————. *Critique of Practical Reason.* Translated by L. W. Beck. Chicago: University of Chicago Press, 1949. Reprinted New York: Library of Liberal Arts, 1956. (The pagination of *Akad.* V is indicated in the margin.)

————. *Critik der Urteilskraft.* Berlin and Libau: Lagarde and Friederich, 1790. Second edition, 1793. Reprinted in *Akad.* V.

————. *Critique of Aesthetic Judgement.* Translated by J. C. Meredith. Oxford: Clarendon Press, 1911 (Preface, Introduction and sections 1–60 of the *Kritik der Urteilskraft,* 1793; the pagination of *Akad.* V is given in the margin).

————. *The Analytic of the Beautiful* [*Critique of Judgment,* §§ 1–22] and the *Feeling of Pleasure and Displeasure* [*Anthropology,* Book II] translated, with an introduction by Walter Cerf. New York: Library of Liberal Arts, 1956.

————. *Critique of Teleological Judgment.* Translated by J. C. Meredith. Oxford: Clarendon Press, 1928 (sections 61–91 of *Kritik der Urteilskraft,* 1793; the pagination of *Akad.* V is indicated in the margin).

————. *The Doctrine of Virtue.* Translated by M. J. Gregor. New York: Harper Torchbooks, 1964 (Part II of *Metaphysik der Sitten;* there is another translation, by James Ellington, in the Library of Liberal Arts series).

————. *Gesammelte Schriften.* Edited by the Royal Prussian Academy of Sciences. 24 vols. Berlin: Reimer, 1902–38 (*Akad.*).

————. *On History.* Translated by L. W. Beck. New York: Liberal Arts Press, 1963.

————. *The Metaphysical Elements of Justice.* Translated by John Ladd. Indianapolis and New York: Bobbs-Merrill, Library of Liberal Arts, 1965. (Abridged version of "Doctrine of Right" from *Metaphysik der Sitten.*)

————. *Metaphysical Foundations of Natural Science.* Translated by James Ellington. Indianapolis and New York: Bobbs-Merrill, Library of Liberal Arts, 1970.

————. *Metaphysische Anfangsgründe der Naturwissenschaften.* Königsberg, 1786. Reprinted in *Akad.* IV.

————. *Metaphysik der Sitten* (1797). Reprinted in *Akad.* VI, 203–493.

————. *Philosophical Correspondence 1759–99.* Edited and translated by Arnulf Zweig. Chicago: University of Chicago Press, 1967.

————. *Prolegomena.* 1783. Reprinted in *Akad.* IV, 253–383. Translated by L. W. Beck. Indianapolis and New York: Bobbs-Merrill, Library of Liberal Arts, 1950.

————. *Die Religion innerhalb der Grenzen der blossen Vernunft.* Königsberg, 1793. Reprinted in *Akad.* VII.

————. *Religion Within the Bounds of Reason Alone.* Translated by T. M. Greene and H. H. Hudson. 1934. New York: Harper Torchbooks, 1960.

Kaufmann, Walter. *Hegel: Reinterpretation, Texts and Commentary.* 2 vols. Garden City, N.Y.: Doubleday, Anchor Books, 1965.

Kimmerle, Heinz. *Das Problem der Abgeschlossenheit des Denkens.* Bonn: Bouvier, 1970 (*Hegel-Studien,* Beiheft 8).

Knox, T. M. and Kroner, Richard S. See Hegel, *Early Theological Writings.*

Kritisches Journal der Philosophie. Edited by F. W. J. Schelling and G. W. F. Hegel. Jena: Cotta, 1801–02. (Reprinted completely in *N.K.A.* IV).

Kroeger, A. E. See Fichte, *Science of Ethics* and *Science of Rights.*

Krug, Wilhelm Traugott (1770–1842). *Briefe über den neuesten Idealismus.* Leipzig: Müller, 1801.

Laube, Heinrich. *Moderne Charakteristiken.* Mannheim, 1835.

Locke, John (1632–1704). *Essay Concerning Human Understanding.* Edited by J. W. Yolton. 2 vols. London: Dent, Everyman's Library, 1961.

Lossius, Johann Christian (1743–1813). *Physische Ursachen des Wahren.* Gotha: C. W. Ettinger, 1775.

Méry, Marcel. See Hegel, *Premières Publications.*

Neuer Deutscher Merkur. Edited by C. M. Wieland. Weimar, 1801.

Nicolin, Gunther, ed. *Hegel in Berichten seiner Zeitgenossen.* Hamburg: Meiner, 1970.

Nohl, Hermann. See Hegel, *Theologische Jugendschriften.*

Pascal, Blaise. *Pensées.* Edited by Léon Brunschvicg. Paris: Hachette, 1897. (Most modern editions show Brunschvicg's numbering in a concordance.)

Pelczynski, Zygmunt A. See Hegel, *Political Writings.*

Plato's Cosmology [*The Timaeus*]. Translated by F. M. Cornford. New York: Liberal Arts Press, 1957.

Politisches Journal, nebst Anzeige von gelehrten und andern Sachen, herausgegeben von einer Gesellschaft von Gelehrten, Hamburg.

Reinhold, Karl Leonard (1758–1823). *Beyträge zur leichtern Uebersicht des Zustandes der Philosophie.* 6 vols. Hamburg: Perthes, 1801–03.

———. *Beyträge zur Berichtigung bisheriger Missverständnisse der Philosophie.* Jena, 1790.

———. *Fundament des philosophischen Wissens.* Jena, 1791.

———. *Versuch einer neuen Theorie des menschlichen Vorstellungsvermögens.* Prague and Jena: Widtmann and Mauke, 1789. Reprinted Darmstadt: Wissenschaftliche Buchgesellschaft, 1963. (These last three volumes make up Reinhold's *Elementarphilosophie.*)

———. *Briefe über die Kantische Philosophie.* New augmented edition. Leipzig, 1790–92. (Originally published in *Deutscher Merkur,* 1786–87.)

———. "Der Geist des Zeitalters als Geist der Philosophie." *Neuer Deutscher Merkur,* 1801, Heft 3, 167–93.

———. "Sendschreiben an Fichte." *Beyträge* I, 113–134.

———. Ed. *C. G. Bardilis and C. L. Reinholds Briefwechsel über das Wesen der Philosophie und das Unwesen der Spekulation.* Munich, 1804.

Rosen, Stanley. *G. W. F. Hegel: An Introduction to the Science of Wisdom.* New Haven: Yale University Press, 1974.

Rosenkranz, Karl (1805–1879). *Georg Wilhelm Friedrich Hegels Leben.* Berlin, 1844. Reprinted Darmstadt: Wissenschaftliche Buchgesellschaft, 1963.

Schleiermacher, Friedrich Daniel Ernst (1768–1834). *Ueber die Religion: Reden an die Gebildeten unter ihren Verächtern.* Berlin, 1799. (Abridged translation: *On Religion: Speeches to its Cultured Despisers.* Edited by John Oman. New York: Ungar, 1955.)

Schelling, Friedrich Wilhelm Joseph (1775–1854). *Briefe und Dokumente.* Edited by Horst Fuhrmans. Bonn: Bouvier, 1962 ff. (2 vols. to date).

———. "Darstellung meines Systems der Philosophie." *Zeitschrift für Spekulative Physik* II, Heft 2, 1801. Reprinted in *Werke* IV, 105–212.

————. *Erster Entwurf eines Systems der Naturphilosophie* and *Einleitung zu dem Entwurf.* Jena and Leipzig: Gabler, 1799.

————. "Fernere Darstellungen aus dem System der Philosophie." *Neue Zeitschrift für Spekulative Physik* I, Heft 1, 1802. Reprinted in *Werke* IV, 333–510.

————. *Ideen zu einer Philosophie der Natur.* Leipzig: Breitkopf und Härtel, 1797 (second edition, Landshut: 1803)

————. "On the Possibility of a Form of Philosophy in General" (1794). Translated by Fritz Marti in *Metaphilosophy* VI, Number 1, 1975.

————. *On University Education.* Edited by N. Guterman. Athens, Ohio: Ohio University Press, 1966.

————. *Sämtliche Werke.* Edited by K. F. A. Schelling. 14 vols. Stuttgart and Augsburg: Cotta, 1856–1861. (The pagination of this edition is preserved in the photo-reprinted *Ausgewählte Werke.* 8 vols. Darmstadt: Wissenschaftliche Buchgesellschaft, 1966–1968.)

————. *System des Transzendentalen Idealismus.* Tübingen: Cotta, 1800. Reprinted in *Werke* III (and in *Ausgewählte Werke,* 1799–1801).

Schelling, F. W. J. "Über das Absolute Identitäts—System." *Kritisches Journal der Philosophie* I, Heft 1. Tübingen, 1802. Reprinted in Hegel, *Gesammelte Werke* IV, 129–73.

————. *Von der Weltseele.* Hamburg: Perthes, 1798. Reprinted in *Werke* II, 345–583.

Schiller, Friedrich. *On The Aesthetic Education of Man.* Translated with an introduction by Reginald Snell. New York: Ungar, 1971.

Schulze, Hans. See Fichte, *Briefe.*

Schulze, Gottlob Ernst (1761–1833). *Kritik der Theoretischen Philosophie.* 2 vols. Hamburg: Bohn, 1801.

Smith, William. See Fichte, *Popular Works.*

Spinoza, Benedictus de (1632–1677). *Chief Works.* Translated by R. H. M. Elwes. 2 vols. New York: Dover, 1951.

————. *Opera Omnia.* Edited by H. E. G. Paulus. 2 vols. Jena: Akademische Buchhandlung, 1802–03.

————. *Opera.* Edited by Karl Gebhardt. 4 vols. Heidelberg, n.d.

Schulz, Hans. See Fichte, *Briefe.*

Schwarz, Hermann. *Immanuel Kant, ein Lebensbild.* Halle: Hugo Peter, 1907.

Tiedmann, Dietrich. *Geist der Spekulativen Philosophie.* 3 vols. Marburg, 1791–97.

Tilliette, Xavier. *Schelling: Une Philosophie en Devenir.* Paris: Vrin, 1970.

Wallace, William. See Hegel, *Logic.*

Zeitschrift für spekulative Physik. Edited by F. W. J. Schelling. 2 vols. Jena and Leipzig: Gabler, 1800–1801; continued as *Neue Zeitschrift für spekulative Physik* (Tübingen: Cotta, 1802–3).

Zimmerli, Walter C. *Die Frage nach der Philosophie.* Bonn: Bouvier, 1974 (*Hegel-Studien,* Beiheft 11).

Zweig, Arnulf. See Kant, *Philosophical Correspondence.*

Analytic Index